Vol. 9

Quick

SIMPLIFIED BIBLE COMM

luke
& john

LIFE THAT LASTS FOREVER

CONTRIBUTING EDITORS:

DR. STEPHEN LESTON
ROBERT DEFFINBAUGH

CONSULTING EDITOR:

DR. MARK STRAUSS

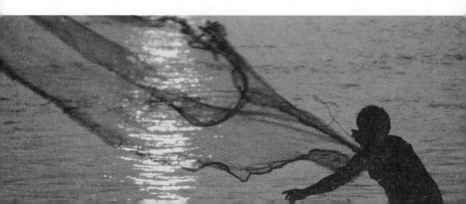

TABLE OF CONTENTS

THE GOSPEL OF LUKE

Introduction to the Gospel of Luke   7
Outline   10
The Gospel of Luke   14

THE GOSPEL OF JOHN

Introduction to the Gospel of John   120
Outline   123
The Gospel of John   127

THE GOSPEL OF
LUKE

INTRODUCTION TO
LUKE

As author of this Gospel and its sequel, the book of Acts, Luke is responsible for over a fourth of the content of the Greek New Testament. He brings a distinctive perspective to the writing as well. While many of Jesus' followers had the reputation of "unschooled, ordinary men" (Acts 4:13 NIV), Luke's writing in his opening paragraph displays the sophisticated style of Greek historians, and then he moves into smooth, everyday vernacular. His eye for detail is evident in numerous places.

AUTHOR

Luke doesn't identify himself in either of the books he wrote, but there has been little dispute that he was the author of both. He was a physician (Colossians 4:14), and notes specifics in several of Jesus' healings that other writers do not. Aside from the Colossians reference, Luke is mentioned only two other times in the New Testament (2 Timothy 4:11; Philemon 24). People have theorized that he might have been Lucius of Cyrene (Acts 13:1), one of the seventy-two disciples sent out by Jesus (10:1–17), one of the Greeks mentioned in John 12:20, or even the other disciple with Cleopas on the road to Emmaus (24:13–35). But there is no biblical or historic evidence for any of these speculations.

More reliable is the assumption that Luke knew Jesus' mother, Mary. Therefore, his Gospel includes the wonderful account of the shepherds visiting the manger, the story of Elizabeth and Zechariah and the birth of John the Baptist, the mention of Simeon and Anna when Jesus was presented in the temple, and the story of Jesus questioning the religious leaders in the temple at age twelve (1–2).

Luke also traveled on some of Paul's journeys, which is evident from passages in the book of Acts that switch from third person to first person. And he must have been more than a mere acquaintance because Paul refers to him as a dear friend (Colossians 4:14).

PURPOSE

Evidence points to Luke being a Gentile believer who wrote for a Gentile audience. The primary recipient of both his books was "most excellent Theophilus" (Luke 1:3 NIV; Acts 1:1), a title that suggests someone of wealth and authority—perhaps a ranking official. Luke tended to give details about Jewish locations that wouldn't have been necessary for Jewish readers. These and other clues suggest that Luke's intent was explaining the story of Jesus to Gentiles.

OCCASION

Theophilus may have been a financial backer for Luke's travels and/or writing. However, while he may have been the first recipient of Luke's words about Jesus, it isn't likely he was intended to be the sole reader. Theophilus had already heard about Jesus; Luke was writing to confirm the authenticity and validity of the gospel. Luke began with eyewitness accounts and then personally investigated them to ensure accuracy (1:1-4). He showed that the faith of Theophilus—and all those who believed in Jesus Christ—had a strong foundation.

THEMES

In his concern for Gentiles, Luke's portrayal of the gospel is more encompassing than that of the other Gospel writers. He stresses an individual's privilege and ability to repent and be forgiven—and the joy that results from each such decision (15:7, 10, 32). Numerous Samaritans, women, children, Roman officials, and other traditional outsiders are shown in a positive light, providing a natural segue into his book of Acts and the worldwide mission of the church. Luke alone tells of the thief on the cross who repents and is promised a place in paradise with Jesus (23:39-43).

Luke had a high regard for women, as seen in stories such as the faith of Elizabeth (1:5-80), Anna in the temple (2:36-38), and the dilemma between Mary and Martha (10:38-42). He records Jesus' gentle words toward women of faith (7:13; 8:48; 13:12, 15-16; 23:28-31), and he credits the women who traveled with Jesus and supported Him (8:1-3). In doing so, Luke introduces his readers to thirteen women who appear nowhere else in scripture.

Luke has much to say about money. More accurately, he records much of what Jesus had to say about wealth that other writers didn't include. For example, Luke is the only source for Jesus' Parable of the Rich Man and Lazarus (16:19-31). He also tells of how first the twelve disciples, and then another seventy-two, were sent out with no provisions in order to see for themselves that God would provide (9:1-6; 10:1-17). And the theme of money is carried throughout the Gospel, as he notes attitudes toward the poor as well as toward the rich.

Though he doesn't usually elaborate, Luke also highlights the prayer habits of Jesus (3:21-22; 5:16; 6:12; 22:41-44; etc.). Because of His example, Jesus' disciples began to ask about improving their own prayer habits (11:1).

HISTORICAL CONTEXT

Luke establishes times within his Gospel by citing rulers of the period (1:5; 2:1-2; 3:1; etc.). However, the actual date of his writing is difficult to determine. Neither of his books makes reference to the fall of Jerusalem (AD 70) or even Nero's persecution of the early Christians (AD 64). It is commonly estimated that Luke was written after Mark, which was probably written in the mid to late 60s.

CONTRIBUTION TO THE BIBLE

Over half of Luke's Gospel contains content found nowhere else in scripture. In addition to what has already been mentioned (Elizabeth and Zechariah, the Nativity stories, Jesus at age twelve, the repentant thief on the cross, the Rich Man and Lazarus, etc.), Luke includes seven miracles of Jesus and nineteen of His parables that are unique to this Gospel.

Were it not for Luke's Gospel, we would miss out on many of the most-read and appreciated portions of scripture: the parables of the Good Samaritan (10:30–37) and the Prodigal Son (15:11–32), Jesus' visit to see Zacchaeus (19:1–10), one of the accounts of a resurrection from the dead (7:11–17), the healing of the ten lepers (17:12–19), the two disciples on the road to Emmaus after Jesus' resurrection (24:13–35), Jesus' "Father, forgive them" prayer from the cross (23:34 NIV), and more.

On a related note, Luke tended to notice and record the artistic, poetic expressions of the people he researched. He alone includes the songs or canticles of Elizabeth (1:41–45), Mary (1:46–55), Zechariah (1:67–79), Simeon (2:29–32), and even the angels announcing Jesus' birth (2:13–14).

STRUCTURE

The commentary for this book is laid out by chapters for ease of use, but here is a look at the broader structure of this book of the Bible:

Jesus' Birth and Preparation for Ministry	1:1–4:13
Jesus' Ministry in Galilee	4:14–9:50
Jesus' Journey to Jerusalem	9:51–19:27
Jesus' Ministry amidst Conflict in Jerusalem	19:28–21:38
Jesus' Arrest, Trial, and Crucifixion	22:1–23:56
The Resurrection and Ascension	24:1–53

OUTLINE

A MIRACLE BIRTH (BEFORE JESUS') 1:1–80

Luke's Salutation 1:1–4
Zechariah's Encounter with Gabriel 1:5–25
Jesus' Birth Predicted 1:26–56
John the Baptist Is Born 1:57–80

THE ARRIVAL OF THE MESSIAH 2:1–52

The Birth of Jesus 2:1–20
The Infant Jesus at the Temple 2:21–40
The Boy Jesus at the Temple 2:41–52

TWO MINISTRIES BEGIN 3:1–38

The Voice of One Calling in the Desert 3:1–6
Q & A with John the Baptist 3:7–20
Jesus' Family Tree 3:21–38

TEMPTATION, REJECTION, AND HEALING 4:1–44

Forty Days in the Wilderness 4:1–13
The Hometown Crowd Turns on Jesus 4:14–30
Jesus Demonstrates His Power 4:31–44

CHOOSING DISCIPLES AND DEFINING DISCIPLINES 5:1–6:11

A Shift of Emphasis 5:1–11
Healing a Leper and a Paralytic 5:12–26
Levi Becomes a Disciple and Throws a Party 5:27–39
Sabbath Issues 6:1–11

A DIFFERENT WAY OF SEEING THE WORLD 6:12–49

Designating the Top Twelve 6:12–16
Blessings and Woes 6:17–26
A Very Different Perspective 6:27–49

SAVING FAITH AND A FAITHFUL SAVIOR 7:1–50

The Faith of a Gentile 7:1–10
Jesus Brings a Widow's Son Back to Life 7:11–17
A Message for John the Baptist 7:18–35
Unusual Insight from a Woman "Sinner" 7:36–50

PARABLES, MIRACLES, AND FAMILY MATTERS   8:1–56
Spiritual Wisdom and the Parable of the Soils   8:1–21
Two Fear-Inspiring Miracles   8:22–39
Two More Amazing Miracles   8:40–56

HIGHS AND LOWS OF MINISTRY   9:1–62
Paired Up and Sent Out   9:1–9
Jesus Feeds Five Thousand   9:10–17
Peter's Confession and Jesus' Transfiguration   9:18–36
Some Shortcomings of the Disciples   9:37–56
Excuses Not to Follow Jesus   9:57–62

SEVENTY-TWO MISSIONARIES, A GOOD SAMARITAN, AND SIBLING RIVALRY   10:1–42
The Seventy-two   10:1–24
The Good Samaritan   10:25–37
Mary and Martha Disagree about What's Important   10:38–42

PRAYER, DEMONS, SIGNS, AND WOES   11:1–54
Lessons on Prayer   11:1–13
Jesus vs. Beelzebub   11:14–36
A Long Series of Woes   11:37–54

WARNINGS AND ASSURANCES   12:1–59
Beware Bad Yeast   12:1–11
Hoarding vs. Trust   12:12–34
Two Contrasting Scenarios   12:35–59

CLEARING UP SOME MISCONCEPTIONS   13:1–35
Why Do Bad Things Happen?   13:1–9
Resentment in Response to a Healing   13:10–17
Two Short Parables   13:18–21
Take Nothing for Granted   13:22–35

BANQUET ETIQUETTE   14:1–35
Dinner Conversation   14:1–14
A Banquet Parable   14:15–24
Seeing Things Through to the Finish   14:25–35

LOST AND FOUND (X 3) — 15:1–32

The Lost Sheep — 15:1–7
The Lost Coin — 15:8–10
The Lost Son — 15:11–32

TWO CHALLENGING PARABLES — 16:1–31

The Shrewd (Dishonest) Steward — 16:1–18
The Rich Man and Lazarus — 16:19–31

FAITH, SERVICE, AND EXPECTATION — 17:1–37

Sin and Forgiveness — 17:1–10
A 10 Percent Return of Gratitude — 17:11–19
Missing the Obvious — 17:20–37

PERSISTENCE AND PENITENCE — 18:1–43

A Persistent Widow vs. an Unjust Judge — 18:1–8
A Pharisee and a Tax Collector — 18:9–14
Little Children and a Rich Ruler — 18:15–34
A Loud Blind Man — 18:35–43

LAST JOURNEY TO JERUSALEM — 19:1–48

A Tax Collector in a Tree — 19:1–10
In the Absence of the Master — 19:11–27
Jesus Arrives at Jerusalem — 19:28–48

QUESTIONS OF AUTHORITY — 20:1–47

By What Authority? — 20:1–18
Taxes and Resurrection — 20:19–40
Son of David or Lord of David? — 20:41–47

THE FUTURE: INDICATIONS AND INSTRUCTIONS — 21:1–38

A Widow's Special Gift — 21:1–4
The Coming Fall of Jerusalem — 21:5–24
Signs and Promises — 21:25–38

BETRAYAL, DENIAL, ARREST, AND ANGUISH — 22:1–65

A Traitor among the Group — 22:1–6
The Last Supper — 22:7–38
Jesus' Arrest — 22:39–65

JESUS' TRIALS AND CRUCIFIXION 22:66–23:56
The Trials 22:66–23:25
Jesus' Crucifixion 23:26–43
Jesus' Death 23:44–56

RESURRECTION AND SECOND CHANCES 24:1–53
The Empty Tomb 24:1–12
Cleopas and His Friend 24:13–35
A Final Training Period 24:36–53

LUKE 1:1–80

A MIRACLE BIRTH (BEFORE JESUS')

Luke's Salutation	1:1–4
Zechariah's Encounter with Gabriel	1:5–25
Jesus' Birth Predicted	1:26–56
John the Baptist Is Born	1:57–80

Setting Up the Section

Luke begins his Gospel of Jesus not with the account of Jesus' birth, but with the announcement of the miraculous, approaching birth of John the Baptist. The Jewish people had been told to expect the coming of Elijah prior to the arrival of their Messiah (Malachi 4:5–6). John the Baptist would fulfill the Elijah role of preparing for and announcing the coming of Jesus (Matthew 11:11–14). And Zechariah and Elizabeth prove to be dedicated and influential parents just as Mary and Joseph were.

📄 1:1–4

LUKE'S SALUTATION

Luke immediately acknowledges that numerous people have been writing about Jesus, but he wants to ensure his readers that they will have a trustworthy account based on eyewitnesses (1:1–2). He personally sets out to investigate carefully before writing. "Most excellent" (1:3 NIV) was a title of respect. While nothing is known of Luke's recipient, Theophilus, he may have been a Roman official who became a Christian. He very well might have been a Gentile, and perhaps even Luke's financial backer. Regardless, since Luke is writing to an individual concerned with the truth of the gospel of Jesus, his Gospel is appropriate for all interested readers.

📄 1:5–25

ZECHARIAH'S ENCOUNTER WITH GABRIEL

The Herod referred to in verse 5 is Herod the Great, who would rule until 4 BC. A number of other Herodian leaders are mentioned in the Bible—all descendants of Herod the Great.

Luke's description of Zechariah and Elizabeth reveals their childlessness as well as the qualities for which they found favor with God, and which were the basis for God's selection of them as the parents of John.

Zechariah (or Zacharias) was not a prominent religious leader, but he was a faithful priest. Unlike later New Testament religious figures who exemplify self-righteousness and completely twist the intent of God's law, Zechariah stands out as someone "upright in the sight of God" (1:6 NIV). His wife Elizabeth is equally righteous. However, their inability to conceive a child may have been seen as a sign of God's displeasure for some offense (an opinion soon to be disproved).

Many priests were available to serve in the temple, so various duties were assigned "by lot" (1:9 NASB). The duties were allocated according to the divisions of priests (1 Chronicles 24). When it came time for the order of Abijah's division to perform the temple duties, Zechariah is chosen for the very high privilege of burning the incense, which he did either in the morning or the evening. This was such a high privilege it might be done by a priest only once in a lifetime. It was a very coveted task. Some of the priests would never have the honor of going into the Holy Place alone and providing fresh incense that burned continually on the special altar before the Most Holy Place. But while Zechariah is there, the angel Gabriel appears to him.

After getting past the initial shock and fear (1:12), Zechariah hears that his wife Elizabeth will soon have a child—a very special child (1:13–17), whose purpose will be to prepare the people for the coming of the Lord. He will be filled with the Holy Spirit from His mother's womb (1:41, 44).

While it's understandable from a human perspective that Zechariah has difficulty believing this amazing thing is happening to him, there were a number of examples of supernatural births in the Old Testament with which he is certainly familiar. Abraham and Sarah had a son in their old age, as did Hannah and the parents of Samson.

Critical Observation

The instructions for John's upbringing as specified by Gabriel are conditions of the Old Testament Nazirite vow (Numbers 6:1–21). Samson and other biblical figures were also Nazirites (Judges 13:2–5).

Zechariah is understandably confused and skeptical because of his and Elizabeth's advanced age. Because of his doubts, and to signify that something special has indeed occurred, Zechariah's ability to speak is temporarily suspended. It will be restored when the promised child is born (1:20).

The people outside the temple are growing restless (1:21). Zechariah is supposed to lead a blessing when he comes out, and it shouldn't have taken very long to light the incense. In addition, the people waiting would be well familiar with the story about the sons of Aaron, who were put to death because they had performed this very function with an improper attitude (Leviticus 10:1–2). Even after Zechariah emerges from the temple, it takes them all a while to determine what has happened. But it doesn't take long for Gabriel's prophecy to come true (1:24–25).

📄 1:26-56

JESUS' BIRTH PREDICTED

Gabriel's announcement to Mary is significant for many reasons, including the declaration that Jesus will be the Messiah who will fulfill God's promise to King David (1:32–33). This promise is recorded in 2 Samuel 7, particularly verses 10–16. Nathan's prophecy from God was that King David's family (of which Jesus would be a descendant) would rule forever.

Mary is quite a contrast to Zechariah in age, gender, and marital status. Yet Gabriel gives her a similar impossible prediction. After her initial surprise at being addressed as "highly favored" (1:28 NIV), she is also confused at how she can be pregnant having never had sex (1:34). This is an additional contrast: Zechariah had been somewhat doubtful, but Mary is only seeking clarification in order to comply with God's message. Mary quickly absorbs what Gabriel is asking her to do, and her response is exemplary (1:38).

Both Mary and Elizabeth are learning that nothing is impossible with God (1:37). Gabriel identifies them as relatives, but their relationship is never explained. We aren't told how much each woman knew of the other's story prior to Mary's visit. Nor do we know exactly when Mary conceived God's child. But no sooner has Mary greeted Elizabeth than Elizabeth's child "leaped in her womb" (1:41 NIV). Filled with the Holy Spirit, Elizabeth immediately recognizes the importance of the child Mary will bear, as well as the significance of the son she is carrying (1:41–45).

We aren't told that Mary, too, is filled with the Holy Spirit, but can assume so. Her song (called the *Magnificat*) reflects a great depth of spiritual understanding. Her praise (1:46–55) is buoyed with numerous Old Testament references and allusions. It begins with her personal expression of humility and expands to reflect God's grace to His chosen people, Israel.

Elizabeth is six months' pregnant when Mary arrives (1:36), and Mary stays three months (1:56). We can speculate that she stays until the birth of John, and then returns home to complete her own pregnancy.

Critical Observation

Luke tends to notice and record creative expression more than other Gospel writers. He alone recorded Elizabeth's Spirit-inspired proclamation (1:42–45). He also included several songs or canticles.

Mary	1:46–55 "The Magnificat," Latin for "magnify," from Mary's opening words.
Zechariah	1:68–79 Called "The Benedictus," which is Latin meaning "blessed."
Angelic chorus	2:14 Called "Gloria in Excelsis," Latin for "Glory to God."
Simeon	2:29–32 Called the "Nunc Dimittis" because these are the first two words of the Latin translation of the prayer. It translates into English as "now depart."

📖 1:57–80

JOHN THE BAPTIST IS BORN

When the time comes for Elizabeth to have her baby, neighbors and relatives gather (1:57–58). But a conflict arises at the baby's circumcision because the crowd of supporters assumes the child will be named after Zechariah. The name, however, has already been assigned by Gabriel (1:13), which Elizabeth knows. But the others resist her and go to Zechariah, who asks for a writing tablet. As soon as he gives written confirmation that the child's name will be John (1:63), he regains his speech and immediately begins praising God.

In first-century Middle East culture, being named after a father or other family member indicated intent to follow in his steps. But John will not become a priest like Zechariah. He will have his own distinct ministry.

Luke also notes that these very important events are not first announced to the religious elite of the day, or even in the temple in Jerusalem. The first to hear of the arrival of the kingdom of God (and to respond in awe) are the simple people in the hill country (1:65). The announcement foreshadows the later ministries of Jesus and John, who come not to the healthy and the righteous, but to the sick and to sinners (Matthew 9:12–13).

As Elizabeth and Mary had done previously, Zechariah uses his renewed power of speech to praise God. His Spirit-inspired proclamation (1:67–79) is more personal and prophetic than Mary's, laying out John's purpose in life as well as his relationship with Jesus. Yet John's individual ministry is seen in the context of the nation of Israel.

Luke's concluding statement for this account (1:80) is short, but summarizes about thirty years of John's life. Zechariah's and Elizabeth's child will grow not only physically, but will also become strong in his spirit. His strength will be developed in solitude for eventual use in public ministry.

Take It Home

In light of the significant events taking place in this passage, the participants all seemed to prepare for their roles in solitude. Mary and Elizabeth went into seclusion. Zechariah found solitude in silence. And John went into the wilderness. To what extent is solitude a part of your regular spiritual growth? Do you make time to be alone with God, or is most of your spiritual commitment tied to fellowship and interaction with others? Are you satisfied with your current balance of time devoted solely to God and time devoted to others?

LUKE 2:1–52

THE ARRIVAL OF THE MESSIAH

The Birth of Jesus   2:1–20
The Infant Jesus at the Temple   2:21–40
The Boy Jesus at the Temple   2:41–52

Setting Up the Section

Luke interweaves the birth stories of Jesus and John the Baptist. In the previous passage he provided the angelic foretelling of both miraculous births, and provided the story of John's birth. In this passage, he moves on to the details of Jesus' birth and early life.

Luke 2 has three major sections. Verses 1–20 depict the birth of Jesus and the worship and witness of the shepherds. Verses 21–40 feature an account of the presentation of Jesus at Jerusalem, and the inspired testimony of Simeon and Anna. Verses 41–52 describe Jesus' visit to the temple, His Father's house, busy with His Father's business.

📖 2:1–20

THE BIRTH OF JESUS

The details of Jesus' birth are surprisingly scarce in the Bible. Mark and John ignore them altogether. Matthew provides a few stories surrounding the birth. Luke is the only Gospel writer to cover the birth itself.

Demystifying Luke

Remember that Luke's recipient, Theophilus, could have been a Roman official. The term "most excellent," which Luke uses in chapter 1 (1:3 NIV), is also used by Luke three times in Acts (23:26; 24:3; 26:25), each time in reference to a political official of high standing. While we may care little that Quirinius was governor of Syria (2:2), this fact would have been significant to Theophilus. Luke was providing facts that showed Theophilus that faith in Jesus had historical validity—something not true of the other "gods" of the time.

The census (2:1–3) not only inconveniently forced people to their hometowns; it was also a painful reminder that the Jewish people were under the rule of a pagan power. Yet it serves to send Mary and Joseph to Bethlehem (2:4–5), the place where the prophet Micah had long ago predicted the Jewish Messiah was to be born (Micah 5:2). The journey from Nazareth to Bethlehem is more than sixty miles and will take at least three days.

Luke properly points out that Joseph and Mary are "pledged to be married" (2:5 NIV) at this point. Matthew calls them husband and wife (Matthew 1:19, 24)—titles used as soon as an engagement was formally announced. But to ensure the purity of the bride, the engagement was followed by a one-year period of abstinence and waiting. At the end of the year, the marriage ceremony would be held, the relationship consummated, and the couple would begin living together. When Mary is found to be pregnant during the waiting period, Joseph's initial instinct is to get a quiet divorce. But after being informed by an angel what is happening, Joseph breaks tradition and takes Mary into his home. However, the official consummation and beginning of their marriage will not take place until after the birth of Jesus (Matthew 1:18–25).

Much of the imagery that has become a part of the Christmas and Nativity tradition has been supplied by our filling in the gaps of Luke's account. What we are told is that there is not room in the inn. In this case, the word *inn* probably refers to a guest room. It was the custom of the day for the Jews of Jerusalem to have enough guest rooms to accommodate their guests. Joseph and Mary must have expected this would be the case, but when they arrive in Bethlehem, such accommodations aren't available.

Joseph and Mary's not having a place to stay results in the baby Jesus being wrapped in rags or strips of cloth and placed in a cattle feeding trough for a crib (2:6–7). We do not know if Jesus is born in a stable or in a cave. The feeding trough could have been borrowed, so if the baby may have been born under the stars. Mary may have preferred the privacy. The trough would have provided a soft place for the baby to sleep and the strips of cloth, wrapped around the child, would have kept his arms and legs tucked in and kept the cold out, especially if the family was camped in the open, out in the elements. In addition, the baby being wrapped in cloths and lying in a manger would be a sign for the shepherds (2:12).

The Egyptians in the days of the Old Testament looked down on shepherds (Genesis 46:33–34), yet Israelite leaders such as David and Moses were shepherds. God Himself is described as a shepherd. The shepherds described by Luke seem to be godly men—men who are looking for the coming of Israel's Messiah. All the others of those who are directly informed of the birth of the Messiah in Matthew and Luke are described as godly people, and so it seems to be true of the shepherds as well. After all, news of His coming would not be good news (2:10) unless they were seeking Him. The haste of these shepherds to the place of Christ's birth (2:15–16) also testifies to their spiritual preparedness and eagerness for the coming of the Messiah.

To these humble shepherds the angel of God appears in a blaze of glory, which causes them to be greatly frightened (2:9). The angel assures them that he brings them good news, and tells them of the birth of the Messiah. This is to be the cause of joy for all the people—all the nations, and not just Israel, would benefit from His birth. Suddenly, the angel is joined by a host, as a divine confirmation of the angel's announcement.

The angel has promised a sign to the shepherds—they will find the child wrapped in strips of cloth and lying in a cattle feeding trough (2:12). The sign is not designed to convince the shepherds of the truth of the angelic announcement. Surely the splendor of the angel, compounded by that of the heavenly host, is convincing enough. This sign is for the purpose of identification. The way that they will recognize God's Messiah is by His swaddling clothes and by His unusual crib. No other child will be found in such a setting.

These signs do even more than simply identify Jesus. They allow Him to identify with the shepherds. One of the names of Messiah is Emmanuel, which means "God with us." The circumstances of our Lord's birth uniquely identify the Lord Jesus with the shepherds. The Lord seemingly has no roof over His head, no house to dwell in. Neither do the shepherds, who, we are told, sleep under the stars as they care for their flocks (2:8). Jesus is poor and of no reputation, as are they. And Jesus is to be both the sacrificial Lamb of God (see Isaiah 53:4–6; John 1:29) and the Good Shepherd (Psalm 23:1; Ezekiel 34:23; John 10:14).

The shepherds' arrival at the manger (2:16) must have been comforting for Mary and Joseph. Both have been told by their own angelic messengers about the significance of the child they will parent, but surely it is reassuring in this faraway place to get confirmation from other sources. And after seeing Jesus, the shepherds spread the word about what they have been told, amazing all who hear them (2:17–20).

📄 2:21–40

THE INFANT JESUS AT THE TEMPLE

Several ceremonies were required after the birth of a child.

1) The circumcision was to take place the eighth day after the birth of a son (Leviticus 12:3) because the mother would be ceremonially unclean for seven days after giving birth. The child was usually assigned a name at this time.
2) A second ceremony was the presentation and consecration of a firstborn son (Exodus 13:1–2, 12).
3) Then there was the purification of the mother, celebrated forty days after the birth of a son or eighty days after having a daughter (Leviticus 12:1–5).

It is the second ceremony, the presentation of Jesus at the temple, which is most prominent in Luke's account (2:27). It is on this occasion that Simeon and Anna appear to attest and announce that the baby Jesus is God's Messiah, the Savior of the world.

Critical Observation

Jesus' circumcision is not prominent in this passage, but it is noteworthy. First, this record attests to the fact that the parents of our Lord did everything according to the Law (2:39). Second, the circumcision of Christ parallels that of John, described earlier (1:59–79). Finally, it was at the circumcision of Christ that His name was formally given.

Jesus' name was predetermined and had been announced by Gabriel (Matthew 1:21; Luke 1:31). The Hebrew form of the name was Jeshua, derived by combining two root words that meant "the Lord" and "to save." So the name *Jesus* means "the Lord is salvation."

During His presentation, the identity and significance of Jesus is twice more confirmed. The first to praise Jesus is an old man named Simeon, who has been told by the Holy Spirit that he will not die before he has seen the Christ (2:26). The only things we are told about Simeon are those which matter most to God—things pertaining to his faith, his character, and his relationship with God. We are told that Simeon is righteous and devout (2:25), which speaks of his personal walk with God and his integrity. He is a man of faith and hope, for he looked for the restoration of Israel through the coming of the Messiah. Finally, Simeon is a man who is filled by the Holy Spirit. It is the Holy Spirit who has revealed to Simeon that he will not die until he has seen the Messiah (2:26). It is also the Holy Spirit that directs Simeon to the temple on the particular day that Jesus' parents bring Him to be presented to the Lord. Finally, in some unspecified way, it is the Spirit of God who reveals to Simeon that this child is indeed the Messiah.

Recognizing Jesus to be the Messiah, this elderly man takes the child in his arms and blesses God. He reveals that He will become a light of revelation to the Gentiles and glory for Israel (2:32). He also is the first to acknowledge the suffering that will come to Jesus and those connected to Him (2:34–35).

Up to this point in Luke's Gospel, all of the inspired utterances pertaining to the Lord Jesus have been very positive, speaking with reference to His ruling on David's throne, setting right the things that are wrong, and bringing peace and salvation to people. But now Simeon unveils the other side of the story, which is also a part of the Old Testament prophecies, such as those of Psalm 22 or Isaiah 53—prophecies of the rejection, crucifixion, and death of the Messiah. More pointedly, Simeon's words prepare Mary for the grief she must suffer, as the rejection of Her Son by men will cause her to witness His death on the cross.

Simeon's revelations are confirmed by Anna, an eighty-four-year-old prophetess who never leaves the temple. While we are told less about what she actually says, we are given more information about her background than Simeon's. Anna is of the tribe of Asher, one of the ten lost tribes of Israel, which were scattered in the Assyrian captivity. She is also a prophetess. She was married for seven years before her husband died, and has lived the rest of her life as a widow. Day and night she is in the temple praying and fasting. She gives thanks to God and speaks of Jesus' role in the redemption of Jerusalem (2:38).

The inspired utterances of Simeon and Anna completely overshadow the ceremony of Christ's presentation. The occasion for the appearance of our Lord at the temple is His presentation, but nothing is actually said about this ceremony. We have no record of the ritual, nor are we given the names of any of the priests involved in the ceremony. We are only told of Simeon and Anna and of their proclamations. It is not the ceremony itself, the ritual of the presentation of Jesus, which is most important, but the proclamation of these two saints.

📄 **2:41–52**

THE BOY JESUS AT THE TEMPLE

Luke's next story fast-forwards twelve years to the only inspired, biblically recorded incident in the life of Jesus between His birth and His adult ministry. After an annual trip to Jerusalem to celebrate Passover, Jesus is found missing on the return trip home to Nazareth. His parents backtrack to Jerusalem and finally find Him in the temple with the teachers, listening and asking questions (2:46).

After a rebuke by His frustrated mother, Luke provides the earliest known words of Jesus: "Why were you searching for me? . . . Didn't you know I had to be in my Father's house?" (2:49 NIV). Or as some translations render it, "Did you not know that I must be about My Father's business?" (NKJV).

Although Jesus' parents don't understand what He means, Jesus is already preparing Himself for His adult mission. At thirteen Jewish males joined the adult community, and Jesus has an opportunity at the temple to learn things His parents can't teach Him. (This is the last time Joseph is mentioned in Jesus' life.)

This story is bracketed by two separate notations about the growth of Jesus (2:40, 52). Just as all humans do, Jesus went through a growth process—not just physically, but spiritually, intellectually, and relationally as well. And even though Jesus had made His point at the temple, He returns with His parents to Nazareth and is obedient to them (2:51).

Take It Home

When people put God first in their lives, they can expect benefits—and occasional problems. Mary and Joseph had the unique privilege of rearing the Savior of the world, but they found themselves homeless in Bethlehem and confused twelve years later in Jerusalem. And even today, those who choose to follow God are sometimes left without explanations for bad events in their lives. Have you experienced problems or disappointments as a believer? If so, how do you deal with them?

LUKE 3:1–38

TWO MINISTRIES BEGIN

The Voice of One Calling in the Desert	3:1–6
Q & A with John the Baptist	3:7–20
Jesus' Family Tree	3:21–38

Setting Up the Section

The first four chapters of Luke's Gospel intertwine the accounts of the birth of both John and Jesus, along with significant childhood events. Thus, when we come to the ministry of John the Baptist in chapter 3, we are finding John in the spotlight, as he has been before, as the forerunner of the Messiah. In fact, all four Gospels begin Jesus' public ministry with the ministry of John the Baptist.

3:1–6

THE VOICE OF ONE CALLING IN THE DESERT

Luke tells us that Jesus is about thirty years old when He begins His public ministry (3:23), and John the Baptist precedes Him. So while John has an important calling and a bold, emphatic message, he is by no means old. He apparently shows much maturity for a young man.

There is not one instance in the Gospels where we are told that John performs a miracle. John does not heal people, like our Lord, so far as the text informs us. Those people who witnessed the ministry of Jesus, in the very place where John had formerly preached and baptized, testified that John never performed signs (John 10:41). This means that it is only John's preaching that attracts the crowds. He must have been some preacher. (No doubt it was the messianic nature of his message that caused such excitement.) John's ministry seems to give hope of the coming of the kingdom, as it is intended to do (3:15–17).

Several of the names Luke mentions at the opening of chapter 3—Pontius Pilate, Herod, Philip, Annas, and Caiaphas—serve to ground Jesus' ministry in actual historical events (3:1–2).

Some people consider John the Baptist the last of the Old Testament prophets. Luke associates the ministry of John with Isaiah's prophecy of the voice in the wilderness, preparing the way for the Lord (3:4–6). He extends the quotation to include Isaiah 40:5—beyond what Matthew and Mark include—which states that all humanity will see God's salvation. This passage is especially significant from Luke's Gentile perspective because it foretold not just the coming of Israel's deliverer, but someone who will enable all humankind to see God's salvation (3:6), which is a key theme for Luke.

Like the prophets of old, John preaches a message of repentance that includes a call to both personal response and responsibility.

📄 3:7–20

Q & A WITH JOHN THE BAPTIST

John stays in remote areas all around the Jordan River (3:3). He doesn't seek out the leadership of the nation or the elite population segments; instead, all kinds of people go out to hear him.

Other Gospel writers provide more complete physical descriptions of John (Matthew 3:4; Mark 1:6) in addition to the essence of his message. But Luke alone shares some of the interaction between John and various groups in his audience.

Surrounded by soldiers, tax collectors, and others, John speaks frankly. Addressing them as poisonous snakes (3:7), he talks of coming wrath and the need for repentance. He also tells the Jewish people in the crowd that they can't count on their national heritage (having "Abraham as our father" [3:8 NIV]) to ensure God's favor. Rather, they are to repent and produce good fruit (3:7–9).

When pressed for specifics, John's responses are simple and straightforward. People with extra food and possessions are to share with those who have none. Tax collectors are to be honest and not collect more money than they are due. Soldiers are instructed to be content with their pay and stop extorting money or falsely accusing people (3:10–14).

Critical Observation

Luke's Gospel will continue to address the proper use of material goods. Many of the parables of Jesus that Luke chose to include in his writing will center on the subject of money and/or wealth.

The crowds seem to take John's message to heart. In fact, John's presentation is so impressive that they are hoping to hear that he is the Messiah (Christ) they have been told to expect. But John makes it quite clear that there will be no mistaking the two (3:15–16). John may have seemed impressive, but Jesus will be more powerful. John will baptize with water, Jesus with the Holy Spirit and fire. Jesus will separate the useful wheat—those with true faith—from the worthless chaff and burn up the chaff (3:17).

Demystifying Luke

A "winnowing fork" (3:17 NIV) was a shovel-like tool used to toss grain into the air so the outer chaff would either fall and be burned or blow away in the wind and only the good wheat would remain. This was a familiar process in an agrarian community of the first century.

John's message may sound harsh to modern ears, yet it was good news for his listeners. However, his boldness will later lead to his arrest and death (Matthew 14:3–12; Luke 3:19–20).

📄 **3:21–38**

JESUS' FAMILY TREE

Although John has publicly declared his unworthiness to even untie the thongs of Jesus' sandals (3:16)—a task designated for the lowest of slaves—Jesus still acknowledges John's ministry and comes to him to be baptized. All four Gospels include Jesus' baptism by John, but only Luke notes that Jesus is praying when heaven opens and the Holy Spirit descends on Him in the form of a dove (3:21–22).

When God's voice from heaven calls Jesus His Son (3:22), the words suggest more than just a Father/Son relationship. As God established kings for Israel in the Old Testament, He invites them into a relationship of sonship (2 Samuel 7:14; Psalm 2:6–12). So here at Jesus' baptism, God designates Jesus as the King of Israel, confirming what Gabriel had told Mary prior to Jesus' birth (1:31–33). And the additional comment, God's approval of Jesus, calls to mind Isaiah 42:1–4, the prophetic foretelling of the coming servant of the Lord who brings God delight.

Verses 23–38 contain Luke's genealogy of Jesus. Matthew provides one as well (Matthew 1:1–16), but the two versions have considerable differences. One obvious distinction is that Matthew begins with Abraham and tracks the line of descent to Jesus—clearly something that would interest Jewish readers. Luke begins with Jesus and goes backward through history to Adam, suggesting a more Gentile-friendly perspective that Jesus' significance was for the entire human race and not just the Hebrew people. In addition, the difference in placement should be noted. Matthew began his Gospel with Jesus' genealogy—His "credentials." Luke waited until he introduced the public ministry of Jesus, placing the genealogy right between Jesus' baptism and His temptation. Another significant difference is that Matthew traces the royal line through David's son Solomon while Luke traces it through David's son Nathan.

Critical Observation

The variations in names used in Luke's version of Jesus' genealogy compared to Matthew's suggest that Matthew may have been tracing the kingly line of Christ through His father, Joseph, while Luke recorded the ancestors of Jesus through His mother, Mary.

The baptism of Christ identifies Christ as Israel's king, and demonstrates that He has the Father's approval and the Spirit's anointing. The genealogy shows that our Lord has the right lineage—that He is indeed of the "throne of David." The temptation proves that our Lord has the godly character to reign. In every way, Luke shows Him to be qualified for the task He has been given.

Take It Home

Luke recorded the specific response of John the Baptist when tax collectors and soldiers asked what they should do in order to "produce fruit in keeping with repentance" (3:8 NIV; 3:10–14).

- To the crowd, he said to share its resources.
- To the tax collectors, he said to be honest and just.
- To the soldiers, he said to not take advantage of their power and to be content with their pay.

Suppose someone from your own profession had been there and asked the same question. What do you think John would have told them?

LUKE 4:1–44

TEMPTATION, REJECTION, AND HEALING

Forty Days in the Wilderness   4:1–13
The Hometown Crowd Turns on Jesus   4:14–30
Jesus Demonstrates His Power   4:31–44

Setting Up the Section

After Jesus' baptism (3:21–22), He is tempted by the devil for a period of forty days. There are several reasons why the temptation accounts are of importance to us. From the standpoint of Jesus' ministry and calling, His mission is contingent upon His victory over every temptation of Satan. Also, by studying the temptation of our Lord by Satan, we learn a great deal about our adversary, Satan, and the means by which we can withstand his attacks.

Afterward Jesus begins a public ministry of teaching and healing, and quickly becomes a well-known and popular figure...except in Nazareth, where He had been raised.

📄 4:1–13

FORTY DAYS IN THE WILDERNESS

Jesus' baptism may have been a high point in His life, with the descent of the Holy Spirit and the voice of His heavenly Father expressing His love and approval (3:21–22). Yet the Spirit immediately leads Jesus into the wilderness to be tempted. It seems safe to presume that these temptations are a barrage by the devil to strike when He is the weakest.

Satan's first temptation appeals to Jesus' physical hunger. After forty days with nothing to eat, Jesus would be more than just hungry. A physical body deprived of food that long, apart from divine intervention, would be weakened to the point of near death. Yet Satan's taunt to turn a stone into bread (4:3) is not effective. We know from Matthew that John the Baptist subsisted in the wilderness on locusts and wild honey (Matthew 3:4) and from Mark that wild animals were in the wilderness (Mark 1:13). So Jesus could find food, but He isn't there to eat, as indicated in His response (4:4).

Jesus had a need for food as well as the power to meet that need. While many people would consider that a formula to immediately satisfy the need, Jesus chooses to remain focused on God rather than fulfill His own desire at the moment.

Critical Observation

Why was Jesus led to be tempted in this passage when He later taught His disciples to pray, "lead us not into temptation" (Matthew 6:13 NIV)? The word *temptation* can be used in two very different senses. One is clearly a solicitation to sin—which is always the case with Satan. But from God's point of view, a better word is *test*, which is an opportunity for someone to be proven righteous. So Abraham was tested when told to offer Isaac (Genesis 22:1–2), and Job was similarly tested (Job 1–2). Although Satan attempted a full-out temptation of Jesus in the wilderness, from God's point of view it was a test (which He passed with flying colors).

The devil's second temptation is an offer of power and authority as he parades all the kingdoms of the world before Jesus in an instant (4:5–7). Jesus and Paul both recognized Satan as the ruler of this world in the sense that he dominates fallen human beings through the power of sin and death (John 12:31–32; 16:11; 2 Corinthians 4:3–4; Ephesians 6:12). The devil may influence kings and kingdoms, yet he is not in control. Jesus is the One who is in sovereign control of history. God could not foretell the future if He did not control it. So Jesus' second response (4:8) is a reminder to keep God foremost in one's thoughts.

Satan's third temptation (4:9–11) reveals his acknowledgement of Jesus as the Son of God. For anyone else, a leap off the pinnacle of the temple would be certain suicide. Jesus has already twice used scripture to refute temptation (Deuteronomy 6:13; 8:3), so this time the devil uses scripture, perhaps attempting to enhance his proposition (Psalm 91:11–12). But Psalm 91 was not a promise of protection for Israel's Messiah. Rather, it was a promise of protection from God's wrath for all who take refuge in God. The devil's motive may be to disqualify Jesus as Messiah, weaken His faith and trust in God, bring about a premature introduction of Jesus as Messiah, or maybe even kill Him. Regardless of his intent, Jesus curtly rejects his proposal with a third quotation from scripture (4:12; Deuteronomy 6:16).

It would be a mistake to assume that Satan's words should be accepted at face value. Scripture calls him the father of lies (John 8:44). It is not at all certain that just because Satan claims to possess all the kingdoms of the world (4:5–6) that he really does have the right to offer them to Christ. Satan is always offering others that which he does not possess. For example, he encouraged Adam and Eve to help themselves to the forbidden fruit of the tree of the knowledge of good and evil and thus to a new level of knowledge. Our Lord offers people what He possesses, what He has purchased (for instance, salvation by His blood), but Satan offers what is not his.

Having failed after trying his best, the devil leaves Jesus alone. But he isn't finished with his temptation. He is merely waiting for another opportunity (4:13).

Demystifying Luke

Luke tells us Jesus' temptation lasted forty days, often a significant number in scriptural accounts. Perhaps most significant, it was the same number of years that the Israelites wandered in the wilderness, a time of testing after their lack of faith to enter the promised land.

Jesus' temptation also drew a significant analogy to the temptation of Adam and Eve in the garden. In the New Testament Jesus is described as the second Adam. Just as Adam was tempted and fell, Jesus was tempted and stood strong. In many ways, Jesus came to undo what Adam did. This parallel is highlighted even more in the fact that Luke refers to Adam as the son of God (3:38) and Satan confronts Jesus as the Son of God (4:3).

📄 4:14–30

THE HOMETOWN CROWD TURNS ON JESUS

It is clear that Jesus has become a much talked about personality (4:14–15). When He decides to return to Nazareth, the town where He grew up, He goes to the synagogue on the Sabbath. There He is called on to read from the book of Isaiah, and the passage is a prophecy of the Messiah who will have a preaching and healing ministry (4:16–19; Isaiah 61:1–2). When He finishes reading, He then declares that He is fulfilling the scripture (4:21). In other words, Jesus is claiming to be Israel's Messiah.

Isaiah 61 was a significant passage for the people to hear from Jesus. They viewed themselves as the poor and oppressed that God was promising to bless with healing and deliverance. First, the people respond very positively to Jesus' claim. Luke informs us that the people are amazed at what Jesus says (4:22). Unfortunately, the warm response to Jesus' words is the result of a distorted concept of the Messiah.

Jesus points out that if His ministry were correctly understood, He would be rejected like all the other prophets of Israel's history. Prophets were not received by Israel, but spurned, persecuted, and even killed, and this without exception (1 Kings 19:10; Jeremiah 35:15; 44:4–5; Acts 7:52). Jesus not only cites the principle that Israel's prophets were never honored by their own people, He shows that the Gentiles received blessings from the prophets (4:24–27). He cites the case of Elijah's stay with the Gentile widow at Zarephath (1 Kings 17:9) and of the healing of Naaman, the Syrian, a military leader of the army that was successfully attacking Israel (2 Kings 5:1–14).

In both cases, the prophet of Israel brought blessings to Gentiles, which the Jews, his own people, did not receive. It is this key point that makes the people of Nazareth furious. They, like the Jews later described by Luke in the book of Acts (13:46, 50; 22:21–22), violently react to Jesus' words. There is not even an attempt to "sanctify" their actions by trumping up false charges, which is what will happen at His trial and crucifixion. Anyone who speaks of the blessing of the Gentiles instead of the Jews is a traitor!

The crowd rushes Jesus from the synagogue and presses Him toward the precipice of a nearby cliff, attempting to force Him to fall to His death. Jesus does not escape by fleeing, or by "taking a back way out." Instead, He walks through the midst of His opponents (4:30). Just as the waters of the Red Sea parted to allow Moses and God's people to pass through, so the angry crowd parts to allow Jesus to pass through its midst, unharmed, untouched. This is the one and only miracle that this crowd will witness.

There is a similar incident recorded by Matthew and Mark that many scholars consider to be descriptions of the same event (Matthew 13:53–58 and Mark 6:1–6).

Demystifying Luke

Luke's prominently Gentile audience would certainly have been encouraged by this account of Jesus. Some must have wondered, How can a Jewish Messiah, dying in fulfillment of Jewish scriptures, obtain salvation for a Gentile? Yet centuries before, God had promised Abraham that "all peoples on earth will be blessed through you" (Genesis 12:3 NIV). The Jews would initially reject Jesus, and the Gentiles would be included in God's invitation of salvation to all people.

📄 4:31–44

JESUS DEMONSTRATES HIS POWER

Jesus moves on to Capernaum where, as in Nazareth, He begins to teach. The people in the synagogue are amazed at His teaching. (There was a similar reaction in Matthew's Gospel, immediately after Jesus had delivered the "Sermon on the Mount" [Matthew 7:28–29].) What is it that distinguished Jesus' teaching from that of the scribes and Pharisees, and made His teaching authoritative, when their teaching was not? The difference does not seem to be a matter of style, so much as of substance. Jesus taught with personal authority. Hearing Him speak would have been more like hearing from someone who authored the book, rather than someone who had simply read the book.

Jesus is soon interrupted by a man with an evil spirit. The demon controls the man's voice, and screams out at Jesus in a loud and disruptive manner. Even so, the evil spirit recognizes Jesus' identity and purpose (4:33–34). With a stern rebuke, Jesus drives the demon from the man and he is not harmed. Between Jesus' teaching and power, news about Him spreads quickly (4:36–37).

Later that day Jesus gives a command to heal the fever of Peter's mother-in-law, allowing her to immediately get up and attend to her guests (4:39). And when the sun goes down, ending the Sabbath, crowds of sick and possessed people seek Him out and He heals them.

Early the next morning Jesus goes to a solitary place, yet the people keep coming. They desperately want Him to stay in Capernaum, but Jesus is committed to a broader teaching ministry to all the villages of Galilee. They want to see miracles, but He has come to proclaim the kingdom of God. The healings and exorcisms are not an end in themselves, but are meant to demonstrate the powerful arrival of the kingdom of God—a message that everyone needs to hear. His fellow townspeople in Nazareth are not interested in this message and even those in Capernaum seem more interested in physical healing than in Jesus' proclamation of the kingdom. So Jesus moves on.

Take It Home

In some of the most stressful conditions possible, Jesus withstood Satan's strongest temptations. And He did so in a manner available to all of us: He simply quoted scripture. Each of His responses to the devil came directly from our Old Testament.

Jesus offers us a model to follow in so many ways. As we observe those who responded to Him, and the wide breadth of their responses, it leaves us examining how we respond to God's presence in our own lives. Do we rejoice? Do we misunderstand? Do we obey?

LUKE 5:1–6:11

CHOOSING DISCIPLES AND DEFINING DISCIPLINES

A Shift of Emphasis	5:1–11
Healing a Leper and a Paralytic	5:12–26
Levi Becomes a Disciple and Throws a Party	5:27–39
Sabbath Issues	6:1–11

Setting Up the Section

If Luke chapter 4 focused on the ministry of Jesus to the masses, chapter 5 begins to focus on the ministry of Jesus with respect to the leadership of Israel. So far in Luke's account, Jesus has been portrayed as a solitary teacher moving from place to place, teaching in the synagogues. In this passage He begins to call disciples to travel with Him in His ministry of teaching and healing. But when He and His disciples don't conform to established norms, they soon encounter opposition.

📄 5:1–11

A SHIFT OF EMPHASIS

Luke's reference to the "Lake of Gennesaret" (5:1 NIV) is what other Gospel writers usually call the Sea of Galilee. With a crowd of people pressing around Jesus at the water's edge, He borrows Peter's boat so He can sit down and teach. When He finishes, He tells Peter to sail out to deep water and drop the nets. Peter doesn't really want to, but does as Jesus instructed.

Critical Observation

Was this Jesus' first encounter with Peter, Andrew, James, and John? Not likely. His progressive calling of the disciples seems to roughly follow this sequence:

1) At the suggestion of John the Baptist, some of his disciples begin to follow Jesus (John 1:36–51).

2) Jesus calls Peter, Andrew, James, and John to follow Him, which they begin to do as they continue their fishing business (Matthew 4:18–22).

3) After the miraculous event in this account, the four fishermen/disciples leave their boats to follow Jesus full time (Luke 5:1–11).

4) Jesus calls Levi, also known as Matthew (Luke 5:27–28).

5) Jesus calls the rest of the Twelve, but the specifics are not recorded in the Gospels.

6) Others wish to follow Jesus, but the cost of discipleship is high (Matthew 8:18–22).

7) Jesus spends a night in prayer prior to appointing twelve disciples as His apostles (Luke 6:12–16).

Peter's words in verse 5 indicate that he and his partners are tired from working all night. Besides that, they have just finished washing their nets. They will have to do it all over again. Also, Peter indicates that their efforts had been futile. Night was the best time to fish. If they had not caught anything at night, why in the world should they catch anything in the daytime, the worst possible time to fish? In addition, there seems to be a hint of irritation here. Jesus' order could have certainly seemed naive.

Yet when Peter's obedience results in a miraculous catch of fish that almost sinks two boats, he humbly acknowledges his sinfulness (5:6–8). Peter thought he was the expert, but now sees that Jesus is Lord of the sea as well. Peter doubted that they would make a great catch, and feared that his efforts would be wasted. Now he sees his Lord's sovereignty and his own sin.

Jesus' response to Peter can seem perplexing. Peter confesses his sinfulness. Why does Jesus tell him not to be afraid (5:10)? Peter is probably fearful because he not only recognizes his own sin but also the Lord's righteousness. His words reveal his awareness of Jesus' greatness.

Ultimately the Lord's provision for Peter's sin is even more abundant than His provision of fish. That provision will be made at the cross of Calvary, where He will die in the sinner's place. Communion and intimacy with God is abundantly provided by the Lord's sacrificial death. It is too early for Peter to know about this, and so he is simply assured, without any specific details being given.

At this point Peter, Andrew, James, and John leave their boats behind to follow Jesus full time. Before calling them to catch people (5:10), Jesus lets them experience every fisherman's dream—a catch of a lifetime. Yet their most significant accomplishments lay ahead.

Take It Home

It's important to remember this text is not teaching that those who are most committed to Christ must leave their secular jobs to be His disciples. The disciples left their jobs, but that was necessary in order for them to be with Jesus while He was physically present on the earth.

After His resurrection and ascension, Jesus is present with all of us through His Holy Spirit. Our calling goes deeper than our physical location or occupation. While we may not need to relocate to be in His presence, we are called—like the disciples—to leave behind all of our other allegiances and follow Him completely in every situation.

📄 **5:12–26**

HEALING A LEPER AND A PARALYTIC

The term *leprosy* could include a number of different skin diseases, but Luke (a doctor) notes that one particular man who approaches Jesus (5:12) is covered with the disease. Normally, a person in this condition would have no contact with those who were "clean" or not infected. Yet Jesus touches the man before healing him (5:13). Jesus is doing several significant things here.

1) He is touching a leper before he is cleansed, showing that He is not tainted by the uncleanness of others, but rather makes unclean people clean.
2) He is instantly producing physical healing of a very serious disorder.
3) He is not only healing the man, but pronouncing him to be cleansed, which was the role of the priest as described in Leviticus 13–14.

Jesus did not always explain His motives. But in this case, by telling the healed leper to show himself to the priests, it is to be a testimony to them (5:14). Jesus also orders the man not to tell anyone else, but how does a healed leper explain his instantaneous recovery without giving credit to the man who helped him? So news about Jesus spreads even more (5:15).

Jesus keeps trying to seek out solitary places where He can pray (5:16). Jesus' retreat for prayer is an expression of His dependence upon the Father. It puts His successes in perspective, for He does everything in obedience to the Father's will and in the power of His Spirit (4:14). These times keep Jesus' perspective and priorities in line with those of the Father.

Jesus is beginning to attract curious religious leaders who critique what He says. This is the case once when He is speaking in a home where four men bring a paralytic to be healed (5:18–19). The house is overflowing with people, including many Pharisees (5:17). Luke includes a detail about these Pharisees—they are sitting, even in a packed room with standing room only. This may be because the sitting position is the position of authority for the teacher. A teacher in those days did not stand to teach; he sat to teach (4:20–21). For these teachers to stand may seem like a concession to Jesus' authority.

The scene might have been a bit comical with the crowd of religious leaders– falling debris and the sudden appearance of a man on a suspended pallet (5:18–19). But it is no joke to Jesus, who sees the faith of the man's friends and tells him, "Friend, your sins are forgiven" (5:20 NIV).

Jesus' response is not what any one of them really want to hear. The man's friends are surely expecting a healing for their friend after all their work and ingenuity. Even more, the Pharisees are taken aback that Jesus would claim to forgive sins. It is blasphemy to them (5:21). Forgiveness of sins is something that only God can do. Thus, to tell a man his sins are forgiven is to claim to be God.

But Jesus knows what they are thinking. He asks which is easier, to heal or to forgive (5:23). There is no visible proof that sins have been forgiven. One can claim that ability without having to prove it. But to command a paralyzed man to walk–the proof is visible. Jesus has set up this circumstance to show that He has both the power to forgive sins and to make the paralyzed walk (5:25–26).

📄 **5:27–39**

LEVI BECOMES A DISCIPLE AND THROWS A PARTY

Luke says little about Jesus' call of Levi (referred to later in 6:15 as Matthew). Jesus calls Levi from his tax booth to follow, and Levi gets up and goes (5:27–28).

Demystifying Luke

Tax collectors such as Levi were not only often dishonest, but they were a painful reminder of the fact that Israel was not a free nation, but subject to Roman rule and authority.

Luke has already revealed one of the evils of which many tax collectors were guilty when he recorded what John the Baptist told the tax-gatherers who came to be baptized—don't collect more than you've been ordered (3:12–13). Thus, at the least we know that many tax collectors were guilty of abusing their position by using the power of the state to charge excessive taxes and keep the profits from their evil deeds. Luke himself will later inform us of one instance in which a sinful tax collector (Zacchaeus) repents and makes restitution for his misconduct (19:1–10).

Since nothing is said of Levi's desire to make restitution for previous dishonesty (as will be the case with Zacchaeus [19:1–10]), perhaps he is an upright and honest person—and maybe that is why Jesus chooses him.

To celebrate, Levi hosts a banquet for Jesus, and the guest list includes both Pharisees and fellow tax collectors. Luke tells us that the guests included "tax-collectors and others" (5:29 NIV). This is different from Matthew and Mark, who identify the guests as "tax-collectors and 'sinners'" (Matthew 9:10 NIV; Mark 2:15 NIV). When the Pharisees see Jesus and His followers drinking and associating with those they consider beneath themselves, they ask the disciples (not Jesus) why Jesus allowed it. Jesus, however, answers their question.

Jesus' answer in verses 31–32 reflects the difference between the heart of God and the heart of Pharisaism. The Pharisees thought that holiness required them to remain separate from sinners, to refuse to have contact with them. Jesus was holiness incarnate, and yet His holiness was not diminished by His contact with sinners. In order for God to call sinners to repentance, God found it necessary to have contact with them, which is the reason for our Lord's incarnation—of His taking on human flesh, living among men, touching and being touched by them.

Apparently Jesus' response isn't what they want to hear, so they press the point (5:33) of Jesus' and John's differencing practices. John the Baptist ate a rather unusual diet of desert foods (locusts and wild honey [Matthew 3:4]) and did not drink wine (1:15). It is quite plain, then, that what John did not drink, namely wine, Jesus did.

Jesus tells two short parables (5:36–39) to explain that sometimes new things must replace old things; trying to incorporate the two just doesn't work. The Pharisees are entrenched in old ways—trying to follow the Law to the letter in order to obtain righteousness. It isn't working, and never will. Jesus and the "sinners" are happy, enjoying life, and developing relationships. The guests are in the presence of the bridegroom, and it is a time to celebrate.

📄 6:1–11

SABBATH ISSUES

Luke is not concerned here with providing a precise chronology. This can be seen by the broad time references ("one Sabbath" [6:1 NIV]; "on another Sabbath" [6:6 NIV]). Luke's purpose is to prepare his readers for the rejection, arrest, conviction, and execution of Jesus by His opponents by laying the groundwork early in the book. The Pharisees reject Jesus because He claims God's own authority (5:17–26), because He associates with sinners (5:27–39), and now, because He does not keep the Sabbath as they interpret it (6:1–11). These issues will dominate the relationship between the Pharisees and Jesus, culminating in His crucifixion.

While in chapter 5 the Pharisees (first mentioned by Luke in conjunction with the pronouncement to the paralytic that his sins were forgiven) object to Jesus' authority to forgive sins, they do not seem to have yet resolved a way to oppose Him. When we come to verses 6–11 in chapter 6, they have their minds made up. They are no longer looking for evidence as a basis for making a decision about Jesus; they are looking for proof to validate their rejection of Him. What began with curiosity, and led to concern, has, by the time we have reached our text, become condemnation and criticism.

In verses 1–5, some of Jesus' disciples begin to strip heads of grain from the field, rub them in their hands to separate the grain from the sheaf, and pop the grain into their mouths. This, to the Pharisees, is technically harvesting and threshing grain, something which one could do on any other day, but not on the Sabbath. Jesus' disciples are breaking the Pharisees' interpretation of "work" on the Sabbath and so the Pharisees challenge them.

In response, Jesus cites an Old Testament story (1 Samuel 21:1–6), where David and his men had eaten food that, according to law, should only be consumed by the priests. But the conditions warranted such an action, and since the Pharisees revered David, they could understand making an exception in that case. However, they don't think much of Jesus, and He and His followers aren't afforded the same tolerance. Yet that doesn't keep Jesus from making it perfectly clear that He is "Lord of the Sabbath" (6:5 NIV). As such, He—not the Pharisees—will have the final say in what is appropriate to do or not do on the Sabbath. Jesus' argument, as outlined by Luke, is based upon a very simple premise: Who you are determines whether you have the authority to define what is and is not a true Sabbath violation.

In Jesus' response, He refers to Himself as the "Son of Man" (6:5 NIV). This term has only once been used previously by Luke, and that at the time of the Pharisees' rejection of Jesus' authority to forgive sins. Jesus' use of the title is drawn especially from its messianic significance in Daniel 7. Jesus begins to use the title for Himself at the first evidence of rejection.

The expression, "Lord of the Sabbath" (6:5 NIV) is also significant. Besides affirming His position as Messiah, Jesus may also be saying that the rest associated with the Sabbath has come in Christ: "Come to Me, all who are weary and heavy-laden, and I will give you rest" (Matthew 11:28 NASB).

The second story in verses 6–11 is even more telling of the Pharisees' legalistic attitudes. The Pharisaical view of the Sabbath would reluctantly allow for one to render aid to a dying man, to one in such dire straits that he would not live till the Sabbath had ended. But Jesus heals a man with the withered hand—this does not fit into the Pharisees' category. The man's malady is not life-threatening. The Pharisees therefore believe that Jesus should have waited to heal this man. Jesus, by His actions, is raising the question, "Why?"

His question highlights the bad logic of the Pharisees. If the Sabbath was for good, then doing good on the Sabbath could hardly be wrong. It is that simple. Why was the Sabbath given, for good or evil?

Jesus could have easily avoided the issue by waiting until they weren't watching to heal the man. But He turns the tables with a piercing question (6:9). It is perfectly permissible to save a life on the Sabbath and, in a sense, His healing of the man is an act of salvation. And since Jesus only speaks, the Pharisees can't even accuse Him of doing any work. Still, they begin to plot against Him. They will continue to confront Him throughout His ministry.

By this point, the Pharisees are the bitter enemies of Jesus. They are not interested in following Him. They are no longer open to the possibility of His being the Messiah. They only wish to be rid of Him, something they will only later be able, in the providence of God, to achieve. The Sabbath controversy is, for them, the last straw. They are deadlocked in an irreconcilable conflict so long as they stubbornly resist.

Take It Home

Numerous debates continue as to whether old ways or new ways are better when it comes to religious things. Are the old hymns better than newer praise music? Is casual clothing in church appropriate? Is worship lessened or heightened by the presence of a band rather than an organ or a cappella? We all have our preferences, and draw lines as to what is inappropriate. Where do you stand in the old-vs.-new debate? How do you prevent Pharisaic legalism from creeping in while holding strong to what you feel Jesus would have you do?

LUKE 6:12–49

A DIFFERENT WAY OF SEEING THE WORLD

Designating the Top Twelve   6:12–16
Blessings and Woes   6:17–26
A Very Different Perspective   6:27–49

Setting Up the Section

This passage contains Luke's parallel to Matthew's Sermon on the Mount. The two versions contain many similarities but more than a few distinct differences. Luke has recently provided a number of accounts of Jesus' encounters with the Pharisees and has shown how legalistic attitudes had twisted the intended meaning of the gospel. Here Jesus provides His own outlook on how people should live.

It's important to read Jesus' words in terms of the principles of the law, not just specific actions. For instance, Jesus' teaching on "turning the other cheek" is not simply a mechanical kind of response to a right cross punch, but a principle that should govern our relationships with our enemies. We honor the sermon best when we apply it in the broad strokes of our lives.

6:12–16

DESIGNATING THE TOP TWELVE

By this time Jesus has attracted a number of followers. (Seventy-two would soon be sent out to various towns [10:1].) Luke regularly notes Jesus' commitment to prayer, as he does here (6:12). After spending a night in prayer, Jesus designates twelve of His disciples to become apostles. Luke has already recorded the call of Peter, Andrew, James, John, and Matthew (referred to as Levi in 5:27–29). At this point he completes the list (6:13–16).

In every biblical list of the apostles, Peter is listed first and Judas last. Yet this does not suggest that Jesus recruited Peter to be "the rock" and Judas a traitor. It takes all the disciples a long while to figure out who Jesus really is and what their roles should be. It is likely during their extended learning process that Peter eventually rises to prominence and Judas falls away to become a thief and betrayer.

6:17–26

BLESSINGS AND WOES

After calling the Twelve, Jesus is surrounded by a great crowd. The extent of Jesus' popularity with the people is evident from two major facts mentioned by Luke. First, the large number of people who are there, even in such a remote place. Second, the great distance from which people are coming. Here, we are told by Luke that they have come from all over Judea, Jerusalem, and even from the coast of Tyre and Sidon (6:17). A large number have come to benefit from Jesus' great power to heal diseases and remove evil spirits. And while the great throng is assembled, Jesus begins to teach the people (although Luke records that He primarily addresses His disciples [6:20]).

Critical Observation

There are a number of differences between Luke's account of the Sermon on the Mount (6:17–49) and that of Matthew (chapters 5–7).

- Luke's version of Jesus' sermon is considerably shorter than Matthew's (Matthew 5–7; Luke 6:17–49).

- Matthew used third person to speak of those who are blessed; Luke uses second person ("you").

- Matthew addressed characteristics that are a bit more spiritual, while Luke's traits are physical (poor in spirit vs. poor, hunger and thirst for righteousness vs. hunger, etc.).

- Matthew's account deals only with blessings, while Luke's includes a list of curses that correspond to each one (rich vs. poor, well fed vs. hungry, etc.)

Care must be taken when reading these passages blessing the poor. Jesus does not attribute any intrinsic benefit to being poor, or any automatic evil in being rich. Jesus says, "Blessed are you who are poor," not, "Blessed are all who are poor." Luke's account identifies the poor as the disciples who have chosen poverty in order to follow Him. So also, those who are rejected and persecuted are treated this way because of their faith (6:22). It is not simply being poor that is blessed, but being poor for Christ's sake. There is no intrinsic merit in being rejected and persecuted, but only in being thus treated on Christ's account (1 Peter 2:20). The joy of serving Jesus will more than compensate for the things disciples give up in order to serve.

Take It Home

The point of the passage is clear. People must make a decision as to their values and their priorities. We must all choose to forsake some things in the pursuit of others. Not everyone must forsake wealth to follow Christ, although all must forsake the love of money. Life involves choices. We must choose what in life to pursue. Every choice has both benefits (blessings) and a price to pay. The gospel of Jesus Christ is the good news of a gift, the gift of eternal life, which is of infinite value (Philippians 3:7–11).

📖 **6:27–49**

A VERY DIFFERENT PERSPECTIVE

Jesus' teaching is 180 degrees different from what people are accustomed to hearing. Not only does He teach love for one's enemies, He even refuses to justify retaliation/revenge for offenses (6:27–30). This is the context for the familiar Golden Rule (6:31). Jesus' challenge is to rise above the status quo of relationships and initiate a higher level of love and care than is being demonstrated by others (6:32–36).

Critical Observation

Measures of grain were sometimes carried in the folds of the loose clothing worn in the Middle East. So if we want to receive a good measure (a lap full) of forgiveness poured out on us, we should not be stingy offering it to others (6:38).

Jesus warns against judging and condemning others. Giving and forgiving are the appropriate antidotes (6:37–38). Status seeking and hypocrisy only cause difficulties in life: The blind have difficulty leading other blind people, students should seek to imitate their teachers rather than seeking higher status, and it's foolish to try to remove a speck of sawdust from someone's eye with a plank in one's own eye (6:37–42).

It is foolish to pretend to be someone you aren't. Just as trees are recognized by their fruit, people are identified by their actions. People with good hearts can't help but produce good deeds, just as evil in one's heart will produce evil in one's life. And whatever is in the heart—good or bad—will certainly be reflected in one's speech (6:43–45).

It's easy to give lip service to Jesus and consider oneself a believer (6:46); it's much harder to love enemies, freely give to someone who is trying to take from you, keep from judging others, and maintain a mind-set of humility. But genuine believers obey even the difficult commands of Jesus. In the closing parable, also recorded in Matthew's account (Matthew 7:24–27), one homebuilder digs a deep foundation on rock (6:48). The other doesn't even bother with a foundation. So when a torrent falls on the two homes, the first one stands firm while the second is completely destroyed (6:46–49).

Take It Home

Jesus called His followers to extraordinary responses. It's a natural and ordinary response for people to love those who love them, but we Christians are called to love our enemies. We are to do so because God has loved us while we were His enemies. We are to do so because God is the One who will bless us for obeying His commands.

LUKE 7:1-50

SAVING FAITH AND A FAITHFUL SAVIOR

The Faith of a Gentile   7:1–10
Jesus Brings a Widow's Son Back to Life   7:11–17
A Message for John the Baptist   7:18–35
Unusual Insight from a Woman "Sinner"   7:36–50

Setting Up the Section

At this point in Luke's narrative, Jesus has been in public ministry for a while. Yet He is still coming across people who stand out from others in the crowd. A Roman centurion displays faith greater than any witnessed in Israel. A woman recognizes the significance of Jesus and anoints Him. And Jesus gives tribute to the faithful ministry of John the Baptist.

📄 7:1–10

THE FAITH OF A GENTILE

After Jesus' famous sermon (6:17–49), He goes to Capernaum where He encounters a delegation sent by a Roman centurion. The official is requesting Jesus' healing of a servant. Although the Jewish people didn't much care for the Romans as a whole, this particular man is an exception. Not only has the centurion shown respect for the Jewish nation and helped with the construction of a synagogue, he also values his servant who is sick—a servant who might very well be Jewish (7:2–5).

Demystifying Luke

There are some differences between Luke's account of the centurion and that of Matthew. It is not difficult to conclude that the accounts in Matthew 8:5–13 and Luke 7:1–10 are a record of the same incident. However, Luke's Gospel makes a point of telling us that the centurion never personally spoke with Jesus, while Matthew's account clearly gives us this impression. How, then, can we explain the apparent contradictions in these two accounts?

It would have been a reasonable explanation that Matthew understood that a delegation sent by this man was the same as the man himself coming to Jesus. But more importantly, we don't always need to feel an obligation to reconcile the differences between accounts, particularly when they are not central to the significance of the story. The Gospel writers were aware of the writings of others (Luke 1:1–2), and yet they felt free to have differences in their accounts—perhaps differences which remind us that we have only partial accounts of any incident in the life of Christ and that each is remembered differently by different people. That doesn't take away the value of understanding what Jesus did.

Jesus accommodates the request. Yet while still on the way to the man's house, additional messengers from the centurion intercept them, explaining that the centurion doesn't need Jesus to actually go to his home. He understands authority, and believes that Jesus can simply speak and heal his servant. The centurion's faith is revealed not just in the fact that he recognizes Jesus' authority, but that he recognizes that Jesus' authority is the result of a higher authority. The centurion's faith attests to Jesus' identity in a way that the religious leaders have yet to understand (7:7). Jesus is amazed that the man has such faith, because no one in Israel has yet shown that level of belief in Him. By the time the messengers get back to the centurion's house, the servant is well (7:9–10).

Critical Observation

The story of the centurion's faith is very similar to the Old Testament account of Naaman and Elisha (2 Kings 5). In both cases, a Gentile official sought help from a Jewish man of God to find relief from a serious illness. (Naaman had leprosy; the Roman centurion's servant was near death.) Yet Naaman had been initially reluctant to follow the course of action prescribed by Elisha, while the Roman centurion showed exemplary faith in Jesus.

📖 7:11–17

JESUS BRINGS A WIDOW'S SON BACK TO LIFE

About twenty-five miles southwest of Capernaum was the town of Nain (7:11). It is there two large crowds converge. One crowd is traveling along with Jesus and His disciples. The other is a group of townspeople in a funeral procession. A widow's only son has died, which in that culture leaves her essentially helpless. As the two crowds merge, Jesus sees what is happening and His heart goes out to the woman (7:13).

Jesus approaches the coffin (which would not have had a top if made according to Jewish tradition), and the pallbearers stand still. Then He reaches out and touches the coffin, an unusual move since it would have rendered anyone else ceremonially unclean for doing so. With no ceremony, Jesus simply instructs the boy to arise, which is immediately evident by his sitting up and speaking (7:15). Not surprisingly, the crowds of people are all filled with awe. They acknowledge Jesus as a great prophet and begin to praise God (7:16–17).

This story, like that of the healing of the centurion's son, also brings to mind the healings of the prophets Elijah and Elisha. Jesus' raising of the dead son reminds us of a similar incident in Elijah's ministry (1 Kings 17:17–24) and in that of Elisha as well (2 Kings 4:18–37). In the case of Elijah, especially, there are parallels to the raising of the son of the woman who lived at Nain. Both boys were the only son of a widow. Both boys were raised from the dead by a prophet of God. Both Elijah and Jesus presented the boys to their mothers. Both raisings proved that a true prophet of God was present. But the more labored and time-consuming resurrections performed by the Old Testament prophets were overshadowed by this instantaneous raising of Jesus.

Critical Observation

These two miracles, the healing of the centurion's son and the raising of the widow's son, serve several purposes in the developing message of Luke's Gospel.

- They testify to the fact that Jesus is who He claimed to be—Israel's Messiah.
- They serve as a backdrop for the questions of John the Baptist, which are to be introduced in the next section.
- They are samples of the kind of faith that we should have today.

📄 **7:18–35**

A MESSAGE FOR JOHN THE BAPTIST

The last Luke has said about John the Baptist is that Herod had imprisoned him (3:20). John is still following the ministry of Jesus through messengers, though. Yet apparently he isn't hearing what he expected. He sends two of his disciples to Jesus, asking directly if He is the promised Messiah or if everyone should be looking for someone else (7:18–20).

Critical Observation

Believers sometimes have a "pious bias" and assume that righteous people don't have the same doubts and difficulties of less religious people. John's lack of certainty that Jesus was the Messiah may seem like a shortcoming. Yet in spite of their spiritual connection, as far as we know John and Jesus had very little physical contact. In addition, Jesus was trying to avoid publicly identifying Himself as "the Messiah" because the term meant different things to different people. He was not planning, for example, to overthrow the Roman government and set up His own kingdom on earth (as many people were hoping).

Perhaps John is encouraging Jesus to declare His spiritual credentials—maybe he is even daring Him to speak up, in a sense. But Jesus doesn't declare Himself the Messiah as John may have hoped. Nor does He go work things out with John. Instead, He merely tells John's disciples to go back and report what they were seeing: blind and lame people healed, lepers cured, the dead raised, and the good news of the gospel preached to the poor (7:22). These were all signs from Isaiah (Isaiah 29:18; 35:5–6) of the coming of God's end-time salvation. In effect, Jesus is simply telling John to do what every first-century Jewish seeker needed to do—compare the prophecies of the Old Testament with the deeds and declarations of Jesus Christ. If Jesus fulfills these prophecies, then the Bible bears witness to the fact that He is the Messiah.

Jesus doesn't appear at all upset that John has questioned Him. Just the opposite: After John's disciples have gone, He gives John a glowing tribute (7:28). However, He adds that the least person in the kingdom of God would be even greater. In other words, John anticipated the kingdom of God. Jesus identified John as the one who had been prophesied to prepare the way for the Messiah. But those who will come after John will understand more clearly Jesus' death and resurrection and the redemption His suffering will bring.

Most in the crowd agree with what Jesus says about John. Only the Pharisees and the experts in the Law have refused to be baptized (7:30). Jesus points out that some people just can't be pleased. They criticize John's ascetic lifestyle, even suggesting he has a demon (7:33). But then they accuse Jesus of gluttony and drunkenness because He eats and drinks with regular people (7:34). Yet spiritually discerning people can see the validity of both Jesus' and John's ministries (7:35).

📄 7:36–50

UNUSUAL INSIGHT FROM A WOMAN "SINNER"

All four Gospels include an account of the washing of Jesus' feet by a woman (Matthew 26:6–13; Mark 14:3–9; Luke 7:36–50; John 12:1–8). Despite a few similarities, the story in Luke seems to be a separate event from the one described in Matthew, Mark, and John.

We are not told precisely when this incident occurs, or the name of the city. The principle characters are Jesus, Simon the Pharisee, and the woman with a soiled reputation. It is interesting that Luke gives us the name of the host, but not of the woman. Omitting her name may have been an act of grace, purposely done.

Jesus may have had a reputation for associating with tax collectors and "sinners," but on this occasion He has accepted a dinner invitation from a Pharisee. The host's intent is not clear because this is during a phase where the Pharisees are increasing their opposition against Jesus (6:11).

While Jesus is eating, an uninvited guest appears with a fancy jar of perfume. Since Jesus and the others eat while reclining at the table, His feet are away from the table rather than under it, as in Western dining. So the woman washes His feet with her tears, dries them with her hair, and then anoints them with the perfume. To make things worse, the host (and perhaps many others) knows of the woman's reputation, and assumes Jesus isn't much of a prophet if He doesn't know as well.

Jesus not only knows all about the woman; He knows what His host is thinking. The story He tells makes the point that those who are forgiven most, love most (7:40–43).

Critical Observation

In verse 47 it would appear that Jesus is telling the woman that she is forgiven because she loved much. To love because you are forgiven is a natural response to grace. To be forgiven because you love could be interpreted as earning forgiveness through works. But that is not what the parable teaches. In the parable, the one who is forgiven much loves much in response. The forgiveness precedes the response of love. A better translation of verse 47 would be "I tell you, her many sins have been forgiven—as her great love has shown" (TNIV).

Jesus' body language in verses 44–47 is significant. All through the dinner, Jesus' back is to the woman, who is anointing and kissing His feet. He is, at the same time, facing His host, Simon. Now, once Simon's rejection of Jesus is revealed, in contrast to the woman's worship, Jesus turns His back on Simon and faces the woman, even though He is still addressing Simon (7:44). Jesus is, by His actions, rejecting Simon and accepting the sinful woman.

This woman's motives are pure and her actions are genuine. (Perhaps it was the host's inattention to Jesus that had motivated her to improvise the washing and drying of Jesus' feet when she had no pitcher of water or towel.) Yet it is her faith that impresses Jesus most of all. He forgives her sins and sends her on her way in peace, leaving the dinner guests wondering if He really has the authority to do so (7:44–50).

Take It Home

Jesus wanted His Pharisee host to realize that those who are forgiven most tend to love most. The Pharisee's accusation that Jesus associated with sinners was good news to the woman who understood the depth of His forgiveness. Even today, the better we comprehend Jesus' forgiveness—and the less we are concerned with proving our own righteousness—the better equipped we are to show love to others.

LUKE 8:1–56

PARABLES, MIRACLES, AND FAMILY MATTERS

Spiritual Wisdom and the Parable of the Soils	8:1–21
Two Fear-Inspiring Miracles	8:22–39
Two More Amazing Miracles	8:40–56

Setting Up the Section

Jesus' ministry has become very active. He is teaching the crowds, training His disciples, healing all kinds of diseases, casting out evil spirits, and even performing an occasional phenomenal miracle or resurrection of the dead. In this passage, Luke records a bit of each of these aspects of Jesus' ministry, along with brief mentions of His supporters and family.

As we look more closely at the description of the ministry of Jesus in the Gospels, we discover that very soon the party that accompanies our Lord becomes quite large. One of the few texts that informs us about this large group is Luke 8. In addition, Luke informs us of the vital role a large number of women play in supporting the ministry of Jesus and His disciples.

SPIRITUAL WISDOM AND THE PARABLE OF THE SOILS

Jesus has spent a year or so wandering around Galilee and preaching. In the early days He was often pictured as alone or with a few disciples. At this point, however, it seems He begins a new phase of ministry, traveling again through Galilee (8:1). But this time He is beset by crowds everywhere He goes, along with a rather significant following of disciples (in addition to the Twelve) and supporters (8:2–3).

Luke names three of Jesus' female sponsors, revealing a great diversity in background and social status: Mary Magdalene (from whom the seven demons had been cast out); Joanna the wife of Cuza, Herod's steward (this may explain one of Herod's primary sources of information about Jesus and His ministry [9:7]); and Susanna, who is not mentioned again in the scriptures (8:2–3). The women all seem to have this in common: Jesus has miraculously delivered (healed) them of conditions for which there is no human solution. Some, like Mary Magdalene, were delivered of demon possession. Others were healed of sicknesses and disease. They went with Jesus to be of help to Him because they had experienced His help in their lives. Luke is clear that these women are not mere "hangers-on." They are active contributors to the proclamation of the gospel of the kingdom.

Jesus uses and encourages women in ministry. Luke's account of these women who follow Jesus and support the Galilean campaign is a tribute to them and to their ministry. It commends the women for their faithfulness and commitment to the Lord and it values their ministry as a partnership in the gospel (8:3).

Critical Observation

Jesus' practice of allowing women to support Him and His followers gave approval to the general principle of supporting those who proclaim the gospel. Our Lord set the precedent that those who proclaim the gospel should be supported by those who benefit from that preaching. This is seen earlier in the Old Testament prophets (1 Kings 17:7ff; 2 Kings 4:8–10), and is taught in principle by the apostle Paul (1 Corinthians 9).

Jesus seems to be making several shifts in the way He ministers:

1) In the first Galilean campaign of our Lord, the emphasis was on His identity as Israel's king. Now, He seems to be concentrating more on the nature of the kingdom itself.

2) There is a change of method. Jesus is now teaching by means of parables—more indirectly than before.

3) Jesus is beginning to spend more time with His disciples. In His first Galilean campaign, it would seem that His disciples were not always present. From now on, Jesus pours more effort into the teaching of His disciples (not just the Twelve but the larger group of His followers).

Why the shift to parables? Parables can reveal God's truth to those with spiritual awareness, even while concealing it from those intent only on opposing Jesus (8:10). Some people aren't as interested in truth as in maintaining their religious status, so they will discover no truth in Jesus' parables.

The Parable of the Soils (8:4–15) makes this very point. It is found in all three of the synoptic Gospels (Matthew 13:1–23; Mark 4:1–20; Luke 8:4–15). It has become quite a familiar illustration to many modern-day believers, but imagine the disciples' confusion after first hearing only the parable without the explanation (8:5–8). The Parable of the Soils describes what becomes of seed that is sown in four different types of soil.

1) Soil that is the hardened soil of the pathway. This seed does not penetrate the soil at all, but is quickly snatched up by the birds of the air.

2) The rocky soil, a shallow layer of earth, barely covering the rock below. The seed that falls upon this type of soil quickly germinates, aided by the warmth retained by the rock, but is hindered by a lack of depth and by a lack of moisture. The seed that germinates quickly also terminates quickly.

3) Soil populated with thorns. The seed falling into this soil germinates and begins to grow, but is eventually crowded out by the hardier thorns.

4) The fruitful soil, which produces a bountiful crop.

Thankfully, Jesus gives His followers a clear interpretation (8:11–15). As He sows the Word of God, His hearers will respond in numerous ways: some not at all (hardened), some enthusiastically at first but soon falling away (rocky), others trying to add His teachings to an already full life rather than changing priorities (thorny). Some, however, will hear the Word, retain it, and become productive for God's kingdom (fruitful).

Yet immediately after using a parable to intentionally cloud the truth from the religious leaders who follow Him, Jesus teaches that light is meant to shine and that everything hidden will be disclosed (8:17). When the time is right—after His death and resurrection—His disciples will be prepared to bring everything He has told them out into the open.

Demystifying Luke

It would not be long after this that the cult of Gnosticism would form. This group proposed that secret spiritual knowledge was attainable by only a privileged few. That's not what Jesus was teaching here. Even while attempting to keep His role as Messiah low key, He was training His disciples and giving them full explanations. They could then provide the early church with all the truth Jesus taught them (Colossians 1:25–26).

Spiritual wisdom is not something to take for granted. It is acquired by careful listening, and can be lost through apathy and inattention (8:18). Indeed, Jesus even begins to define relationships in terms of those who hear God's Word and put it into practice (8:19–21). Those who practice such spiritual disciplines are considered family by Jesus, even more so than His flesh-and-blood family, which doesn't yet believe in Him (Mark 3:21; John 7:5).

8:22–39

TWO FEAR-INSPIRING MIRACLES

The account of the stilling of the storm is the first of three miracles recorded by Luke in chapter 8. It is followed by the healing of the demoniac, then the raising of Jairus's daughter, interrupted by the healing of the woman with the issue of blood. The two central threads that run through these miracles are fear and faith.

Every biblical account of Jesus' calming the storm is surprisingly short and succinct (Matthew 8:23-27; Mark 4:35-41; Luke 8:22-25). What comes through clearly, however, is Jesus' expectation that by now the Twelve should have faith in Him. Even a raging storm that could terrorize experienced fishermen is no problem for Jesus' power. After He speaks, not only does the storm dissipate, but the sea immediately becomes absolutely calm. In response, the disciples are amazed and fearful (8:25). It would seem that their reaction to what Jesus has just done is even more startling than the life-threatening storm itself. They are beginning to catch on that maybe they are scared of the wrong things.

Failing to trust in Christ dishonors and displeases Him and is detrimental to men. The disciples' lack of faith does not please our Lord here, nor does it do so elsewhere (Matthew 14:31; 16:8). It is dishonoring to Christ, for it shows that the disciples do not trust Him as the Son of God. In addition, the disciples' lack of faith causes them much unnecessary consternation and fear.

Faith involves a decision for which people are responsible. Our Lord's rebuke of His disciples, regardless of how gentle it was, indicates that the disciples were expected to have faith, and are held accountable for failing to have faith. While faith is, in one sense, a gift of God, it is also a gift that may be accepted or refused. Faith involves choices—though sometimes it means moving and sometimes it means waiting.

Yet no sooner have they landed than they have another frightening encounter. In a relatively remote stretch on the other side of the Sea of Galilee, they find a demon-possessed man living among tombs (8:26-39). He no longer wears clothes. People have tried to secure him for his own protection, but chains cannot hold him.

Critical Observation

The Bible never explains how people became demon-possessed. But it addresses possession by evil spirits as a very real and distinct problem, not merely a form of mental illness.

When Jesus asks his name, it is the demons who answer. The name Legion suggests a multitude of demons (8:30). Yet they recognize Jesus and His power to determine what happens to them (8:28, 31). Take note of the fact that although the demoniac falls at Jesus' feet, it is not an act of worship, as it will be when the demons are cast from the man. The demons do recognize Jesus' identity, and they also acknowledge His superiority and authority over them. They recognize, for example, that He can do with them as He pleases. Their petitions are addressed as those of inferior beings to One who is infinitely superior to them, but not in devotion or worship; only in fear.

It seems that the demons need to be embodied in something, if not someone, and beg Jesus to allow them to go into a nearby herd of pigs. Jesus grants the request, but the pigs immediately rush down a steep bank into the sea and drown (8:32-33).

The men who are watching the pigs, run into town to report what has happened. By the time they get back, the previously possessed man is dressed and rational. Seeing him there and fully cured, the townspeople are overwhelmed with fear (8:34–37). They desperately want Jesus to leave, and the cured man begs to go with Him. But Jesus tells him to go home and tell what God has done (8:38–39). Who better to not only describe but also to demonstrate the healing power of God?

This account is important for us for several reasons. First, it teaches us much about the demonic forces that oppose our Lord and His church. It reminds us of the supernatural forces at work contrary to the Christian. It reminds us, as well, that Jesus Christ has power over the demonic forces, indeed, even over an entire "legion" of demons. This description of Legion provides us with a kind of "untouched photo," unmasking Satan's deception and destruction. Second, the deliverance of the demoniac draws our attention to a fear of God, which is unholy and unhealthy, one which causes men to draw away from God, or, as in our text, to ask the Son of God to withdraw. Finally, the townspeople's response reveals the resistance and fear that can come against the good that Jesus can do.

8:40–56

TWO MORE AMAZING MIRACLES

Although Jesus has sailed across the Sea of Galilee, enduring a storm and facing off with a demon-possessed man, a crowd is still waiting for Him when He gets back to shore. A ruler of the synagogue named Jairus meets Him, pleading for Him to come and heal his dying daughter. Jesus agrees, and they head for Jairus's home, but the going is slow because of the crushing crowds surrounding Jesus (8:42). So imagine the disciples' surprise when Jesus stops and asks who touched Him (8:45).

They aren't aware that a woman who has suffered from a bleeding disease for twelve years has sneaked up and, in faith, touched the edge of Jesus' cloak. She shouldn't be there because the bleeding makes her unclean. It is very likely a menstrual problem, so even if she can get Jesus' attention in the crowd, it will be horribly embarrassing to request healing.

But Jesus will not allow the woman's faith to go unnoticed. She is a positive example for everyone. In addition, she might feel guilty about "stealing a healing" later on, or afraid that in telling the story to others they might interpret the results as magic rather than faith. So Jesus waits until the woman comes forward (trembling) and explains what she has done (8:47). He acknowledges her faith and sends her home in peace.

In the meantime, however, word arrives that Jairus's daughter has died. Jesus isn't fazed, and He encourages Jairus to believe that she will be healed (8:50). When they arrive, mourners are already wailing, and they laugh when Jesus suggests the girl is only sleeping (8:52–53). They don't laugh long, though, because the girl stands up at Jesus' command. He tells her parents to feed her and not to tell anyone what has happened. Perhaps Jesus' command for silence is primarily directed to the faithless scoffers who wait outside (Matthew 9:23–25). Not only do they miss seeing this outstanding miracle, they also will be denied hearing about it firsthand. Lack of faith has any number of drawbacks.

Much is said about fear in this passage: the disciples during the storm, the people who knew the demon-possessed man, the woman standing before Jesus, etc. In particular we should notice Jesus' admonition to Jairus not to fear, even after hearing the worst about his daughter. Can you think of a time when it seems God has been slow to act? If so, how did you respond while waiting for Him? What is your initial response to crisis situations: fear or faith? How might you increase your faith so that such times will feel less stressful in the future?

LUKE 9:1–62

HIGHS AND LOWS OF MINISTRY

Paired Up and Sent Out	9:1–9
Jesus Feeds Five Thousand	9:10–17
Peter's Confession and Jesus' Transfiguration	9:18–36
Some Shortcomings of the Disciples	9:37–56
Excuses Not to Follow Jesus	9:57–62

Setting Up the Section

Any business or ministry that undergoes rapid growth will almost always experience corresponding problems. Jesus' ministry is no exception. In this passage the apostles are given more responsibility, resulting in some successes as well as some failures. Some of them are beginning to see Jesus for who He really is, yet argue about which of them is the greatest. Jesus is still popular with crowds, but now has Herod's attention as well. Meanwhile, His miracles continue.

📄 9:1–9

PAIRED UP AND SENT OUT

One day Jesus gathers the apostles, puts them in pairs, and sends them out to preach about the kingdom of God and to heal (9:2). He gives them "power and authority to drive out all demons and to cure diseases" (9:1 NIV), and He forbids them to take any provisions. They are to go village to village, in each place finding a willing host to allow them to stay and do their work. If none is found, they are to "shake the dust off [their] feet" (9:5 NIV)—a gesture that demonstrates complete separation and disdain.

While there are people in the remote villages who may not have heard much about Jesus or His message, Herod certainly has. He is curious about Jesus (9:9). He is a Jew and probably knows something about the Messiah. He might have heard talk of the kingdom of God and feels threatened. He could be haunted by guilt and fear that John the Baptist (whom he has killed) has risen. Or maybe he just wants to see a miracle (23:8).

📖 9:10–17

JESUS FEEDS FIVE THOUSAND

When the disciples return from their ministry, Jesus tries to provide them a place and time for a little retreat (9:10). But the crowds find them and gather, so Jesus continues to teach and heal.

When the crowds don't go home, and it is time to eat, the disciples tell Jesus to send everyone away. But He tells the disciples to feed the crowd. They have just returned from living day to day by the provision of God, yet they balk at this challenge. They see five thousand men (plus women and children) and only see five loaves and two fish. They see no way to feed the crowd without going out to buy food for everyone (9:13–14).

So Jesus takes over. He gives thanks for the food and begins to divide it. Envision at least one hundred groups of fifty people each, with the twelve apostles distributing the seemingly never-ending source of food from Jesus' hands. It is not likely a coincidence that there are twelve baskets of leftovers—one for each of the still spiritually short-sighted apostles (9:17).

📖 9:18–36

PETER'S CONFESSION AND JESUS' TRANSFIGURATION

Luke's next story shows that the apostles are beginning to glean some insight about Jesus that the masses are missing. There is no clear consensus about who Jesus is. Everyone seems to agree that He is a specially designated man sent from God, but no one is saying He is the Messiah (9:19).

It can be safely said that Luke places a heavy emphasis on prayer. He is careful to link prayer with great manifestations of God's grace and power. This is true in both the Gospel of Luke and the book of Acts. Look at these instances, including verse 18, when the disciples make their confession, in which prayer shortly precedes a great event.

In Luke's Gospel:		
Text	**Prayer**	**Event**
1:5–20	Prayer of Zechariah	Announcement of John's birth
3:21–22	Jesus prays at His baptism	Father appears, speaks (3:21–22)
4:42	Jesus' private prayer	Galilean ministry (4:43 and following)
6:12	Jesus in prayer	Choosing the twelve disciples
9:18	Jesus in prayer	The great confession
9:28–29	Jesus in prayer	The transfiguration

In the Book of Acts:		
Text	**Prayer**	**Event**
1:14	Disciples in prayer	Pentecost
4:31	Prayer of church	Powerful witness in Jerusalem
7:59–60	Stephen's prayer	Saul's conversion
9:11	Saul in prayer	Saul's sight regained and filled with Holy Spirit
10, 11	Prayer of Peter, Cornelius	Gospel spreads to Gentiles
12:5	Church in prayer for Peter	Peter's release
13:1-3	Fasting and prayer	First missionary journey
16:25	Prison prayers	Earthquake, release, conversion of jailer

So Jesus asks the Twelve, "Who do you say I am?" (9:20 NIV). Peter usually gets credit for the answer, but he is probably speaking for the group. He identifies Jesus as "the Christ of God" (9:20 NIV), a bold proclamation that Jesus is the Messiah.

Peter has recognized that the teaching and actions of Jesus have shown Him to be the Messiah. And yet the apostles are far from a complete understanding of their Master. Jesus instructs them not to tell others about this. He wants to provide them with a fuller understanding of a Messiah who will (for now) be a suffering servant rather than a military victor or political figure. And He begins to prepare them for their own suffering: denial of self, taking up a cross, and possibly even loss of life (9:23–27). But He also promises that some of them will personally witness "the kingdom of God (9:27 NIV)."

Eight days later, three of them find out what He means (9:28). He takes Peter, James, and

John up a mountain to pray with Him, and they witness His transfiguration. Jesus' clothing, and even His physical appearance, changes. He becomes "as bright as a flash of lightning" (9:25 NIV), and Moses and Elijah appear and speak about His departure (9:29–31).

Both Moses and Elijah had departed the earth with some mystery. Moses was buried by God (Deuteronomy 34:6). Elijah was carried to heaven in a whirlwind (2 Kings 2:11). These men speak to Jesus about His departure, meaning His exit from earth and return to heaven. The word translated "departure" harkens back to Moses' exodus from Egypt when he led God's people to freedom, an apt parallel for the work of Christ.

The disciples have been very sleepy, but when awakened, see the full glory of Jesus. As the two heavenly visitors begin to leave, Peter proposes building shelters for them, possibly in an attempt to extend their stay. Or maybe he thinks if Jesus' kingdom is established now, they all could skip the suffering, rejection, and death that Jesus has been talking about. Whatever Peter's intent, Luke tells us he doesn't know what he is saying (9:33).

Even as Peter is speaking, he is interrupted by the voice of God (9:35). After the voice has spoken, Jesus is again alone, and the three disciples keep it to themselves (9:36).

📄 9:37–56

SOME SHORTCOMINGS OF THE DISCIPLES

Meanwhile, the other nine apostles have been asked by a desperate father to cast an evil spirit out of his son (9:38–40). Although Jesus has given His disciples authority to drive out demons (9:1), they are unable to help this young man. Jesus merely speaks, the spirit comes out, and the boy is healed (9:42).

Luke doesn't specify to whom Jesus is speaking when He expresses frustration with lack of faith (9:41). Very likely, He is referring to the entire "generation" (9:41 NIV), which would include the father, the people in the crowds, and even His disciples. And when Jesus tries to tell the disciples about His impending betrayal and death, they are still clueless about what He means (9:44–45).

The apostles may not have completely understood Jesus' teaching about His kingdom, but that doesn't stop them from arguing about who will have the highest position in it (9:46). In response, Jesus calls forward a small child as an example of the least on earth who will become the greatest in the estimation of God (9:48).

This act must have reminded them of a stranger they had seen driving out demons in the name of Jesus. They had tried to stop him (9:49). (Quite an irony: They had been unable to cast out a demon, and equally unable to stop someone who could!) Jesus tells them not to interfere with people who are working toward the same goals they are (9:50).

Critical Observation

Verse 51 marks a turn in Luke's Gospel. This is a critical narrative turning point as Jesus resolves to go to Jerusalem. It is the beginning of what some scholars refer to as Luke's travel narrative, which will run through chapter 19. This next section of Luke also shows Jesus preparing His disciples for their second mission.

Luke notes that the time is approaching for Jesus to be taken to heaven (9:51). This is a reference beyond Jesus' death and resurrection to His ascension. Luke's Gospel describes the ministry of Jesus before His ascension; the sequel, Acts, reports what happens after Jesus' ascension through His disciples (Acts 1:2).

The disciples are far from ready, yet Jesus sets out for Jerusalem. When denied permission to stay in a Samaritan village, James and John express indignation and ask Jesus if they can call fire from heaven to destroy the offending village. Jesus rebukes them and simply goes elsewhere.

Demystifying Luke

The spiritual and ethnic differences between Jews and Samaritans created problems on a regular basis. This tension was even stronger when the Samaritans realized that Jews were on their way to Jerusalem. Jewish travelers would frequently go around Samaria, but Jesus hadn't chosen to do so.

📄 9:57–62

EXCUSES NOT TO FOLLOW JESUS

Along the road Jesus meets a series of people who want to follow Him. . .sort of. The first person seems to give up the idea when faced with uncertainty (9:57–58). Two more want to put off following until they can attend to other matters—important matters to be sure, but things that prevent them from going with Jesus.

At first reading, Jesus may seem cold and heartless. But in reality, essentially everyone who chooses not to follow (or not to do so wholeheartedly) can come up with a really good reason to justify his or her actions. As Jesus has resolutely set out for Jerusalem, He expects people to decide if they're with Him or against Him.

Take It Home

What are some of the excuses you've heard about why people don't want to follow Jesus? To what extent do you think each excuse is valid? Can you detect any excuses that you sometimes use in order to justify not doing as much as you might feel you ought to do?

LUKE 10:1–42

SEVENTY-TWO MISSIONARIES, A GOOD SAMARITAN, AND SIBLING RIVALRY

The Seventy-two	10:1–24
The Good Samaritan	10:25–37
Mary and Martha Disagree about What's Important	10:38–42

Setting Up the Section

Luke chapter 9 is the immediate backdrop for our text in chapter 10. It began with the sending out of the twelve disciples. The report of Herod's concern with the identity of Jesus is followed by the feeding of the five thousand. After this, Peter's great confession is recorded, followed immediately by the transfiguration of Jesus.

The first words of verse 1 in chapter 10 ("After this. . ." NIV) show the close link between the sending out of the seventy-two and the preceding context. The sending out of the disciples is thus related both to the sending out of the Twelve (9:1–6) and the Lord's instruction on discipleship (9:37–62).

Just as Jesus has sent out the Twelve in pairs to experience firsthand ministry (9:1–6), He now sends out seventy-two more. They are thrilled with what they learned from this teaching method. Jesus also teaches an expert of the Law with a classic parable and teaches two sisters an important lesson on priorities.

☐ 10:1–24

THE SEVENTY-TWO

Jesus' sending out of the apostles in pairs (9:1–6) is described in three Gospels, but only Luke tells of the subsequent sending out of seventy-two in pairs. (Some manuscripts say that seventy went out rather than seventy-two.) And considerably more is said about the appointing of the seventy-two than the mission of the Twelve.

While there are similarities between the two groups that were sent out, there are significant differences in the instructions given.

The Twelve Luke 9	The Seventy-two Luke 10
The Twelve are known individuals.	The seventy-two are not.
Sent out in Galilee	Sent along the route Jesus will be taking to Jerusalem
Told specifically not to preach to the Gentiles or the Samaritans	There is a clear hint of this sending including the Gentiles. This seems to be a more Gentile territory, and there would be no need to speak of what is eaten if they were only in Jewish homes.
This sending seems to conclude Jesus' ministry in Galilee.	This sending seems introductory.
Sent out in place of Jesus	Sent out as forerunners, sent ahead of Jesus, who would be passing by this way (10:1)
Sent out from village to village, and the impression is that they went to those remote, previously missed places. This seems to have been a rural, remote mission (9:6).	Sent to the towns and cities (10:8, 10, 12)

Jesus tells the larger group not to speak to people along the road (10:4) and to eat whatever is set before them (10:8). Seemingly, Jesus is intentionally expanding His ministry—not only going to larger cities than previously, but also beginning to include Gentile territory. (Otherwise, there would have been no need to address the food issue [10:7–8].) But still He instructs His messengers to go only where they are welcomed (10:10–16).

It can seem strange that Jesus would command the disciples to refrain from the normal social amenity of a friendly greeting on the road. His instruction actually implies the urgency of the task: Don't stop for chitchat; get to the business of spreading the good news. Just as Jesus is resolved to go to Jerusalem, so the disciples must be resolved to proclaim the message.

Jesus perceives the world as a vast harvest, with only a few workers (10:2). He makes it clear that the seventy-two are "like lambs among wolves" (10:3 NIV), but He gives them power to heal and authority to preach (10:9, 16).

Demystifying Luke

Korazin and Bethsaida (10:13) were cities on the north side of the Sea of Galilee—the area where Jesus conducted a number of miracles early in His ministry. Capernaum (10:15) was Jesus' home base during His adult life. Jesus contrasted these cities with Tyre and Sidon (10:13–14), two predominantly Gentile cities where He had not taught or worked miracles.

The experience must have been very positive because they return with joy, reporting to Jesus that even demons submitted to them in Jesus' name (10:17). It would seem that their ability to cast out demons was the ultimate evidence of the power and authority they exercised in the name of the Lord Jesus. It is easy to see how they would have come to this conclusion. After all, the nine disciples had been unable to cast a demon out of a boy (9:37–41). If the nine were the "A squad," and they could not cast out a demon, and the seventy-two, the "B squad," were successful, this was cause for great joy. The casting out of demons is proof to the disciples that they have great authority in Jesus' name.

Jesus tells the overjoyed disciples that their ability to cast out demons is evidence of even greater issues than they have imagined. They see their success only in terms of their having authority over the demons; Jesus is also watching their success, seeing Satan in the beginnings of his demise (10:18). Satan is falling down lightning fast. The coming of Christ, and more specifically the cross of Christ, is Satan's defeat, and the mission of the seventy is but a preview of what is to come.

Jesus doesn't want to diminish their joy, but He does try to redirect it. If the destruction of Satan is good news and cause for rejoicing, their salvation is even better news and cause for deepest joy. In a very gentle way, Jesus tells them that they should rejoice in the fact of their salvation, rather than the fact of Satan's downfall and defeat (10:20). On another occasion He will speak of those who have the power to cast out demons, yet He calls them evildoers (Matthew 7:22–23).

Jesus is also full of joy. Although He has "resolutely set out for Jerusalem" (9:51 NIV) to die, He is filled with the Holy Spirit at this point and praises God for the opportunity, at last, for people to witness what the seventy-two have seen. He tells them privately that they have witnessed what prophets and kings have long wished to see (10:23–24), and that God is revealing spiritual insights to them that will remain hidden from the wise and educated (10:21). How can they not feel joy?

📖 10:25–37

THE GOOD SAMARITAN

One day Jesus is approached by "an expert in the law" (10:25 NIV). He asks Jesus about the scriptural prerequisites for inheriting eternal life. Jesus turns the question back on the man, who cites commands from Deuteronomy 6:5 and Leviticus 19:18—to love God with all one's heart, soul, strength, and mind, and to love one's neighbor as oneself. Jesus agrees with the man's answer, adding, "Do this and you will live" (10:28 NIV).

But in order to justify himself, the man asks a second question: "And who is my neighbor?" (10:29 NIV). In response, Jesus tells the Parable of the Good Samaritan. The Jewish priest and Levite, both of whom hold respected religious positions, choose to ignore a severely injured man on the road. The fact that they are going down the road (10:30–32) suggests they are coming from Jerusalem and aren't rushing to some important obligation at the temple. They even go out of their way to cross the road to avoid close contact.

In contrast, a Samaritan—a man who would have been despised by the Jews— sees the same man. He stops, treats his wounds, transports him to an inn, cares for him, and pays the innkeeper to watch over the injured man until he can return. He does everything he can possibly do. So Jesus asks the lawyer which of the three men acted as a neighbor.

The expert in the Law can't even bring himself to say, "The Samaritan." Rather, he responds, "The one who had mercy on him." And Jesus says, "Go and do likewise" (10:37 NIV).

That's twice that the man asks Jesus a question, answers his own question, and is told by Jesus to do what he has said. He thought he was doing a good job of justifying himself by his works, but Jesus quickly shows him it isn't as easy as he thought. Love for God is demonstrated by love for others—all others.

It might appear from the story of the Good Samaritan that Jesus is advocating salvation by works. Jesus is, in reality, doing the opposite. He is attempting to show this expert in the Law that in order to be saved through law-keeping, he will have to do that which he has not been able to do (that is why he felt the need to justify himself), and that no one can do, for salvation through the Law requires perfect, progressive obedience to the Law, without one failure.

Critical Observation

Luke has briefly mentioned the tension between the Jews and Samaritans (9:51–56), but the problem had existed for centuries. When the Assyrians defeated the Israelites in the mid-700s BC, they took many people into exile and brought their own people in to resettle Samaria and other areas. The remaining Israelites eventually intermarried with the Gentiles. When the Jews came out of captivity and returned to their homeland, they faced opposition from the inhabitants, and the mutual dislike of Jews and Samaritans continued from that point forward. But the hostility reached its peak around the time of Jesus' ministry.

📖 10:38–42

MARY AND MARTHA DISAGREE ABOUT WHAT'S IMPORTANT

In another story recorded only by Luke, Jesus is invited to have dinner at the home of Martha, who has a sister named Mary. (They also have a brother named Lazarus [John 11:1–2], whom Jesus raised from the dead.) Martha appears to be the older of the two sisters. In Luke 10 verses 38 and 40, Martha is depicted as the hostess, who invites Jesus into her home. Martha seems not only to be the older, but the more aggressive and outspoken of the two women. It is she who went out to meet Jesus after Lazarus died, and to inform Him that this would not have happened if He would have been there sooner (John 11:20–21).

Mary sits at the feet of Jesus while Martha is busy preparing a meal in the kitchen, which finally aggravates Martha to the point where she goes and asks Jesus to tell Mary to help her (10:40). It's easy to assume that Mary is clearly the more spiritual of the two, yet Martha has a point. This is no small meal. Jesus has His disciples with Him (10:38), which at the time might have been a number much larger than twelve. Who can blame Martha for wanting help? For Luke's first-century audience, Martha's role seems much more understandable than Mary's. They would have been shocked by Mary's behavior—in Judaism, women did not learn at the feet of a rabbi.

Still, Martha seems more angry than jealous. It must be hard to hear that Mary has made the better choice (10:42). Jesus shows no anger toward Martha. Nor does He impose a stereotypical "woman's role" on either of the women. He merely tries to clarify what should have been the highest priority at that moment. And He deals more with their attitudes than their actions.

The story of Martha and Mary underscores the importance and priority of learning at the feet of Jesus, that is, being His disciple. It was not the frantic activity of Martha that won Jesus' commendation, but the quiet activity of Mary, who sat at the feet of her Savior, listening intently to His teaching.

Take It Home

Are you by nature more like Mary or Martha? At church meetings or similar gatherings, are you more attentive to the needs of the group or the content being discussed. . .or are they equally important to you? Regardless of your natural tendencies, how can you ensure that you stay focused on what is better—the one thing that is needed (10:42)?

LUKE 11:1–54

PRAYER, DEMONS, SIGNS, AND WOES

Lessons on Prayer	11:1–13
Jesus vs. Beelzebub	11:14–36
A Long Series of Woes	11:37–54

Setting Up the Section

People are beginning to respond to Jesus' ministry in various ways. He has preached and healed, but has also taught by personal example. Now His disciples begin to ask about how to pray. Onlookers speculate as to how He casts out demons. People start to expect fantastic signs from Him. And the Pharisees increase their opposition to Him.

Up to this point, the emphasis of Luke has fallen on the prayer life of Jesus. But here a certain unnamed disciple sees the Lord's practice as a pattern, one which each disciple should follow, and thus Jesus is asked to teach the disciples to pray as well. The prayer life that characterizes our Lord will, in the book of Acts, characterize the disciples as well. Luke is paving the way, laying the foundation for that constant communion with God in prayer.

📄 11:1–13

LESSONS ON PRAYER

One day when Jesus had just finished praying, one of the disciples asks Him to teach their group to pray. Perhaps the curious disciple had previously been a follower of John the Baptist (11:1). In response, Jesus provides what has become known as the Lord's Prayer (11:2–4), although Luke's version is a bit shorter than the more familiar version found in Matthew 6:9–13.

The prayer Jesus gives to His disciples as a pattern is a short one. This prayer does not include all of the elements of prayer. The prayer is a skeletal one, one which can be filled in with much greater detail, but it is also one that does outline the essential elements of our prayers. It underscores three areas of need:

1) The coming of the kingdom of God. This is a desire for the authority of the Father to be fully established on the earth, and for His glory and splendor to be revealed.

2) Physical needs. The Father is the provider for His children, and thus the disciples are taught to ask Him for their daily needs. The bread represents not just food in a general sense, but all of the areas of physical need.

3) The spiritual needs of saints who still sin. Salvation delivers one from the penalty of sin, but only the return of Christ will rid the saint of the presence of sin. Thus, Jesus taught His disciples to pray for forgiveness for their sins. In order to enjoy fellowship with God, the barrier of our sins must be removed by His forgiveness. There is an ongoing need for this, and it is for this that Jesus taught us to pray.

In this case Jesus does not initiate the discussion of prayer. He has modeled it enough for others to notice and become curious. When asked, He follows His model of prayer with additional instructions. Having provided a model, Jesus moves to the motivation for prayer. To do this He tells two parables. The first parable deals with one's request of a friend (11:5–10); the second with the request made of one's father (11:11–13).

The parable in verses 5–8 demonstrates the need for persistence in prayer. If people can be swayed to change their minds in response to their friends, even at inconvenient times, then how much more is a loving God willing to respond to His followers? The result of persistence is receiving as much as one needs. Yet it is important to ask, seek, and knock (11:9–10) rather than assume God will drop all we need into our laps with no thought.

In the second parable, Jesus teaches that God is like a father who wants only the best for his children (11:11–13). Human fathers give their children good things when asked, rather than potentially harmful substitutes. So a loving, heavenly Father who knows our needs will certainly provide much more for His children. But rather than give us everything we ask for (much of which is not necessarily needed or helpful), God provides the Holy Spirit to those who ask. With the wisdom, strength, and comfort provided by God's Spirit, there is little else we actually need (11:13).

📄 11:14–36

JESUS VS. BEELZEBUB

Jesus has cast out evil spirits from people on numerous occasions. So have the apostles (9:1) and the seventy-two disciples (10:17). Even people they didn't know were driving out demons in the name of Jesus (9:49). But on this occasion, Jesus' onlookers decide to challenge Him.

They can't deny that a miracle has taken place, because a previously mute man is speaking clearly after the removal of the spirit (11:14). So Jesus' critics (Pharisees and teachers of the Law, according to Matthew 12:24 and Mark 3:22) try to question the motive behind the miracle. They accuse Jesus of having the power of Beelzebub, "the prince of demons" (11:15 NIV).

Demystifying Luke

The Old Testament Philistines had worshiped their god Baal under the name Baal-Zebub. The Greek version became Beelzebub, meaning "lord of flies." Perhaps it was an intentional variant spelling of Beelzeboul, which meant "lord of the dwelling." Beelzebub came to be used as a name for Satan (11:18).

Jesus immediately points out the illogic of their speculation. Why would anyone working in league with Satan go around removing evil spirits (11:17–18)? In addition, asks Jesus, how about other Jewish people who drive out demons, or for that matter, the Jewish belief that the power of God could remove evil spirits (11:19)? Is their work of the devil? And even more important: What if they are wrong about Jesus? If indeed He is using the power of God, they are guilty of resisting the kingdom of God (11:20).

Jesus' response quickly shows how foolish such a conclusion is. It was as if Jesus had said, "Who willingly and knowingly shoots himself in the foot?" Satan would not do harm to himself, would he? The opponents of Jesus are foolish to make such a charge against Him. Not only is it false; it isn't even logical.

Jesus has probed their logic (which is faulty), and He has pressed it to a very uncomfortable conclusion (their disciples or followers are operating by Satan's power, too, for they also cast out demons). Now, He gives them one more logical thrust: If they are wrong and He is operating in the power of God, then they must admit that the kingdom of God has come and that Jesus is the Messiah. This is the very thing they most dread, and Jesus has just reminded them of what good logic must conclude: He is the King, whom they refuse to receive.

The second argument of Jesus is just as forceful as the first. Not only are Jesus' opponents wrong in attributing His power to Satan because Satan would not attack himself, but they are also wrong because the One who would attack Satan must be more powerful. No one can take away the possessions of a powerful man without first overpowering the person. The powerful man must first be overpowered, then disarmed, and finally bound, so that his goods can be plundered. Satan is indeed strong (11:21); he takes possession of certain people. But Jesus is stronger (11:22), capable of overpowering him and freeing those who have been bound.

So Jesus soundly refutes the supposition that He might be using the power of the devil, but He also responds to numerous other speculations in this passage. When a woman tries to praise Jesus' mother, He again shifts the focus from His flesh-and-blood relatives to a broader sense of family—all those who hear the Word of God and obey it (11:28; 8:21).

For those in the crowd who may have been trying to remain neutral on the issue, Jesus warns what can happen to those who try to cleanse themselves using their own power. The power of God is necessary to effectively and lastingly deal with the problem of sin and evil (11:24–26).

Then there are those who are asking for a sign (11:16)—probably one of the day-of-the-Lord signs foretold in the Old Testament (such as Joel 2:30–31). Even when John the Baptist had sought additional confirmation about Jesus, He had simply said to look at what He was doing (7:22). If the cure of a mute man is not enough, what else do they want?

Jesus has very strong words for those who request a sign from heaven. His words inform us that this is evidence of a wicked generation of Israelites, and so much so that the "belief" of two

Old Testament peoples puts them to shame. The people of Nineveh accepted the "sign of Jonah" (11:29 NIV) and repented, and the Queen of the South believed the reports about Solomon's wisdom (11:31). For this, they will testify in the day of judgment against this generation for their unbelief (11:32).

Critical Observation

Jesus' mention of the Ninevites (Jonah 3:5–10) and the Queen of the South (1 Kings 10:6–9) is telling. First, because both are Gentiles, and they, because of their belief, condemn the unbelief of this generation of Israelites. Second, both parties believed with much less evidence than what Jesus' audience had seen. The Ninevites repented at the preaching of Jonah, which, as we find it recorded in the book of Jonah, may have been only one short proclamation that they had forty days to straighten up or they would perish. The Queen of the South also was convinced of Solomon's wisdom when she merely heard his words.

The responses of all of these people within the crowd that witnessed Jesus' deliverance of the demoniac were varied, but the end result and the problem was the same in every case: They did not believe in Jesus as their Messiah. And this unbelief was rooted in their rejection of Jesus' words, which led them to a misinterpretation of His works. These who looked beyond the clear manifestations of God's power would receive no other signs (11:29–32).

In the final paragraph of this section, Jesus now exposes the real problem. In verse 33 Jesus says that the purpose of a lamp is to illuminate, and thus a light is put in a prominent place. Since He came to illuminate people (Luke 1:79; John 1:4–18), He does not speak or act in secret, but in the open. His light, as it were, is brightly exposed to people. His generation will not perish for lack of light.

The eye, Jesus says, is the gateway to the person's entire being, his whole body. If the eye is good, if it lets in the light, the whole body is illuminated. If the eye is defective, if it lets in little light, the whole body is dark. Jesus is saying that everyone who fails to interpret the evidence of this miracle as they should has done so because of a defect in their ability to see the truth, not because of any deficiency in the evidence (11:34).

11:37–54

A LONG SERIES OF WOES

It seems odd that after refuting the Pharisees so soundly, one of them invites Jesus to eat with him (11:37). The washing that Jesus decides to forego is not the kind of washing up that mothers insist on before a meal, the washing required by good hygiene. The concern here is not dirty hands but ceremonial defilement. This is a washing that is required by the traditions of the Pharisees, rather than by the Law itself (Mark 7:1–4). It seems He may have intentionally passed on the opportunity in order to challenge the Pharisees on their habits. They remain highly focused on looks and external matters, but have lost sight of the inward purity God desires for His people (11:39–41).

Critical Observation

The word *Pharisee* may very well be derived from a term that means "to separate." The origin of the Pharisees as a sect seems to have been in or around the second century BC. They were not known as a primarily political group as much as the zealots who wanted change through revolution. The Pharisees sought to produce spiritual holiness and spiritual reformation. They recognized that Israel's condition was the result of sin, specifically a disobedience to the Law. It was their intention to identify, communicate, and facilitate obedience to God's law, thus producing holiness and paving the way for the kingdom of God to be established on the earth.

The problem with the Pharisees is not in what they believed, and not even in what they hoped to do, but in what they actually became and did. Their goals were noble and their presuppositions were essentially correct, but they were sidetracked. Instead of being the first to recognize Jesus as the Messiah, they were the first to reject Him. Rather than turning the nation to Him, they sought to turn the nation against Him.

Jesus' response to the Pharisee (11:39–41) is an answer to his surprise at the Lord's avoidance of ceremonial washing. While our Lord is addressing His host, He is also confronting the evils of the whole Pharisaic system (11:39), of which this man is a part.

Jesus' words here can be difficult to follow because the imagery changes so quickly and so often. The overall thrust is the contrast between the outside, which is secondary, and the inside, which is primary. Jesus begins by talking about the washing of the outside of a cup or a dish, but then moves to the inside of a man. He then moves back to the dish imagery and tells His host that He can make the dish clean by emptying its contents and giving them to the poor.

The overall impact of Jesus' words is clear. Jesus differs from His host and the other Pharisees by seeing the inside as more important than the outside—the heart more important than appearances, one's attitudes and motives more important than one's actions. The Pharisees believed that a man is made holy by working from the outside, in. Jesus believed that holiness (and defilement) came from the inside, out.

When it becomes obvious that His host is uncomfortable with His refusal to wash, Jesus unleashes a series of three "woes" on the Pharisees as a group.

1) They emphasized minute points of law while missing the basic fundamentals (11:42).
2) They were preoccupied with position, prestige, and praise (11:43).
3) They had become a source of defilement rather than purification (11:44).

Similarly, the experts in the Law, who should have been the elite subset of the Pharisees, are offended. But Jesus proclaims three woes for them as well.

1) Their teaching resulted in burdens rather than blessings on the people (11:46).
2) They had the same attitude as their forefathers who had persecuted and even killed God's prophets (11:47–51).
3) These self-proclaimed experts had not only lost sight of God's knowledge, but they were hindering others from discovering it as well (11:52).

Not surprisingly, after Jesus addresses the Pharisees and experts of the Law, they get together in fierce opposition to Him (11:53).

Of what did the Pharisees accuse Jesus?	Of what were the Pharisees accused in the Gospels?
1) Eating/associating with sinners—Matthew 9:11; Mark 2:16; Luke 5:30; 7:39; 15:2	1) Hypocrisy—bring forth fruit worthy of repentance—Matthew 3:7–8
2) Not fasting as they did—Matthew 9:14; Mark 2:18; Luke 5:33	2) Honoring God with mouth, but heart far away—Matthew 15:7–20
3) Operating in power of Satan—Matthew 9:34	3) Justifying selves in men's sight, but God knows hearts—Luke 16:15
4) Disciples violating Sabbath by eating—Matthew 12:2; Mark 2:24; Luke 6:2	4) Self-righteousness—Luke 18:10–14
5) Jesus violating Sabbath by healing man with withered hand—Mark 3:1–5; Luke 6:6–10	5) Not having works sufficient to get them into kingdom—Matthew 5:20
6) Healing man with dropsy on Sabbath—Luke 14:1-6	6) Placing their traditions above the Law—Matthew 15:1–20
7) Violating Sabbath, He cannot be Messiah—John 9:16	7) Focusing on externals, not internals—Luke 11:39–41
8) His disciples didn't wash their hands ceremonially—Matthew 15:1–20; Mark 7:1–9	8) Demanding a sign—Matthew 16:1-4; Mark 8:11-12
9) Under what conditions can a man divorce his wife? —Matthew 19:3–12; Mark 10:2–12	9) The leaven of/in their teaching—Matthew 16:5-12
10) Claiming, by inference (sins forgiven) to be God—Luke 5:17–25	10) Being ignorant of the scriptures—Matthew 19; 21:42, and of power of God (Matthew 22:29).
11) Testing Jesus as to what to do with woman caught in adultery/application of the Law—John 8:3–11	11) Elevating themselves and seeking prominence—Matthew 23:2, 5-6
12) Jesus appearing as His own witness—John 8:13–19	12) Shutting off kingdom of heaven from men—Matthew 23:13
	13) Using technicalities as excuses for disobedience of law—Matthew 23:16-24
	14) Focusing on trivial but missing the main points—Matthew 23:23–28
	15) Being lovers of money—Luke 16:14
	16) Disdaining the crowds, who knew not the Law—John 7:49

Take It Home

One of the temptations we face as Christians, and which our text clearly exposes, is to focus on outward acts or appearances rather than on inward motivation. We are often guilty of taking new Christians aside and trying to rid them of their evil behaviors, as though cleaning up the outside purifies the inside. Jesus teaches us that when we clean up the inside, when our attitudes and our motives are pure, our outward lives will clean up. Often, cleaning up only the outside tends to corrupt the inside more. Now, having cleaned up the outside, we find pride and self-righteousness to be added to our list of inner evils. Let us learn from our Lord that holiness begins inside and works out, and not the reverse.

LUKE 12:1–59

WARNINGS AND ASSURANCES

Beware Bad Yeast	12:1–11
Hoarding vs. Trust	12:12–34
Two Contrasting Scenarios	12:35–59

Setting Up the Section

After having just publicly confronted the Pharisees and teachers of the Law, Luke moves to an instance where Jesus gives specific instructions to His apostles about the problems of hypocrisy. He also addresses proper stewardship of the gospel, possessions, and the use of our time.

📄 **12:1–11**

BEWARE BAD YEAST

Jesus and His followers are surrounded by a trampling crowd of thousands (12:1). Yet Jesus seems to ignore the masses and speaks directly to the disciples.

Jesus states clearly that the "yeast" (12:1 NIV) of the Pharisees is hypocrisy—and the danger is that it permeates and spreads like yeast throughout the entire lump of dough. They tend to know little about true religion and act as if they do. On the outside, they look fine. They have long, pious-sounding prayers, and they have all of the trappings of men of dignity and holiness. But inside, Jesus says, they are full of greed and wickedness (11:39). But how can the disciples possibly be tempted to be hypocritical, like the Pharisees?

Critical Observation

Hypocrisy can take many forms:

- Hypocrisy can be a conformity to the values and expectations of someone else, bowing to the idol of other people's values, which are not really our own. Hypocrites adjust and accommodate their appearance to what other people think or feel.

- Hypocrisy can be an inconsistency. It's the discrepancy between what appears and what is, between the way things seem and the way they are. The Pharisees appeared to be righteous on the outside but, in reality, they were wicked.

- Hypocrisy can be a deception by our actions or our words, acting in such a way that people will come to the wrong conclusion. This, to a large degree, was true of the Pharisees.

Hypocrisy is a problem no matter what the motivation. Whether we are hypocritical either to achieve men's praise as the Pharisees or to avoid their persecution, perhaps as the disciples, Jesus calls us to something different.

Jesus seems to suggest that a more likely problem for His disciples is knowledge of the complete truth yet being reluctant to speak out. Perhaps that's why He speaks of hidden things being made known (12:2–3) and fear of those who can physically threaten (12:4). But He also makes clear each person's worth and God's awareness of each person and situation (12:6–7). He tempers His comments on the fear of God by addressing His listeners as "friends" (12:4 NIV).

Jesus challenges His followers to stand firm for Him when the time comes, promising that He will be their heavenly advocate (12:8–9). The unforgivable sin of blasphemy against the Holy Spirit is better defined in Matthew 12:31–32, and Mark 3:23–30 as attributing the work of the Holy Spirit to Satan. If someone does not acknowledge the role of the Holy Spirit in faith and salvation, no other course of forgiveness exists. Indeed, it is the Holy Spirit who will instruct believers on what to say during times of trial and persecution.

We see a number of examples of those who stand firm in the power of the Spirit in the book of Acts. Peter and John, when arrested, boldly preach the gospel as their defense (Acts 4). Stephen, when arrested and charged before the crowd, powerfully preaches the gospel as his defense (Acts 6–7). So, too, with Paul (Acts 22). The Holy Spirit gives people under duress a special sense of God's presence (Acts 7:55–56), thus comforting and assuring them. He also gives them the words to speak and the power to speak them boldly.

📄 **12:12–34**

HOARDING VS. TRUST

Still surrounded by a great crowd, a voice breaks through while Jesus is talking to His disciples (12:13). Jesus is a rabbi, a teacher. He has not come to oversee probate court, and He lets the man know (12:14). It is unclear to whom the following parable is directed, whether the disciples, the crowd, or maybe even the questioner and his brother who are disputing their inheritance. Yet Jesus clearly identifies the root of the problem: greed (12:15).

The Parable of the Rich Fool (12:16–21) teaches that a person's view of the future determines his or her present conduct. The rich man does well to think in terms of the future; his failure is in not recognizing where his wealth has come from. Jesus clarifies that it is the ground that produces a good crop (12:16). God has provided the wealth, but the man is seeking to cash it in and store it.

Critical Observation

Modern readers of the Parable of the Rich Fool may be a bit discomfited to realize that his plans for the future are not very different from many people's goals for retirement. Jesus' teaching in the following passage (12:22–34) helps put the teaching of this parable in context. Whether wealthy or poor, we should keep our focus on real treasure (12:33).

The rich man is a fool because he perceives his possessions as his security. He has great wealth, but doesn't use it for anyone except himself. However, Jesus is not condemning wealth per se in this parable. His own interpretation is that this is how it will be for anyone who stores up wealth but is not rich toward God (12:21). Concern for the future, He says, should not escalate into worry (12:22). Just as rich people can become preoccupied with accumulating wealth, so can those of lesser means.

Jesus' statement that life is more than food (12:23) reflects His rebuke of the devil during His temptation (4:4). When we worry about clothing or food we fail to focus on what is most important in life. Additionally, such worry is foolish when we consider God's marvelous provision for His creatures in nature (12:24–28). Believers should put God's kingdom first, and everything else will fall into place (12:30–31).

It seems that Jesus isn't putting His disciples into the category of poor people, because He tells them to sell their possessions and give to the poor (12:33)—a general rule, not a broad-sweeping command. What is in one's heart is inextricably connected to his or her idea of treasure. In the long run, heavenly things endure as earthly ones deteriorate (12:33–34).

📖 12:35–59

TWO CONTRASTING SCENARIOS

Jesus then tells two parallel stories, both of which emphasize the importance of readiness for His coming, yet with vastly different results. In the first (12:35–38), a master has attended a wedding banquet and his servants are anticipating his return. Keeping the lamps burning (12:35) was important in a culture without electricity or streetlights. And when the master gets home and finds his servants faithfully waiting, he serves them (12:37). Keep in mind how counter-cultural this image would be in the first century—a master serving his slave!

In contrast, Jesus speaks of a homeowner who has no interest in visitors (12:39–40). In this case, the return of the Son of Man is described in terms of an unexpected thief who breaks into the house.

In both stories the coming of someone is unscheduled. The difference, however, is the relationship between those in the house and the one who will be arriving. The faithful servants—those that are alert and ready—are rewarded for their watchfulness.

The disciples are confused, and as usual, it is Peter who speaks up to ask Jesus to clarify (12:41). Jesus doesn't respond directly, but gives additional clues to what He means (12:42–48). If directed to individuals, Jesus' words are uncomfortably severe. Another interpretation, however, is that the nation of Israel is the servant who knows what his master wants (12:47). Because they are not ready to receive Jesus, the Jews are cut to pieces (dispersed) and assigned a place with the unbelieving Gentiles (12:46). The Church (including both believing Jews and Gentiles) will eventually be put in charge of the Master's possessions (12:44). Whether eagerly anticipated or dreaded, one's attitude toward the Lord's second coming is the result of his or her response to His first coming.

Demystifying Luke

Throughout the Bible, fire is closely associated with the presence and power of God. It is figuratively and literally an instrument of divine wrath exercised against sinful people—both Jews and Gentiles. Biblical prophecy speaks of fire yet to come, including the fire of divine judgment linked with the Messiah. At the outset of his ministry, John the Baptist spoke of the coming Messiah as bringing fire (3:16–17).

Jesus continues with some additional alarming statements in verses 49–59. He speaks of coming fire (12:49), division of families (12:52–53), and the possibility of prison for those who don't reconcile with the magistrate (12:58). Jesus' ministry will not bring peace to everyone. He is going to judge sin, and unrepentant sinners will be punished before God's kingdom can ultimately be established. Yet the passing of judgment will not only be painful to sinful people; it is painful to God as well. In addition to God not wanting to see anyone perish (2 Peter 3:9), there will be the literal pain Jesus will experience. It is a baptism He dreads (12:50). His love for humankind will motivate Him to go through with it, yet not all the consequences will be positive.

Take It Home

Opposition in the disciples' day took the form of the raised fist; today it frequently takes the place of the raised eyebrow. People don't want to be looked down on, or even questioned as to their motives when it comes to spiritual things. To what extent are your own religious beliefs (or more specifically, your public statements of faith) influenced by the actions and attitudes of others? Do you detect any hypocrisy? Greed? An air of superiority?

LUKE 13:1–35

CLEARING UP SOME MISCONCEPTIONS

Why Do Bad Things Happen?	13:1–9
Resentment in Response to a Healing	13:10–17
Two Short Parables	13:18–21
Take Nothing for Granted	13:22–35

Setting Up the Section

In this passage Luke describes Jesus in a number of settings. He is still healing and teaching, but the tone of His message has changed. He speaks of punishment, weeping, gnashing of teeth, and the coming desolation of Jerusalem. Yet He also tells of God's patience and the ongoing opportunities for people to participate in God's rapidly growing kingdom.

📖 13:1–9

WHY DO BAD THINGS HAPPEN?

Verses 1–9 seem to take place in the same setting as before, where Jesus and His disciples were surrounded by a crowd of thousands (12:1). Some of those present bring up news of a recent tragedy: Pilate had ordered people killed while they were offering sacrifices in the temple (13:1). This was more than a mere statement of fact; it was an assumption that the people killed were somehow more guilty of sin than others, and God had allowed them to die. Similarly, a common belief was that a person's prosperity was proportional to his or her piety.

In response, Jesus speaks of a different tragedy—the collapse of a tower inside the wall of Jerusalem that had killed eighteen people (13:4). The two tragedies are quite similar. In both cases, people had died suddenly and unexpectedly at places where they probably felt most secure. One group was offering sacrifices to God; the other was adjacent to a structure that had been erected for the group's defense.

In both cases, Jesus emphatically refutes the assumption that the victims had done anything to expedite their deaths. Rather, He teaches His listeners to view the two events as symbolic of the kind of death that everyone who doesn't repent will face (13:3, 5).

He follows His comments with a parable about a fig tree (13:6–9). The lack of fruit certainly applies to Israel, as confirmed by other statements and parables Jesus has been teaching. Yet in spite of the nation's stubborn rebellion and sin, the parable emphasizes God's patience and an extended period of grace (13:7–9).

Demystifying Luke

A fig tree was a common biblical symbol for the nation of Israel, which is likely the case in Jesus' parable (13:6–9). Many gardens in the area were planned with a fig tree planted in the center. If the tree failed to produce fruit, it only made sense to remove it to use the space for something more productive.

📄 **13:10–17**

RESENTMENT IN RESPONSE TO A HEALING

The setting for this section changes from that of a crowded street to a synagogue where Jesus is teaching. (This will be Luke's final mention of Jesus teaching in such a location.) While there, He sees a woman who has been crippled for eighteen years, calls her forward, and heals her. It is the Sabbath, and the synagogue leader becomes upset.

Previously, Pharisees who had opposed Jesus' healings on the Sabbath had challenged Him personally. The synagogue leader uses a different tactic: He starts telling the people to come for healings only on the six days suited for work (13:14).

Jesus calls him on his hypocrisy. First, how likely will it be that anyone will be healed there on a workday if Jesus is not present? Second, as the healed woman and numerous onlookers are praising God (13:13, 17), the very person in charge is trying to shut down their enthusiasm. And finally, Jesus points out that the man isn't even giving the woman ("a daughter of Abraham" [13:16 NIV]) the same respect he would give his ox or donkey (13:15–16 NIV).

📄 **13:18–21**

TWO SHORT PARABLES

The Parable of the Mustard Seed (13:18–19) is frequently interpreted as showing how quickly the kingdom of God would grow. However, another interpretation is possible. In the original language, the seed was not so much planted as thrown, or cast aside. Perhaps the mustard plant wasn't planned or provided for, yet grew surprisingly large and strong. If this is the case, perhaps Jesus is suggesting that His rejection by the Jewish people is like being cast aside, yet the end result will be a strong kingdom that provides for all believers, including Gentiles. In contrast to the well-tended but fruitless fig tree in danger of being destroyed (13:6–9), the mustard plant will thrive.

Similarly, the next parable (13:20–21) can have different interpretations. It may be that the woman mixed the yeast into the flour. Or perhaps her intent was to hide the yeast (another acceptable translation). If the latter, the woman's efforts certainly backfired because a little yeast would quickly permeate a large amount of dough. If, like the synagogue leader in verse 14, the leaders of the Israelites are attempting to hide the gospel—especially from the Gentiles—their efforts are futile.

📖 **13:22–35**

TAKE NOTHING FOR GRANTED

Jesus is continuing toward Jerusalem (13:22), where He knows He will be put to death. A voice in the crowd calls out, "Lord, are only a few people going to be saved?" (13:23 NIV).

Jesus doesn't respond to the question directly, but rather begins to speak in terms of a door and limited time to enter (13:24–25). The door is narrow, but at least it is currently open.

Salvation will involve more than mere association with Jesus, such as sharing a meal or listening to His words (13:26). Some people who assume entitlement to God's kingdom are considered "evildoers" by Jesus (13:27 NIV). In the kingdom of God, many who consider themselves first will be last, and those who are last will become first.

At this point in His ministry, Jesus is not to be deterred from His mission—not even by rumors of Herod's desire to kill Him (13:31). While Herod is hoping to meet Jesus (9:9) he also fears Him, thinking He might be the resurrected John the Baptist, whom Herod himself had executed (9:7-9). Jesus isn't swayed. He gives the Pharisees a return message, though it is doubtful they will have the courage to deliver it (13:32-33).

Jesus knows exactly what to say, and again He expresses sorrow for what He sees. He concludes this section of His teaching with a fondness for Jerusalem and her people (13:34-35). Yet He keeps moving in that direction to do what He has come to do.

LUKE 14:1-35
BANQUET ETIQUETTE

Dinner Conversation   14:1–14
A Banquet Parable   14:15–24
Seeing Things Through to the Finish   14:25–35

Setting Up the Section

In recent passages, Jesus has been teaching some difficult lessons, and He continues in this one—once at a dinner and again while beset by crowds as He travels. Much of what He says is easy to understand, even though His listeners might be reluctant to acknowledge it. Some of His teachings are, and have always been, a bit difficult to comprehend without considerable thought and reflection.

📄 **14:1–14**

DINNER CONVERSATION

If it seems suspicious that Jesus is invited to eat with a prominent Pharisee, such suspicions are confirmed when we read He is carefully being watched (14:1). Also quite dubious is the diseased man coming to Him on the Sabbath (14:2). Jesus is clearly aware of what is going on because He asks His fellow diners whether they believe it is lawful to heal on the Sabbath. Since the Sabbath forbade work, the rabbis typically debated whether it was lawful to do good, such as healing, on the Sabbath. Different rabbis had different opinions. Generally it was considered that only life-threatening disease or injury could be treated on the Sabbath.

When no one is willing to speak up, Jesus heals the man with dropsy and sends him on his way (14:4). Jesus is aware that the Pharisees wouldn't hesitate to make an exception to their traditions about "work" if one of their sons, or even one of their animals, needed help on the Sabbath. Still, they try to impose their legalistic standards on others, so Jesus doesn't hesitate to call them on their hypocrisy. Even after Jesus' miracle they have nothing to say (14:6).

Demystifying Luke

Dropsy (14:2) was a medical condition noted only by Luke (a doctor) in the New Testament. Now called edema, it occurs when fluid accumulates in the body and causes soft tissue to swell. If prolonged, the problem can be terminal.

The Pharisees' air of superiority is reflected in their table manners as well.

Certain seats, usually those nearest the host, were considered places of honor. (This was true not only for the Pharisees, but throughout the Greco-Roman world.) It had become something of an art to secure one of the better seats at any occasion. It wasn't unlike musical chairs as grown men jockeyed for the best positions at social functions. Jesus points out that it would be much more preferable to be asked by the host to move up rather than be humiliated by being asked publicly to yield your seat to a more distinguished person (14:7–11). Ironically, Jesus is probably in the lowest position as He tells the group that "everyone who exalts himself will be humbled, and he who humbles himself will be exalted" (14:11 NIV). In other words, the way up is down. Those who wish to be honored must be humble. The ways of the kingdom of God are not man's ways.

Critical Observation

In Israel the meal table played a very important role, not only in the family, but in society as well. When an Israelite provided a meal for a guest, even a stranger, it assured him not only of the host's hospitality, but of his protection.

Jesus also challenges the dinner guests to provide meals for those who cannot afford to throw parties—the poor, crippled, lame, and blind (14:12–14). When planning a banquet, the temptation is to invite those who are most likely to benefit us in return. Thus, one thinks first of inviting family members or rich friends, who will reciprocate in kind. We are tempted to give in order to get. Jesus teaches that this practice should not only be revised, but reversed. In this world, people invite their friends and the rich, in order to gain from their reciprocal invitations and hospitality. In God's economy, people should be gracious to the helpless and to those who cannot pay them back, and when the kingdom of God is established on the earth, they will receive spiritual rewards. Rather than seeing one's hospitality repaid as it would be by family or friends, the more satisfying result would be blessings and eternal rewards.

📄 14:15–24

A BANQUET PARABLE

The ambience of the dinner party is probably a bit tense at this point, so perhaps the man's comment in verse 15 is an attempt to lighten the mood. However, it also emphasizes the Pharisaical belief that they will be the ones around the table in God's kingdom.

Demystifying Luke

The mention of a feast that would happen in God's kingdom (14:15) is a reference to Isaiah 25:6–8. God's salvation is portrayed as a great final banquet with the Lord as the host. This is actually an important theme that runs through Luke—look at all the meal scenes!

The parable Jesus tells in response (14:16–24) confirms that, indeed, the leaders of Israel should be at the banquet. The invitations have been sent out well in advance of the event, and it appears that the recipients have responded that they will be coming. But when the big day arrives and a messenger is sent to escort them to the banquet hall, they all give reasons why they cannot attend. They are expecting the master of the banquet (which certainly must represent God) to excuse them.

The excuses cited by Jesus are telling. Staying home with a new wife (14:20) is a poor enough excuse, but the others are even more ludicrous. One person wants to go see a field he has apparently bought sight unseen (14:18). The second person has supposedly bought a pair of oxen without even trying them out (14:19). Not only are these people making last-minute excuses, the excuses aren't even good ones!

The master becomes angry when he receives his servant's report. He sends the servant right back out with instructions to bring in all the street people he can find. The servant rounds up all the poor, crippled, blind, and lame people he can find (14:21 [also see 14:13]), but there is still room. So the master sends him to the outer roads and country lanes to gather enough to fill the house. The original elite who declined the invitation are no longer welcome. But the others who would normally be considered outsiders (probably an allusion to the Gentiles) are compelled to come. For them, the master will not take no for an answer.

The Pharisee's dinner guest is correct. It will be a blessing to eat at the feast in the kingdom of God (14:15). But the guest list will be very different from what any of those present can imagine.

📄 14:25–35

SEEING THINGS THROUGH TO THE FINISH

It is customary for people to follow Jesus wherever He goes (14:25), but in this instance Jesus begins to talk about what it means to really follow Him as a disciple. His expectations are high—and perhaps seem exceptionally high at first. Since Jesus has been teaching love of enemies and the importance of peacemaking, His instructions to "hate" one's own family must sound peculiar indeed. But a true disciple will not put anything before a relationship with his master. . .not even parents, a spouse, or children (14:26). In addition, discipleship includes a cross of one's own (14:27).

Jesus' two examples help make sense of what He is saying. Anyone who begins a building project but runs out of money (14:28–30) has only a monument to his incompetence. And any king who is outnumbered two to one (14:31–33) is well advised to make peace before fighting begins, or he is likely to have to surrender and be at the mercy of his enemy.

In His conclusion (14:34–35), Jesus makes it clear that He expects commitment and dedication from His disciples. He is very honest and up-front about His expectations. Better to have a few followers who finish what they start than a great number who lose their "saltiness" (14:34 NIV) before getting the job done.

Jesus' closing words, "He who has ears to hear, let him hear," (14:35 NIV) are found several times in the Gospels. The words are used in a context where our Lord is not understood by the majority, and where Jesus encourages His listeners to ponder His words carefully to learn their meaning. They serve as a reminder to contemporary readers as well, to dig deep and understand the broad applications of Jesus' teachings, and to apply them, however painfully, to our own lives.

LUKE 15:1–32
LOST AND FOUND (X 3)

The Lost Sheep	15:1–7
The Lost Coin	15:8–10
The Lost Son	15:11–32

Setting Up the Section

Jesus' debate with the Pharisees continues in this passage. They cite a complaint, and Jesus responds by telling three seemingly related parables, including what has become known as the Parable of the Prodigal Son. But on closer examination, the three parables—each of which describes the finding of a lost item, and each of which describes the joy and celebration that resulted—aren't as similar as they first appear.

THE LOST SHEEP

As Jesus continues to move toward Jerusalem, teaching as He goes, He begins to attract a crowd of tax collectors and sinners (15:1). Jesus treats them with respect, and His willingness to associate with them draws criticism from the Pharisees (15:2).

Jesus' rebuke of the Pharisees in Matthew 23 sheds some light on the constant conflicts Luke describes between them:	
The Pharisees loved to draw attention to themselves (Matthew 23:5).	Jesus spent time with people that held no prominence, thus would not enhance the image of the Pharisees (14:7–11).
The Pharisees took an elitist view as to who could enter God's kingdom (Matthew 23:13).	Jesus, by association with the masses, threatened to pollute this pure group of pious people.
The Pharisees focused on the technicalities (Matthew 23:16–24) based (to some degree) upon their expertise in very complex rules and regulations that left everyday people in a fog.	Jesus taught simply. He threatened to undermine the complicated, technical teaching of the Pharisees, and thus they opposed people pursuing Him to hear His teaching.
The Pharisees protected and promoted their own hypocrisy by concentrating on external sins (behaviors), rather than inner attitudes and motivations (Matthew 23:13–14, 25–36).	Jesus emphasized the internal aspects of sin (Matthew 5–7).

So Jesus tells a series of three stories. The first asks His listeners to put themselves in the place of a man who has one hundred sheep, but loses one. So he leaves the ninety-nine to go find the single lost sheep. When he finds it, he carries it home on his shoulders and then calls his friends and family, asking them to celebrate with him (15:5–6).

This is a story the Pharisees can relate to. Most people have experienced the joy of finding something valuable they had considered lost. Jesus is using this universal feeling to explain that there is rejoicing in heaven when even one sinner repents (15:7).

THE LOST COIN

Jesus' second story is very similar to the first. This time a woman owns ten coins and loses one. She sweeps and searches the house until she finds it. Then she, like the man in the first story, calls together her friends and neighbors to celebrate. And again Jesus observes that, "there is rejoicing in the presence of the angels of God over one sinner who repents" (15:10 NIV).

So far so good. Aside from the fact that the celebrating might seem a bit excessive in both cases, Jesus has said nothing to upset His listeners.

Critical Observation

The critical difference between Jesus and the Pharisees is that the letter cared about possessions, while Jesus cared about people. The Pharisees grumbled that Jesus could eat with and gladly receive repentant sinners and rejoice in their return, yet the Pharisees would diligently search for lost possessions and celebrate when they found them. Among other things, these first two parables indirectly expose the misplaced compassion of the Pharisees. The stories also contrast the kind of love for that which was lost in the Pharisees with that of the Lord Jesus.

The Pharisees were out of sync with heaven. Why were they unwilling to seek out sinners and unable to rejoice at their repentance? Why were they unwilling to associate with them? This is what the third parable will tell us. The third parable depicts the loving and forgiving heart of God (in the father), the repentance of the sinner (in the younger brother), and the sullen joylessness of the Pharisees (in the older brother).

📖 **15:11–32**

THE LOST SON

Although this passage has come to be known as the Parable of the Prodigal Son, it would be more appropriately titled the Parable of the Two Sons. The younger son who asks for his share of the estate (15:12) might have received a third of the father's wealth. (The older son would have been entitled to a double portion.) The assets shouldn't have gone to either son until the death of the father, yet the father grants the son's request.

It doesn't take long before the younger boy has "squandered his wealth in wild living" (15:13 NIV). Not only does he become the hired hand of a pagan landowner, but his work involves feeding pigs—one of the most degrading jobs a Jewish person could think of. So he eventually comes to his senses and decides to return home with a different attitude. Meanwhile, the father appears to have been watching for him because he spots his son "while he was still a long way off" (15:20 NIV). The boy is repentant and ready to work as a servant, but is instead immediately restored to full status as a son.

It is not until this point in the story that Jesus begins to reveal the thoughts and attitudes of the older son: He is incensed that his brother is back home and having a party thrown in his honor. The older brother had worked hard and is upset that he never had such a celebration. The father tries to point out that their relationship is supposed to be reason enough to celebrate (15:31), but the story ends without the older brother being satisfied.

The closing terminology of this story (15:32) echoes the first two: The younger son had been just as "lost" as the sheep and the coin. And now that a personal relationship was at risk, the celebration at finding what was lost should have been even greater. Luke doesn't record the response of the Pharisees, but surely they see their own attitudes reflected in that of the older brother.

Demystifying Luke

Sometimes the Parable of the Prodigal Son is perceived primarily as a source of comfort for all parents with wayward children, and in one sense it is. But in the context of the two preceding stories, this last parable shocks the readers with the grace of the father compared to the lack of grace of the brother (representing the Pharisees). This last parable emphasizes the theme of joy at finding the lost, and by doing so it reveals the Pharisees' lack of concern for the lost.

It is interesting to note that Jesus' story never attempts to minimize the foolishness or serious offense of the younger son. Yet his repentance is equally serious and sincere. If heaven rejoices over one sinner who repents (15:7, 10), the son's return would indeed be a time for such rejoicing. Yet the Pharisees would throw parties for retrieved sheep and coins but not celebrate the "finding" of an actual human being who had been "dead" but was made alive again (15:32).

Whether or not His listeners detect it, Jesus points out a number of similarities between the two sons. Both want a celebration that doesn't include the father (15:13, 29). Neither has a genuine love or appreciation for the father, even though he loves them both. Both sons were slaves—the younger because he squandered his money in a faraway land and the older because of his attitude while working for his father. Both are materialists. And both are sinners.

Only one, however, is on record as being repentant and restoring a good relationship with the father. It is not a lack of love on the father's part, but a lack of repentance on the part of the older son (and the Pharisees) that will prevent receiving all the father has to offer.

Take It Home

The message these three parables brought home to the Pharisees and scribes is painfully clear: They cared too little for lost people. The Pharisees wrongly believed that it was good works that merited God's favor, rather than His grace manifested toward sinners. The older brother was angry with the father because he felt he did not get what he deserved (a banquet), while the younger brother got what he didn't deserve (a banquet). The older brother's works didn't work, but the younger brother's repentance did. That is the way God's grace is—it is bestowed on unworthy people, sinners, who do not trust in their good works but in God's grace.

Part of the Pharisees' logic in not caring for people like the lost son is that they seemed to believe their degree of holiness was measured by the distance they kept from "sinners." The Bible actually speaks of holiness in terms of the closeness we keep to Christ. In the Gospels we find Christ closely associating with, and having compassion on, people whose behavior the religious establishment took exception to. This can be a challenge to us to understand our own ideas of holiness in a different light. Do we shun the very people Christ engaged, invested in, and celebrated the return of?

LUKE 16:1–31

TWO CHALLENGING PARABLES

The Shrewd (Dishonest) Steward	16:1–18
The Rich Man and Lazarus	16:19–31

Setting Up the Section

The entire 16th chapter of Luke revolves around one's attitude toward and use of material possessions. This subject is one that Luke has been speaking to throughout this Gospel. What we find in chapter 16 is not the final word on the subject, but it is more specific in its application than previous references.

Jesus continues to teach His disciples, aware that the Pharisees are listening in on everything He is saying. The Pharisees are lovers of money, so Jesus tells two parables about rich men. One man has a crooked employee he is about to fire, and the other finds himself suffering in hell after a lifetime of selfish luxury.

🖹 LUKE 16:1–18

THE SHREWD (DISHONEST) STEWARD

Luke has had a lot to say about wealth and possessions so far in his Gospel: attitudes toward tax collectors, blessings on the poor, sending disciples out without provisions, invitation lists to banquets, and more. In this passage the topic begins to get more emphasis.

The rich man's steward has been "wasting his possessions" (16:1 NIV)—not unlike padding an expense account or perhaps even embezzling. In effect, he is asked to first give an account of his management and then turn in his resignation.

The steward is panicked at first. He is too proud to beg and not cut out to do manual work. So instead he comes up with a plan to make allies who will help him after he is out of work. He offers deep discounts to his master's clients, pulling each one of them into a knowing co-conspiracy against the business owner (16:5–7). Then, in a surprise ending to the parable (16:8), the master commends the steward because he has acted shrewdly.

How can a man who has just been "ripped off" by his employee, a man who has suffered a substantial and irretrievable loss, commend a crooked employee? The answer to this question is in verse 8.

Our Lord's words here indicate several important realities.

1) Both the unrighteous steward and his master valued the same thing—shrewdness. You don't commend a man for something you disdain.

2) Both the unrighteous steward and his master were members of the group that our Lord characterized as people of the world rather than people of the light. The contemporary expression, "it takes one to know one" fits here.

3) Neither the master nor his steward is a member of the group identified as sons of light. We are accustomed to assuming any master in a parable is a symbol for God. Did Jesus tell

this parable because He, too, commended such behavior? After all, He had told His disciples to be "as shrewd as snakes" (Matthew 10:16 NIV). Is He encouraging His followers to be like this crooked businessperson?

Not at all. Jesus makes His purpose clear: His disciples are to use worldly wealth wisely to achieve eternal ends (16:9). If believers are to follow the steward's example at all, it should be to make friends by the use of material possessions (16:9). The unjust steward saw that his days were numbered, and that he would not be able to take his master's money with him. He then began to use his master's money in such a way as to make friends, because they would outlast his master's money. While we should have an eternal motivation over mere survival, we can use money in such a way that will last forever by building relationships with people who will gratefully receive us in heaven.

Demystifying Luke

The proper interpretation of a Greek or Hebrew word always depends on its context. Just as "being tempted" and "being tested" sound much alike to us but are very different biblical concepts, the word *shrewd* also has quite diverse interpretations. Jesus' use of the word in Matthew 10:16 had a positive connotation of being "wise." The serpent in the Garden of Eden was also shrewd, but the meaning there is closer to "crafty." Most commentators would say that Jesus is saying here that the children of God should be just as shrewd in preparing for their eternal welfare as the sinful children of this age are in protecting their welfare in this life.

The rest of Jesus' commentary seems to be a direct contrast with the actions of the steward. Anyone who can't be trusted with little certainly can't be trusted with much (16:10). If we're not trustworthy with worldly wealth and other people's property, how can we expect to be responsible with really important things (16:11–12)? Even though the master in the parable commends the actions of his steward, Jesus makes it clear that following God is an either/or decision. If He doesn't have our complete hearts, we aren't really serving Him (16:13).

Although Jesus has been speaking to His disciples (16:1), He has critics among the surrounding crowd (16:14). Luke clearly states at this point that the Pharisees loved money, so it's not surprising that they are scoffing at Jesus' comments. Jesus has previously pointed out their hypocrisy at various times, and here points out their underlying problem—the Pharisees are seeking approval from the wrong source, and they are seeking to be judged according to the wrong standard. They are striving to be justified by men, so their standard has to be that which people can see and evaluate—outward appearances (16:15).

This simple observation explains the actions and reactions of the Pharisees. To get the approval of people, they acted in a way that would attract attention to themselves and make them look righteous, as people might judge it. Their actions included:

- long prayers
- obvious fasting and contributions
- places of prominence at banquets and ceremonies
- ostentatious clothing
- a proud distance from anyone considered sinful, thus beneath them
- meticulous ceremonial washings

In all of this, Jesus says they are hypocrites because their hearts are not really righteous at all. Understanding this about the Pharisees also explains why they value money so highly. It was an external proof of piety. After all, had God not promised to prosper His people Israel if they kept His laws (Deuteronomy 28:1–14) and to bring them great poverty and adversity if they disobeyed (Deuteronomy 28:15–68)? The Pharisees' love of money is an indication of their attachment to external standards and appearances, so that they can obtain the approval of other people. But in the process of seeking men's praise, they also obtain God's condemnation.

Critical Observation

Jesus' mention of "the Law and the Prophets" (16:16 NIV) was a reference to the entire Old Testament. In this context, His use of the phrase was significant. The Pharisees highly regarded the Law—the five books of Moses. But it was the section of the Prophets that spoke of the coming Messiah. The prophets also had much to say about the "heart issues" of life. God's revelation in the Old Testament was not seeking mere outward conformity, but inward conformity to the will of God. The Pharisees were overlooking a lot of the significance of that portion of scripture.

Jesus also affirms that He is not attempting to do away with the Law that the Pharisees hold in such high esteem (16:17). Including both the Law and the prophets was a way of referring to the complete Old Testament scriptures, not simply the first five books of the Law. The Pharisees had always seen themselves as the keepers of the Law. But after hearing the message of John the Baptist and then Jesus, people are responding to the news of the kingdom with force, in other words, they are so eager they are forcing their way in (16:16).

The reference to divorce at this point (16:18) seems abrupt, but is just one example of how the usually conservative and legalistic Pharisees have adopted a liberal interpretation to justify their own actions, expanding the parameters of the acceptable reasons for divorce until their customs don't reflect what the Law of God taught. Men of this culture and era have come to enjoy the freedom to change wives, and the Pharisees, the self-proclaimed custodians of the Law, function in this area as its corrupters.

📄 16:19–31

THE RICH MAN AND LAZARUS

Jesus begins this parable exactly as He has the previous one: "There was a rich man. . ." (16:1, 19 NIV). Most parables don't provide names for the characters; this is the sole exception. The description of poor Lazarus couldn't be more different from that of the rich man. But only three verses describe their lives. The majority of the parable takes place after their deaths, when the contrast is exactly reversed. Lazarus is carried to "Abraham's bosom" (16:22 KJV), a term Jewish rabbis used for the home of the righteous. From hell (Hades), the rich man can see Lazarus in the distance, and can even communicate with Abraham, but a great chasm prevents any other interaction.

The rich man first appeals for brief relief from his agony, and then for a messenger to be sent to his family members so they can avoid the same dreadful experience in the afterlife. Both requests are denied. He is told that those who would ignore "Moses and the Prophets" (16:31 NIV) would not even be swayed by a personal message from beyond the grave.

We aren't told the Pharisees' response after Jesus' second parable, but after hearing His opening descriptions of the two characters (16:19–21), based upon appearance alone, one can see how the Pharisees would have judged these two men. Since the Pharisees equated prominence with the blessing of God, they would have justified the rich man and condemned Lazarus.

The fate of the two men after their deaths shows the Pharisees' judgment to be wrong. Not only that, it is an indirect blow to the Pharisees. Since they would have related more to the rich man's role in the parable, the fact that God rejects the rich man is an indictment of them (16:24–26).

Take It Home

The two parables in this passage both involve rich characters who don't have God's perspective on life. And Jesus made it clear: "You cannot serve both God and Money" (16:13 NIV). But that doesn't mean Jesus stood opposed to all wealthy people. What do you think is the appropriate balance for us to maintain regarding money and the kingdom of God?

LUKE 17:1–37

FAITH, SERVICE, AND EXPECTATION

Sin and Forgiveness	17:1–10
A 10 Percent Return of Gratitude	17:11–19
Missing the Obvious	17:20–37

Setting Up the Section

At first this passage may not seem to have much coherence between the topics:

- **Not causing your brother or sister to sin—17:1–2**
- **What to do when your brother or sister sins—17:3–4**
- **Faith and the disciple—17:5–10**
- **The healing of the ten lepers and the gratitude of one—17:11–19**
- **The coming of the kingdom of God— 17:20–37**

It takes some effort to determine what the relationship is between these "parts" of the whole. Yet, in the context of Jesus' recent debates and confrontations with the Pharisees, it is likely that His teaching and healing is being done here in full awareness of their prying eyes and listening ears. So what He says and does can be interpreted in light of increasing opposition from Israel's religious leaders.

LUKE 17

☐ 17:1–10

SIN AND FORGIVENESS

Many times, sin is not a solitary problem. Temptations often arise when we get around other people. Jesus seems to acknowledge this problem in verse 1. And He holds accountable those who lead others into sinful actions. His words as recorded by Luke (17:2) are ominous, but a similar statement following His Parable of the Weeds (Matthew 13:40–42) is even worse.

When people acknowledge their sins against others, forgiveness is important. When offended by someone's sin, it is appropriate to rebuke the person (17:3). Yet if he or she repents (apparently, a verbal expression should be sufficient), forgiveness should be extended. And even if the same person commits seven offenses in the same day and repents seven times, forgiveness should be offered in each instance.

The term "brother" (or "sister," 17:3 NIV) refers to a fellow believer. By using this expression, Jesus may well be implying a couple of important truths.

1) He may be informing His disciples that they are not responsible to correct and rebuke mankind in general, but only those whom they know, with whom they closely identify. The Pharisees (not to mention many of us) seemed to love to condemn those outside of their own circles. Jesus tells us that we are responsible to correct those whose sins are personally known to us.

2) He may be reminding the disciples that their sinning brother is still their brother. We cannot, like the self-righteous older brother in the Parable of the Prodigal Son, disown those close to us who sin.

3) The fact that we are responsible to rebuke and to forgive our brother implies that we must also be alert to the kinds of sin that he is most likely to commit. If this brother is close to us, then he is also like us, which means that we must begin by being sensitive to those sins that so easily can beset us. How easy it is to focus on the visible sins of others, rather than on the perhaps more socially acceptable sins of which we are guilty.

From the wording of verse 3, one may wonder if Jesus taught that forgiveness should only be granted if the sinner repents. Does repentance precede forgiveness? Certainly not in the case of our Lord. On the cross, He cried out, "Father, forgive them. . ." (23:34 NIV). Forgiveness is first granted, and then it is experienced by those who repent. Jesus taught that forgiveness was to be granted if the sinner repented, not because we are to withhold forgiveness, but because not all sinners repent. Repentance may not occur, but when it does, we dare not withhold forgiveness. The point here is also that this forgiveness is to be verbalized at the time the sinner repents.

In response, the apostles ask Jesus to increase their faith (17:5). Note the subtle shift from "disciples" (17:1) to "apostles" (17:5).

Critical Observation

Remember that Jesus had already given His apostles power and authority for all kinds of healing and driving out demons (9:1). Yet when He started giving instructions about forgiving one another, they asked for an increase of faith (17:5). This suggests not only the importance but also the difficulty of forgiveness.

The apostles' request implies that what Jesus required necessitated great faith, and that their supply was deficient. Thus, they ask Jesus for more faith, assuming they do not have enough. Jesus' answer is that it takes only a very little quantity of faith to achieve much. With the quantity of faith equivalent to that of a mustard seed—a very small seed indeed—they could uproot a tree and transplant it into the sea (17:6). Did they then need more faith—really? Jesus' answer seems to question their premise that they had too little faith.

The story Jesus tells about the servant and the master (17:7–10) seems to suggest that in addition to faith is the necessity of doing one's duty. In the first instance, it is the master who is not obligated to have gratitude toward the obedience of his slave. Good servants simply do what they are expected to do without fuss or expectation of praise. Perhaps that attitude is lacking among Jesus' apostles.

Demystifying Matthew

If Jesus were making up the parable about the servant and master (17:7–10) in a contemporary setting, He might have told the story of the man who filled out his income tax form. The form was neatly filled out, with all the supporting facts and figures. Along with the form, mailed before April 15th, there was a check for the taxes that were due. Surely, Jesus might say, this man would not expect a call or a thank you note from the IRS or from the president of the United States, expressing the government's gratitude for obedience to the laws of the land. Paying taxes is our duty—one for which we expect no gratitude if we obey exactly as required, but one for which we expect punishment for failing to perform.

Jesus' words in verses 6–10 serve to correct the erroneous thinking of the apostles, who asked for greater faith. The important thing, Jesus says, is not the amount of faith, but the attributes of faith. Here faith is not a matter of quantity, but of quality. The disciples' thinking is that they lack sufficient faith. Jesus' answer is that they lack an accurate understanding of the nature of faith. It appears Jesus is condemning what we might call Pharisaical faith, which is based more upon the possessor of it than its object, a faith based more on one's performance than on God's character.

A 10 PERCENT RETURN OF GRATITUDE

If Jesus had the Pharisees in mind (even while addressing His disciples [17:1]), they would have rankled at being compared to servants who had to clean themselves after working in the fields before preparing and serving supper. And it is at this point that Luke inserts the story of the healing of the ten lepers. (The Gospel writers did not always write chronologically, but frequently recorded various accounts around a particular theme.)

Of the ten lepers, two things set the one who returns apart from the others: He praises God in a loud voice and thanks Jesus, and he is a Samaritan (17:15–16). The inference is that the others are Jewish. And it isn't that their actions are rude or malicious. After all, Jesus has told them to show themselves to the priests, who need to make an official ruling on the healing (17:14). Yet Jesus' questions suggest that taking the time to stop and express their gratitude would have been appropriate (17:17–18). Again, following the law to the letter—but not taking the spirit of the law into their hearts—was indicative of the Pharisees.

All ten lepers are healed. But only one—the Samaritan who returns to acknowledge Jesus for who He is and thanks Him—is told, "Your faith has made you well" (17:19 NIV). Jesus' comment suggests salvation in addition to physical healing.

Luke, of course, has a special message in this, for the one man is not a Jew at all but a Samaritan. Jesus makes a point of referring to this one grateful leper as a "foreigner" (17:18 NIV). Once again, we are being prepared for the gospel to be proclaimed and accepted by the Gentiles, while spurned by the Jewish religious leaders. This one grateful Gentile is a prototype of the many Gentiles who will believe and will praise God.

Take It Home

Jesus' story of the ten lepers is one to think about. It's easy to look down on the nine lepers who didn't stop to express their thanks to Jesus for what He had done for them. Yet today it is still possible—and perhaps too easy—to fall into a rigid obedience of all the things God tells us to do while losing the joy, gratitude, and spontaneity that ought to be involved in the abundant life promised to Christians. Can you think of any such examples in your own life, or in the lives of friends or family members? What can be done to ensure a response more like the Samaritan from now on?

MISSING THE OBVIOUS

Whether or not the previous events had a specific application for the Pharisees, what happens next is clearly directed to them. They approach Jesus and ask about the timing of the coming of the kingdom of God (17:20). He tells them that they won't be able to figure it out with their careful observation. In fact, they have already missed it because it is within (17:21). Perhaps Jesus meant it was a spiritual, inner matter. Others think the word *within* is better translated "among," and that Jesus meant that the kingdom of God was already in the midst of both the Pharisees and the disciples through His own presence and actions, though neither group was yet capable of realizing that fact.

Jesus' answer meant that they would not be able to simply point to the Messiah or the kingdom and say, "Here it is," or, "There it is." Why? Probably because the expectations of what the kingdom would be like were so distorted that the holders of those expectations would never recognize the real thing. The concept of the kingdom was so secular, so earthly, so materialistic, that the kingdom of our Lord was never seriously entertained as an option. Jesus simply did not fit the preconceived expectations of the Pharisees, and on the whole, they seemed to have no thought of changing those expectations. And this was in spite of the fact that Jesus did produce many signs, attesting His identity as Messiah (John 9:16; 11:45–47; 12:37).

While it was difficult to recognize Jesus for who He really was, it had been done. Luke has already told of how Mary, Elizabeth, Zechariah, Simeon, Anna, and John the Baptist had honored Jesus as the Messiah. The words and works of Jesus should have been evidence enough for others, too, but people's hearts are hard and don't always see the obvious.

Demystifying Luke

Luke's term "careful observation" (17:20 NIV) was a phrase used at the time to describe a doctor who closely monitored the symptoms of a patient over time. Since Luke was a physician, the term is quite appropriate.

Jesus speaks to the Pharisees about His first coming (17:20–21) and to the disciples about His second coming (17:22–37). He knows that eventually His followers will be looking for Him in earnest, and tells them not to waste their time chasing down every rumor and impostor (17:22–25). When He comes again, people will know! Yet His coming will be sudden, and humankind will not be prepared any more than it was for the judgments that took place in the days of Noah and Lot (17:26–32).

Some people interpret Jesus' words in verses 34–36 as a reference to the rapture, when believers are called into heaven to be with the Lord and spared the judgment of God:

- Some translations mention two men in the first scenario. Others render the phrase to be a man and wife. The Greek is not gender specific, but simply refers to "two" people. Keep in mind that this passage is not commenting on sexuality, but on the day-to-day events that will be affected by this "taking." In those days there were no bedrooms as we know them today. Often thus the whole family slept together on the floor, on what must have been mats, at best.
- The second case is that of two women, both of whom are going about their daily duties in the grinding of grain. One is taken, and the other is left. But where is the one taken to?

It is possible here to see these scenarios as references to the rapture, but the surrounding context makes it much more likely that the ones taken will be those who are being ushered off to face their final judgment. This interpretation would explain why, when the disciples seek additional information (17:37), Jesus' response is bleak.

The discussion is dropped abruptly. But Jesus will return to the topic of what to expect in future times in Luke 21.

LUKE 18:1–43

PERSISTENCE AND PENITENCE

A Persistent Widow vs. an Unjust Judge   18:1–8
A Pharisee and a Tax Collector   18:9–14
Little Children and a Rich Ruler   18:15–34
A Loud Blind Man   18:35–43

Setting Up the Section

In this section Jesus continues teaching His disciples about the kingdom of God. He uses a number of contrasts to teach some important lessons. He contrasts a persistent widow with a self-centered judge, a Pharisee and a tax collector, little children and annoyed adults, and the priorities of the kingdom of God with those of a wealthy young man. He also continues to heal the sick as He approaches Jerusalem to face His death.

📖 18:1–8

A PERSISTENT WIDOW VS. AN UNJUST JUDGE

Sometimes Jesus would tell a parable that left even His closest followers confused about what He meant. Here Luke first explains why Jesus is telling the story—to show the disciples "that they should always pray and not give up" (18:1 NIV)—before actually recording the parable.

This story is sometimes called the Parable of the Unjust Judge, and sometimes the Parable of the Persistent Widow. After an initial reading, it is clear that the woman is the one who models the lesson of persistence that Jesus intends to teach. But a closer look also shows that He directs His listeners (the disciples) to the words of the judge (18:6).

Jesus' point is that even a self-centered, uncaring person could bring about justice if pestered enough to do it. How much more surely, then, would a loving God respond when asked persistently by His "chosen ones" (18:7 NIV)? God surely stands ready to act on behalf of the ones He loves. We never pester Him with our prayers; indeed, our repeated prayers remind us that He is there and in charge. It is only if we give up that we stand to miss out. When Jesus returns He will be looking for faithful people who are ready for Him (18:8).

There is another inference from this paragraph we need to note carefully. The words of our Lord indicate there will be no real, complete, and ultimate justice on the earth until He returns and establishes it on the earth. We must persistently pray for justice and not lose heart because there will be much injustice until He comes again. There are some who seem to be saying these days that Christ will only come to the earth after we (the church) have established justice. That is not true, either to this text or to the rest of the scriptures pertaining to the coming of His kingdom. The Sermon on the Mount speaks of present pain, mourning, persecution, and sorrow, and of ultimate blessing when He comes with His kingdom.

A PHARISEE AND A TAX COLLECTOR

Still on the subject of prayer, Jesus tells the Parable of the Pharisee and the Tax Collector. But His focus has changed. Rather than addressing the disciples (18:1), He addresses a group of self-righteous people (18:9). In the first parable, it is the character of the one who is petitioned that is in focus; here, it is the character of the one praying who is highlighted. In the first parable, it is justice that is sought; in this second parable, it is mercy and forgiveness. This story is for those who trust in themselves rather than God—who look down on others and prefer their own righteousness to God's mercy and grace.

The Pharisee's words in this parable (18:11–12) are a stark contrast to the tax collector who can't even hold his head up before God. But Jesus is also able to speak for God, and declares the second man justified rather than the first (18:14). This parable helps explain why those are blessed who weep and mourn (6:21).

The previous parable taught persistence in prayer; this one emphasizes humility. According to Jesus, no one is too sinful to be saved—only too righteous. The Pharisee not only does not want God's grace, He disdains it. The reason, in his mind, is that he does not need it, for his righteousness (in law-keeping as he defines it) is sufficient, indeed, more than enough. The penitent sinner goes away justified by grace, while the Pharisee goes away condemned by his own works and words.

Critical Observation

This is not to say that self-righteous Pharisees are beyond saving. They are not! By his own confession, one of the most self-righteous of all Pharisees—Saul of Tarsus—was saved to become an apostle to the Gentiles. But in order to be saved, Saul, who became Paul, had to render all of the things in which he had formerly taken great pride as worthless.

LITTLE CHILDREN AND A RICH RULER

Some commentators believe the theme of humility is continued into the account of the children brought to Jesus to be blessed (18:15–17). But humility doesn't seem to be the characteristic Jesus is referring to (18:16–17). Children can be quite demanding. Others suggest it is faith, yet children are more gullible than faithful. Luke provides an insight missing in the other Gospels. He reveals that the little children brought to Jesus are actually infants.

There are several questions that are essential to understanding this incident, its meaning, and its application:

1) Why did Jesus react so strongly to their efforts to hinder the children from being brought to Him? The gospel itself is at issue. The way in which children were freely accepted by Jesus was similar to the way in which all people must enter into the kingdom of God.

2) Why did the disciples seek to prevent the parents from bringing their children to Jesus? Probably for the same reason Jesus welcomed them—they had nothing to offer but themselves.

3) What is the specific characteristic of childlikeness to which our Lord is referring, which is necessary for anyone to enter into the kingdom? While many claim it is the humility or the faith of these children, since they were merely infants, it is more likely the fact that they are helpless to save themselves. They can't earn any bit of the grace bestowed on them. Throughout Luke's Gospel, it is the lowly and the outcast who receive salvation blessings. The fact that these children had almost no status in first-century society made them an apt image of those that Jesus came to reach.

The next account, that of the rich young ruler, drives home the point that we can do nothing to earn our place in the kingdom of God. The young man tries to justify himself to Jesus because of behavior and attitudes he has held since he was a boy (18:21). Jesus deals with the rich young ruler by focusing his attention on the matter of goodness. Jesus' point is not to affirm whether he himself is good or not, but to challenge the man's concept of what is good. True goodness is perfection, so only God is good. We are all therefore dependent on God for salvation.

Critical Observation

The accounts of the children being brought to Jesus and His discussion with the rich young ruler are found in Matthew, Mark, and Luke—paired together in each instance (Matthew 19:13–26; Mark 10:13–27; Luke 18:15–27). The contrast between childlikeness as a positive trait and wealth as an impediment to following Jesus seems to be a clear thread that ties these two stories together.

To his credit, the young man seems to realize that following the law (as he is convinced he has done) is not enough for salvation. Jesus doesn't really answer the young man's original question. Instead, He tells him what he needs to do to become a disciple. In that event, his earthly treasure will be gone—distributed to the poor—but he will have treasure in heaven (18:22).

That certainly isn't the answer the young man anticipated. It is the one thing he is unwilling to do. The man is unwilling to give up that which gives him security (his wealth) and trust wholly in God. His failing is self-trust over trust in God.

The disciples are still thinking like the Pharisees, assuming that wealth and privilege are signs of God's favor. So this man, who is rich and religious and also seems to be genuinely seeking involvement in God's kingdom, appears to be more than qualified. So naturally they ask, if he can't be saved, then who can (18:26)?

Some may interpret Jesus' answer—with God all things are possible (18:27)—to mean that salvation for the rich is impossible without God's help. But the truth is, God's power is necessary for anyone to be saved no matter their possessions or wealth.

Peter's response (18:28) receives Jesus' commendation (18:29). But Jesus' words to His disciples in verses 31–34 are intended to put their sacrifice into perspective. Do they think that they are giving up everything for the kingdom of God? In reality, they are not giving up, but gaining. There is really only one sacrifice on which the kingdom of God is based, and that is the sacrifice that the Lord Jesus will make.

In Luke's Gospel there is a progressively revealed indication of Jesus' suffering. Luke has informed us that Jesus will be

• rejected by the Jewish leaders (9:22–23)

• betrayed by one of His own (9:44–45)

• rejected by His generation (17:24–25)

• rejected and crucified by the Gentiles (18:31–34)

Luke, in writing this Gospel for a Gentile audience, points out the non-Jews' own role in the rejection and crucifixion of the Messiah. The prophecy of His suffering and death given in 18:31–34 is very specific and detailed.

Yet with such a specific prophecy, the disciples don't understand (18:34). The reason for their lack of understanding is given in our text: The meaning was hidden from them—God deliberately withheld it. They were not ready for it. They would only understand Jesus' rejection, crucifixion, and death after His resurrection.

Jesus had already made specific statements recorded in Luke, directly referencing His death. Yet, as with 18:31–34, the disciples were not ready to understand the full implications.	
Luke 9:20–31	When Jesus questioned His disciples about His own identity, and Peter made his great confession, Jesus made it clear that He would "suffer many things and be rejected by the elders, chief priests and teachers of the law, and he must be killed and on the third day be raised to life" (9:22 NIV).
Luke 9:43–45	After Jesus stepped in and drove a demon from a little boy who the disciples had failed to heal, He told them that He would be "betrayed into the hands of men" (9:44 NIV).
Luke 17:24–25	Jesus told His disciples that before He could return again, He "must suffer many things and be rejected by this generation" (9:25 NIV).

18:35–43

A LOUD BLIND MAN

As Jesus walks toward Jericho, a blind man (Bartimaeus, according to Mark 10:46) hears He is passing. Although he is told that Jesus of Nazareth is passing by, he calls out for "Jesus, Son of David" (18:38 NIV). "Son of David" is a title for the Messiah, suggesting that Bartimaeus isn't spiritually blind.

This is a scene that is both tragic and comic at the same time. Bartimaeus is sitting by the road as it leads into Jericho (18:35). Beggars always have certain spots picked out where the traffic is more frequent, and where, for some reason, there seems to be more generosity expressed (e.g. outside the temple). He cannot see, so his begging is triggered by what he hears—a footstep, the sounds of passers-by talking, etc.

He keeps yelling for Jesus until he annoys everyone around him. But it works. Jesus calls him forward, restores his sight, and declares that his faith has healed him (18:39–42). At this point, the Gospel of Mark exposes the hypocrisy of those who once tried to silence Bartimaeus, for now they tell him to take courage (Mark 10:49). Mark also tells us that the man jumps up, throws off his coat, and goes to Jesus (Mark 10:50).

And as soon as Bartimaeus can see where he is going, the blind man starts following Jesus—quite a contrast to the rich man who had sadly walked away (Mark 10:17–22; Luke 18:18–23).

Take It Home

This passage has much to say about the prayer life of a believer. We are to be persistent in our communication with God, all the while exercising humility. The power of Jesus to save and heal is an ongoing source of hope, even as His willing sacrifice gives renewed meaning to any relationship with Him. Which of these areas needs the most attention in your life? How can you improve your prayer habits and better connect with the One most concerned for you?

LUKE 19:1–48

LAST JOURNEY TO JERUSALEM

A Tax Collector in a Tree   19:1–10
In the Absence of the Master   19:11–27
Jesus Arrives at Jerusalem   19:28–48

Setting Up the Section

Not even halfway through his Gospel, Luke wrote: "As the time approached for him to be taken up to heaven, Jesus resolutely set out for Jerusalem" (9:51 NIV). All the events of Luke 10–18 have occurred along the way.

The subject of the coming kingdom of God has been in view since the Pharisees first asked about when it would come in chapter 17. In chapter 18, the focus changed from the timing and circumstances of the coming kingdom to who would enter into it. Jesus taught that those who would enter His kingdom would not be those who expected to enter. And so the self-righteous Pharisee is not justified, but the penitent tax collector is (18:9–14). Jesus taught His disciples that while the rich young ruler, and those like him, would have much difficulty getting into the kingdom (18:18–27), those who were child-like would possess it (18:15–17).

And in this section, Jesus finally arrives in Jerusalem. As the time of His death nears, His teachings and actions seem to become more intentional and direct.

📄 19:1–10

A TAX COLLECTOR IN A TREE

Jericho (19:1) was about seventeen miles from Jerusalem. At this point in His ministry, Jesus is still beset by crowds as He travels. A tax collector named Zacchaeus desperately wants to see Him, but is very short and doesn't have much of a chance among the hordes of people. So even though he is a man of wealth and position (19:2), he decides to climb a tree so he can get a better view.

Unlike the blind man in the previous story (18:35–43) who had yelled until he got Jesus' attention, Zacchaeus seems to desire anonymity. Yet when Jesus surprisingly stops beneath him and invites Himself to dinner, Zacchaeus welcomes Him (19:6).

Jesus had associated with tax collectors throughout His ministry, yet He never stopped receiving criticism for it. We might even wonder if the people who complained (19:7) included the apostles. Jesus doesn't demand that Zacchaeus sell all his possessions to benefit the poor as He had the rich ruler (18:18–23), but Zacchaeus's response is voluntary and generous (19:8). And regardless of the attitudes of others, Jesus celebrates the salvation of Zacchaeus (19:9–10).

Jesus explains to Zacchaeus that He has come to seek and save what is lost (19:10). Jesus did not come to associate with the rich and powerful. He did not come to provide positions and power for the disciples. He came to save sinners, people like Zacchaeus, the hated and evil tax collector. To do so, He had to associate with sinners. Thus, while it may offend the sensitivities and the social mores of His day, Jesus would go where sinners were, so that the gospel could come to them and they could be saved. If one's goal is to save sinners, then associating with sinners is simply a means to that goal.

Jesus' climactic statement about seeking and saving the lost provides a beautiful summary of this whole Gospel—it is the lost (the outcast, the sinners, the Samaritans, etc.) He has come to save. Those who recognize their need of salvation are being saved, while the self-righteous are losing out.

Critical Observation

When you compare Zacchaeus's story with the story of the blind man named Bartimaeus (18:35–43) you see an interesting picture of the tension that is maintained here between the sovereignty of God and the responsibility of humanity. The blind man called out to the Savior for mercy and received it. Zacchaeus did not call upon the Lord, but the Lord called to him. The scriptures clearly teach that no one who truly comes to Jesus for mercy, on the basis of faith, will be turned away. The scriptures also teach that anyone who comes to Christ for salvation does not come on their own initiative, but is drawn by God. Both of these perspectives are true. God seeks us, and we give ourselves to Him, and it all happens only through the faith that He enables in us.

IN THE ABSENCE OF THE MASTER

Jesus' Parable of the Ten Minas (19:11–27) is usually considered another version of the Parable of the Talents found in Matthew 25:14–30, although there are considerable differences. In Luke's account, Jesus reveals the attitudes of the people toward the nobleman who left and came back as king (19:14–15). And in this version, the servants are given the same amount of money (19:13) and told to put it to use. (A "mina" was a wage one could earn in about 100 days.)

The first servant, who earned a tenfold return on his mina, is rewarded with responsibility over ten cities and verbal praise from his master. The second servant, with a profit of five times the original amount, receives charge of five cities (though no praise is noted). But the bulk of the parable dwells on the third servant. He expresses fear of the master to justify his inaction, and is judged by his own words. His fear should have at least motivated him to invest the money in a bank account to get interest. Consequently, he loses his portion of money to the one who had proven to be faithful with the ten minas. And as for the citizens who bad-mouthed their leader, they are put to death (19:27). (Perhaps the servants represented Jesus' followers while the citizens symbolized unrepentant Israel who rejected Jesus.)

Jesus tells this parable as He is just about to enter Jerusalem. He will soon be going away and leaving responsibility for His ministry to others. When He returns, it will be as King. Clearly, what His followers do in the meantime will be important. Those who are faithful will be rewarded.

Perhaps the third servant may have failed to do business with his master's money simply because he felt that time was too short to engage in business. At the beginning of this parable, Luke tells us that Jesus spoke the parable in addition to His other words, because the people were looking for the kingdom to come immediately (19:11). One of the things a short-term mind-set does is discourage long-term planning and investing. If you receive a check for $10,000 but know that you will have to write a check for that same amount in a day, you generally will not seek to buy a certificate of deposit with it, or to buy a savings bond, or to put the money in your savings account. You will deposit the money in your checking account simply because you know that it will only be a short time before it will be gone.

In the context of Luke's Gospel, this parable now begins to make sense. Jesus is nearing Jerusalem. Expectation is at an all-time high. Everyone expects the kingdom to commence upon our Lord's arrival. This parable is then given by our Lord. The departure of the king to a distant land, and his later return, signals a time delay in the arrival of the kingdom of God. The people expect the kingdom to be established almost immediately, but this parable teaches that there are some intervening events which must take place first.

Take it home

Here is a very real tension in Christian living. We must hold two truths in tension as we seek to apply them. On the one hand, we must live in the light of Jesus' imminent return. Christ may come at any moment, and we should be both ready and watching for His return. But we must also live wisely, making good investments for His kingdom, knowing that His return may not be as soon as we think or hope. Many foolish things have been done by those who feel that the kingdom was imminent. On the other hand, many foolish things have been done by those who feel Jesus' coming is distant. We can count on the return of our King, yet there is ample opportunity to be productive for Him as we are waiting.

📄 **19:28–48**

JESUS ARRIVES AT JERUSALEM

Jesus' arrival in Jerusalem comes at a time of heightened emotions. People close to Him have heard numerous comments about kingdoms and the Messiah and such. Maybe they are hoping for something eventful to occur. After all, everyone knew from Old Testament writings that Jerusalem would be where the Messiah would be enthroned as king. In addition, it was Passover when pilgrims gathered in Jerusalem and fueled the fires of spiritual and messianic expectations. The crowds have no idea how right they are—and how wrong.

One can hardly grasp the mood of many at this moment in history. They are looking for the Messiah, and Jesus is a likely candidate. The moment is right. They look for Him, watching carefully for any indication of His identity. In contrast, the Pharisees and religious leaders are determined that He is not the Messiah, and that He will have no opportunity to be acclaimed such by the masses who wish He was their King. They are intent on putting Him to death, and are only looking for the right opportunity. These opponents of our Lord fear the crowds, and seek to do away with Jesus out of their sight.

Jesus sends two disciples ahead to secure a colt (19:28–31). The fact that it had never been ridden would have qualified it to be used as an offering to God (Numbers 19:2; Deuteronomy 21:3–4). The willingness with which it is given up suggests both a foreknowledge of Jesus and the owners' awareness of who the "Lord" is who needed it (19:32–35). And the fact that it is secured by the disciples acting on the authority of Jesus is a preview of how the church will operate after Jesus' physical departure.

The remaining distance to Jerusalem is negligible, and nothing is said of Jesus riding an animal at any other point. So why now? Jesus is not only declaring Himself to be the king that has been foretold, He is also fulfilling prophecy to the letter (Zechariah 9:9).

His ride into Jerusalem has come to be known as the "triumphal entry." A great crowd of people praise Him with its words and actions (19:36–38). Yet the crowd surrounding Jesus is likely comprised of His followers—not the city as a whole. And even among that crowd, no one fully understands what is going on. Just as Jesus will say that those who crucified Him didn't really understand what they were doing (23:34), so we see that the people in the crowd do not know what they are doing here, either.

The triumphal entry serves to publicly identify Jesus as the king of Israel. Many were wondering if He were the Messiah. His act of riding into Jerusalem on a donkey is His way of affirming His role as king of Israel and Son of God, thus His right to be worshiped by all people.

The Pharisees ask Jesus to silence the people, but Jesus says that praise will come from the very stones if nowhere else (19:39–40). Still, Jesus doesn't seem to consider His entry "triumphal." Rather, He weeps for the city of Jerusalem. What a contrast between the joy of the crowd and the sorrow of the Savior. Jesus knew what lay ahead for this wayward, wrong-thinking nation. Instead of the Messiah's coming bringing about the demise of Rome, the rejection of Jesus as Messiah meant the destruction of Jerusalem, at the hand of Roman soldiers. Jesus therefore speaks of the coming destruction of Jerusalem, which takes place in AD 70 (19:41–44).

It was neither by the Messiah's use of force and power, nor by the death of the Messiah's enemies that the kingdom was to be brought about, but by the Messiah's death at the hand of His enemies. It was not triumph that would bring in the kingdom, but the tragedy (from a merely human viewpoint) of the cross. God's ways are never man's ways. Man would have brought about the kingdom in many ways, but man would never have conceived of doing so by a cross, by apparent defeat and the suffering of the Messiah Himself, for the sins of His people.

Demystifying Luke

Jesus' deity is implied in a number of ways in this passage: His right to use the possessions of humankind (19:29–35), His right to receive praise and worship from humankind (19:36–40), His right to repossess the temple (19:45–48), and His right to institute His kingdom the way He sovereignly chose (suffering that leads to a cross) rather than using the means humankind might prefer (overthrowing enemies that leads to a crown).

Did the Israelites expect Jesus to immediately wage an attack on Rome and on its rule? Jesus does not do so. What Jesus does is attack the Jewish religious system itself and renounces its evils. He marches on the temple and casts out the money changers. This was the holiday season—Passover—and business there in the temple area must have been booming. But instead of using the temple for a place of prayer and worship, the religious leaders made it a place for personal gain.

Jesus' attack on the religious system of His day is strongly reacted to by those with a vested interest—the chief priests, the teachers of the Law, and the leaders of the people. They are not yet able to kill Jesus, due to the crowds, but they are intent on putting Him to death at the earliest possible moment. The battle lines are drawn, but it is not between the Messiah and Rome, but rather between the Messiah and religion. In spite of Jesus' popularity with the people, the religious leaders are more determined than ever to kill Him. They just can't come up with a workable plan—yet (19:47–48).

LUKE 20:1–47

QUESTIONS OF AUTHORITY

By What Authority?   20:1–18

Taxes and Resurrection   20:19–40

Son of David or Lord of David?   20:41–47

Setting Up the Section

Jesus has arrived in Jerusalem to spend the final week of His human life. He has, by His actions, announced His identity as Israel's Messiah. He possessed the donkey (19:29–35), the praises of the people (19:36–40), and finally His temple (19:45–48).

Up to this point, the principle source of opposition to Jesus has been from the party of the Pharisees, who seem to have been dogging the heels of the Savior from very early on in His ministry (see 5:21 and following). Both the Pharisees and Sadducees (teachers of the law or scribes) were political/religious parties, and members from both groups served on the Sanhedrin (the official leadership of Israel). The Sadducees had their primary powerbase in Jerusalem and among the priestly hierarchy, and the Pharisees appear to have been more influential among the synagogue communities, but both were present in Jerusalem.

It is at the Lord's possession of His temple in Luke 19:45 that we see the torch of opposition to Jesus being passed from the Pharisee party to the priests, the scribes, and the elders (20:1). The Jerusalem leaders may not have been overly concerned with Jesus' ministry and influence in the outlying parts of Israel, but became threatened when Jesus invaded their turf. They wanted to stop Him, but the Lord's popularity with the masses was too great to ignore or to challenge (19:48). Thus, they waited for their chance. Their first attack came in the form of an official challenge to the authority by which Jesus did the things He had done (20:2).

The issue that underlies this entire section of scripture is that of authority.

BY WHAT AUTHORITY?

After arriving in Jerusalem, Jesus spends a lot of time in the temple both teaching the people and preaching the gospel (20:1). The religious leaders, who had tolerated His ministry through gritted teeth as long as He had been a wandering rabbi, are now more concerned because He is in their center of operation. This is their territory, their turf, the Jerusalem leaders believe, and thus they confront Jesus in the temple in the context of His teaching there. Their question in verse 2 is two-pronged, not simply one question put differently the second time. There are two questions in view:

1) Just who do You think You are to do these things, anyway?
2) Who gave You the authority to do these things?

The first question has to do with Jesus' personal authority. Jesus is acting as though He owns the place, and so He does. The simple answer is, "I am the Messiah." But while the people are entertaining this at least as a possibility, the leaders reject the thought out of hand. No way! The second question has to do with Jesus' official accreditation—Who sent Him? These leaders seem to think that they are the accrediting agency. Jesus has not received their permission to come to town as He has, or to accept men's praise, or to take over the temple. If the nation's highest spiritual leadership has not authorized Jesus, then who has? That is the issue. It is the issue of authority, both Jesus' innate authority and His delegated authority.

Jesus' reply (20:3-4) isn't an attempt to change the subject. The issue is broader than Jesus, for John the Baptist had introduced Jesus to Israel as the Messiah. If the Jerusalem leaders are going to pronounce on Jesus' authority, they also have to deal with John's, for if John was a divinely appointed prophet, a spokesman for God, then Jesus is the Messiah. Furthermore, if they refuse to accept John's witness, then they surely will not receive Jesus, either. Let them declare themselves, then, on the authority of John. What authority did he have? Who sent him? If they answer this question, then Jesus will answer theirs.

Luke provides the heart of the religious leaders' discussion (20:5-6), which is both comic and tragic. They don't bother discussing the right answer to Jesus' question. Instead, they spend their time trying to justify their answer. When they cannot safely say what they really think, they have to say they don't know (20:7), which must be very frustrating for such self-proclaimed authorities. And because they refuse to answer, so does Jesus (20:8).

Jesus continues by telling the Parable of the Tenants (20:9-16). It seems clear that the vineyard represents Israel, and the owner, God. In time, the tenants decide to take possession of what they are only renting. Each time the owner sends servants (the prophets) to check and collect some of the fruit, they beat the messenger and send him away empty-handed. The owner finally sends his son (Jesus), thinking they will surely respect him. But they see the son's visit as an opportunity to take complete control by killing him.

This parable builds a powerful picture. Men like John the Baptist were prophets, and thus had the authority to speak for God. John, as a divinely appointed spokesman for God, proclaimed Jesus to be the Messiah. But just as Israel's leaders had rejected other prophets, so they had done with John as well. Jesus, in this parable, is telling His audience that He is not just a prophet; He is the Son. That is the basis of His authority. He owns the vineyard. He has been sent by His Father to possess what is His. But they will reject Him and put Him to death.

And they do so with the full knowledge that He is the Son. They kill Him because He is the Son. This, we recall, is what Jesus' opponents have already purposed to do (19:47). It is not so much that they do not know who Jesus is, but that they will not accept His authority.

The people hearing the parable are horrified. But in verses 17–18, Jesus cites another prophecy to verify His meaning (Psalm 118:22; Isaiah 8:14, 15). The stone that is overlooked and rejected by the builders of the nation will eventually become the capstone (or cornerstone). The stone will also be an object of judgment (20:18)—one that opponents to the gospel will continue to stumble over.

20:19–40

TAXES AND RESURRECTION

The religious leaders know Jesus is talking about them (Matthew 21:45), but He is so popular with the people that they can't do as they wish—arrest Him on the spot (20:19). Instead, they resort to stealth and subversion. They watch Him closely and send spies to act nice and try to catch Him saying something they can use against Him. Then they can turn Him over to the government (20:20).

Their plan shows how desperate they have become. To begin with, all that would be needed to "get some dirt" on most people is to watch their actions and catch them doing something wrong. They realize, however, that this will not work with Jesus. Instead, the goal of the leaders of the people is reported here by Luke:

- They purpose to catch Jesus in His words. It was by His words that Jesus put these leaders to shame. It is by Jesus' words, the leaders suppose, that Jesus will be eliminated. It is significant that the leaders of the people cannot and will not attempt to discredit Jesus in any of His actions.
- They seek to deal with Jesus politically. The solution to their problem, as the Jewish leaders reason, is a political one, not a spiritual one. They do not seek to deal with Jesus in any way prescribed by the Old Testament law. They turn instead to a secular government that has the power to execute, the very government that they despise, rather than have Jesus govern them.

The spies go right to a sensitive topic: the payment of taxes (20:21–22). By their thinking, if Jesus is posing as the Messiah and they get Him to say there is no further need to pay taxes to Caesar, then they can alert Rome, get Him charged with treason, and He will trouble them no more. But Jesus sees through them (20:23).

Jesus' response surely takes everyone by surprise. No one expects Him to advocate paying taxes to support the Romans. He acknowledges a distinction between government and God, but doesn't assume they have to be in opposition to one another. Indeed, Jesus will soon give Caesar His very life, so taxes are a small matter. While tax money may belong to governments, people belong to God (20:24–25).

Critical Observation

The denarius Jesus used in His response to the tax question was not just referencing money, though it was that. In Jesus' day there were different kinds of money. The denarius was the form of money used for paying taxes to Caesar. Matthew told of how Jesus paid the two-drachma temple tax (Matthew 17:24–27). The tax was not paid with a denarius, but with the drachma. This is the reason why the money changers were exchanging money in the courts of the temple—the temple tax could not be paid with a denarius. When Jesus asked to see a denarius, it was with a specific purpose in mind.

After the spies fail to trap Jesus and are silenced, the Sadducees come along with another question (20:27–33). This question revolves around a command found in Deuteronomy 25:5-6. If a man died without having sons, his brothers had a responsibility to marry the widow and give her sons. If a brother did so, the son born to the widow carried on the deceased brother's heritage.

The purpose of this legislation was to assure that each family and tribe in Israel was perpetuated by the bearing of children. When the oldest brother married, but died before having any children, the younger brother was to take the widow as his wife so that the first son would carry on the name and the leadership of the deceased. Other legislation assured that the inheritance of land would remain in the tribes and families. Here was a very practical law, given to assure future generations. One can especially see the importance of this legislation when you recall the fact that the Messiah would be born of a woman (Genesis 3:15), from the tribe of Judah (Genesis 49:9-10), of the line of David (2 Samuel 7:8-16). How crucial it was for the tribes of Israel to perpetuate, for from such the Messiah would be born.

Since the Sadducees didn't believe in the resurrection, their query is almost certainly contrived and theoretical, meant to be a stumper. The argument of the Sadducees is based on this premise: Life in the kingdom of God will be just like it is on earth. Consequently, the present institution of marriage is assumed by the Sadducees to continue on in the kingdom. Thus, a woman who was married to seven brothers would be in a terrible predicament in heaven, for she would have to choose one of them to live with.

Demystifying Luke

This is Luke's first mention of the Sadducees, a priestly aristocracy who focused more on political matters than religious ones. In addition to not believing in resurrection of the dead, they downplayed the existence of angels and spirits, and they only viewed as authoritative the books of Moses (the first five books of the Old Testament). The traditions and interpretations of the Pharisees meant little to them. Because of their refusal to believe in resurrection, we hear more about them in the book of Acts—after the death and resurrection of Jesus. We also hear about them more in Acts because their power base was in Jerusalem, where the church was established, rather than Galilee, where most of Jesus' early ministry was conducted.

Jesus' response is concise, yet points out two major errors in the Sadducees' thinking. First, He distinguishes between this age and that age (20:34–35). He specifically mentions the resurrection from the dead (20:35), when people neither experience death nor participate in marriage. Second, He even goes back into the books of Moses to show that, in fact, God had made reference to resurrection at the burning bush (20:37–38). The Sadducees' mistaken assumption was that Moses rejected the doctrine of the resurrection of the dead. Jesus demonstrates that Moses was a believer in the resurrection of the dead, contrary to the belief of the Sadducees.

Jesus' answer is so powerful, His adversaries have to commend Him. The Pharisees enjoy the way that Jesus has silenced their opponents, the Sadducees, when they sought to entrap Jesus in such a way as to give credence to their rejection of the resurrection of the dead. Thus they cannot restrain themselves from praising Jesus for His response (20:39), even though they have set out on a course of trying to catch Jesus in His words. The praise of the Pharisees will be short-lived, however, for in the next question, raised by our Lord Himself, Jesus will show the Pharisees they do not understand the scriptures.

📄 **20:41–47**

SON OF DAVID OR LORD OF DAVID?

After answering the Sadducees' tricky question, Jesus asks one of His own: If David called the Messiah "Lord," then how could the Messiah be David's son? (20:41–44). "Son of David" was a messianic title all Jesus' listeners would have been aware of. So Jesus asks how it is that David had referred to his descendant as "Lord."

By citing this passage from Psalm 110, Jesus makes it clear that they not only have a grievance with Jesus, who claims to be both human and divine, but more so, they are inconsistent with the Old Testament scriptures, even those written by King David. The citing of Psalm 110 by our Lord brings the central issue into focus, and shows it to be a truth taught clearly by the scriptures. The question that Jesus raises in this conundrum is how can the Messiah be greater than his "father" David? There is no explicit claim to deity, but rather the intriguing point that the Messiah must be more than David's son, and so more than Jewish expectations about the Messiah.

Throughout his Gospel, Luke stresses both the humanity and messiahship of Jesus. It is only by the miracle of the incarnation that the Messiah can be both human (a descendant of David) and divine. Jesus never fully answers His own question, but the religious leaders know the source He provided and are aware of what He is saying to them.

Critical Observation

Jesus' choice to refer to Psalm 110 over all other available texts worked well for several reasons:

1) Since the Messiah was commonly understood to be a "son of David," who could speak with more authority on his son than David?

2) The 110th Psalm went far beyond the issue of the Messiah's humanity and His deity, referring to His coming in power to overthrow His enemies.

3) Psalm 110 reveals the attitude of David, as Israel's leader, to the superiority of his son.

4) Psalm 110 clearly teaches both the humanity of the Messiah (a son of David) and His deity (David's Lord).

One question Jesus doesn't ask, yet would be implied from the passage He quoted, is, "Who are the enemies of the Messiah?" If Jesus is the Messiah, as He claims and as John had testified, then they are His enemies. They are the ones whom God will overthrow. And this is precisely what Jesus had suggested in the parable of the vineyard and the vine-growers earlier in this chapter (20:9–18).

Jesus addresses His disciples, but knows that everyone else is listening. His indictment of the teachers of the Law (20:45–47) must be leaving them with their ears burning. They had hoped to catch Jesus in something He said (20:20), yet they can't deny the truth of His charges.

Take It Home

We, too, have to decide what we will do with God's authority. When we reject it, we do not become the masters of our souls and the captains of our fate. When we spurn God's authority, we place ourselves under the dreadful authority of sin, and ultimately of Satan himself. Imagine it. The people of Jesus' day rejected Him, saying they had no king but Caesar (John 19:15). They gladly traded a traitor (Barabbas) for the sinless Son of God. When we reject God's authority, God's rule, we consign ourselves to the dominion of sin and of Satan. The "freedom" that Satan offers people is the freedom from a righteous life, and the bonds of sin and death.

We must deal with God's authority both personally in our own lives and in our lives as a community, the church. We, like these first-century Jewish leaders, can forget that the church belongs to Christ. It is His church, not ours, and He is the one who is to benefit from it. But how often church leaders begin to look on the church as their own, and to protect their power and positions rather than use them as avenues of service. And how often we all go to church expecting (even demanding) to gain from it, but forgetting that it is God who has the right to expect and to get gain. The church, like Israel, belongs to God, and its ultimate reason for existence is not our gain, but His.

LUKE 21:1–38

THE FUTURE: INDICATIONS AND INSTRUCTIONS

A Widow's Special Gift   21:1–4
The Coming Fall of Jerusalem   21:5–24
Signs and Promises   21:25–38

Setting Up the Section

Jesus and His disciples have arrived in Jerusalem, and Jesus has begun to teach at the temple every day. His time is short, and He is trying to give special attention to His followers. Yet each day large numbers of people arise early and show up at the temple to hear what He has to say.

It seems these first four verses (21:1–4) are placed here by Luke in contrast to the Pharisees, to show how God's ways differ so greatly from those of men. The Pharisees loved riches, and they viewed wealth as an evidence of piety. God, in their minds, would be impressed by the wealthy, and would be especially pleased by the size of their contributions.

📄 21:1–4

A WIDOW'S SPECIAL GIFT

Jesus has just been warning His disciples about the abuses of the teachers of the Law and their misplaced priorities. Among His specific charges are that, "they devour widows' houses" (20:47 NIV), indicating a certain level of deceit in their dealings with helpless people. Then, almost as He is speaking those words, He looks up and points out a widow making an offering. Her two small coins, each worth about one-eighth of a cent, surely seem pathetic in contrast to the showy gifts of the wealthy.

Demystifying Luke

The temple treasury was in the court of women, where thirteen collection bins received the gifts of worshipers. The two tiny coins of the widow must have seemed a puny gift, but Jesus was well aware of the sacrifice being made by the woman.

Yet Jesus is pleased with her offering, realizing she is trusting God with all she has to live on (21:4). It's interesting that although Jesus points out the woman's complete selflessness to His disciples, it doesn't seem that He says anything to the woman. Nor are we told the disciples' response to Jesus' comment. But we soon discover their minds aren't on simplicity and sacrifice.

There is an implied contrast between the widow's offering in verses 1–4 and the disciples' admiration for the temple in verse 5 and following. Jesus is impressed with what took place in the temple—with the widow's offering. The disciples are impressed with the temple itself—with its beauty and splendor. Man truly looks on the outward appearance and God on the heart, here, as always.

🖹 21:5–24

THE COMING FALL OF JERUSALEM

The disciples, who may not have come to Jerusalem often, are not unlike tourists taking in the sights. The tax collector, fishermen, and others are simple men who find themselves in one of the greatest architectural achievements of their day (21:5). Luke alone among the Gospel writers informs us that some of these adornments were the result of gifts that were donated.

The disciples are understandably impressed. Was it possible that the disciples' attachment to the temple was based upon some false assumptions concerning it? For example, if the disciples believed that Jesus was about to establish His throne in Jerusalem, would He not make the temple His headquarters? Did this not mean that their offices would be in the temple? If such was their thinking, then no wonder they are impressed with this building. What great facilities this building would provide them.

But this is not at all to be the case. Jesus is aware of the not-too-distant fall of the holy city. Even though the temple is still under construction, Jesus tells the disciples of a time "when not one stone will be left on another" (21:6 NIV). They immediately want to know when the destruction will take place and what to look for. But rather than merely satisfy their curiosity, Jesus instead addresses their conduct—how to respond when the time comes.

Critical Observation

The construction of Herod's temple was not only a magnificent work of architecture but was also built to accommodate Jewish sensitivities. Since only priests were allowed in certain parts of the interior, one thousand of them were trained to do the masonry and carpentry in those portions. Temple service was never interrupted from the beginning of construction in 20–19 BC through the completion of the surrounding buildings and courts in AD 64 .Yet all that beautiful white marble fell in ruins in AD 70.

His warning is widespread (21:8–24), including both the soon-to-come fall of Jerusalem and His considerably later second coming, and what to expect for both believers and nonbelievers. Yet rather than distinguish the events, Jesus is intent to intertwine them. Some of the predicted events will even occur more than once, such as the trampling of Jerusalem by the Gentiles (21:24). It falls in AD 70, and the book of Revelation predicts another similar event (according to many interpretations, at least) at a point in the future (Revelation 11:2).

Jesus provides three primary instructions for His followers:

1) Watch out for false messiahs (21:8). When times get bad, people always arise with answers. But the bad times He is describing will be the judgment of God, and no human solution will remedy the situation.

2) Don't be frightened by wide-scale world events or personal persecution (21:9–19). Jesus will provide words and wisdom to get His disciples through such times (21:15). Yet Jesus' promise that "not a hair of your head will perish" (21:18 NIV) must be viewed in light of His statement in verse 16, that some of the disciples will be put to death. (His predicted betrayal by parents, brothers, relatives and friends [21:16] helps explain Jesus' previous

insistence on putting Him even before family members [14:26].) Followers of Jesus will not perish eternally, though they may pay a high price for discipleship. Luke, in his second volume, the book of Acts, gives a historical account of some of the sufferings of the saints in the days after our Lord's ascension.

3) Do not flee to Jerusalem for safety when it is under siege (21:20–24). Normally people would flock to fortified cities during wartime, but Jerusalem will not stand. This will happen in the lifetime of the disciples who are with Jesus. In Acts, Luke writes, "a great persecution began against the church in Jerusalem, and they were all scattered throughout the regions of Judea and Samaria, except the apostles" (Acts 8:1 NASB).

Jesus' words surely redirect the disciples' thoughts.

- They should lay to rest the disciples' visions of an immediate kingdom, with Jerusalem and that temple as its headquarters.
- They spell out hard times ahead for those who will follow Him, rather than happy days, as nearly all, including the disciples, hope for. This is true for the disciples and for the early church (see Acts), but it is just as true for saints of all ages (2 Timothy 3).
- While it may not seem so, times of adversity are legitimate times for continuing to spread the gospel. The gospel is light to those in darkness, and it offers hope to those in despair.

But Jesus still has more to say.

📄 **21:25–38**

SIGNS AND PROMISES

From the predictions for what will happen in and around Jerusalem, Jesus moves on to heavenly signs (21:25). Here He appears to be speaking specifically to His second coming (21:27), so the same signs produce quite different responses. Those who don't know Christ will "faint from terror" (21:26 NIV), while believers should stand with their heads lifted up in anticipation of their final redemption (21:28).

Jesus intentionally doesn't give His followers a list of specific times and dates. His Parable of the Fig Tree (21:29–31) explains why. Farmers and gardeners don't operate by calendar dates, but in response to the conditions they observe. Jesus expects His disciples to have sensitivity to the season of His return. He doesn't want them ignorant of what to expect, but neither does He want them to suspend their watchfulness until some specified date in the future.

Ongoing debate takes place over Jesus' promise that "this generation will certainly not pass away until all these things have happened" (21:32 NIV). His second coming is included in "all these things," so how can a single generation span such a time period? Some people redefine *generation* more broadly to mean "humankind" or "Israel," although that seems to stretch the context of Luke's writing (and the very definition of *generation*). Another possibility is that "all these things" will occur twice—once for the disciples in Jesus' generation and again for disciples at a future time. Thus, Jerusalem is sacked in AD 70, in fulfillment of our Lord's words. And so, too, Jerusalem will be trodden under the feet of the Gentiles again, during the tribulation (Revelation 11:2).

Jesus' second promise is that His "words will never pass away" (21:33 NIV). He speaks with an authority far greater than even the prophets had. He speaks as God. His words are divine revelation.

Jesus concludes three specific evils that will distract His followers from watching for the signs and understanding their significance (21:34). (These warnings are reminiscent of what He already taught in 12:22–34.)

- Dissipation is the hangover after drinking too much. It would be tempting, in light of the difficulties of life ahead, for Jesus' followers to overindulge in many ways, and then be rendered dull and insensitive to what is really going on around them.
- Drunkenness, directly related to dissipation, would also be a temptation for the suffering, afflicted, persecuted disciple, who is also aware of the chaos taking place in the created universe and who wishes to blot out the danger and the pain by anesthetizing his brain.
- Worry, or the preoccupation with the anxieties of life, would seem justifiable. According to Jesus, though, worrying about the details of life only misappropriates our energies to worthless efforts.

The antidote for all three will be to always watch and pray (21:36). An ongoing relationship with Jesus is the only way really to face all that will take place.

Biblical teachings about the last days can be confusing and a source of fierce debate. But at this time, Jesus' words are eagerly received by crowds of people at the temple (21:37–38). Yet His teaching days are almost at an end.

Take It Home

What is your understanding of the last days and second coming of Jesus? When you read passages like this one, are you more comforted, scared, or confused? The day of the Lord should be a truth that radically changes the Christian's lifestyle. Knowing that the material world will vanish, we should not place too much value on material things. Knowing that the Word of God will never pass away, we should find it of infinite, eternal value. Rather than tempting us to dull ourselves or worry ourselves to death, Jesus' return should motivate us to live a mindful life marked by self-control and a sense of mission.

BETRAYAL, DENIAL, ARREST, AND ANGUISH

A Traitor among the Group   22:1–6
The Last Supper   22:7–38
Jesus' Arrest   22:39–65

Setting Up the Section

Luke's Gospel moves abruptly from Jesus' teaching in the temple after His triumphal entry to the events leading to His crucifixion. Remember the broader setting in which the Last Supper is found. The Jewish religious leaders in Jerusalem have already determined that Jesus must die. After He cleansed the temple, the sparks really began to fly, with the religious leaders making every effort to discredit Him or to get Him into trouble with the Roman authorities (20:19–20). When these efforts, as well as their attempts to penetrate the ranks of our Lord's disciples, miserably failed, the chief priests were delighted to have Judas approach them with his offer. It was only a matter now of waiting for the right chance.

📄 **22:1–6**

A TRAITOR AMONG THE GROUP

Luke's version of Judas's betrayal of Jesus is considerably more concise than that of the other Gospel writers. Prior to this point, Luke has said nothing about Judas by name other than including him (last) in the list of disciples (6:16).

Critical Observation

Other Gospel writers provide a bit more insight into Judas's nature. He was not only the treasurer of the group, but also a thief (John 12:4–6). It was Judas's offer to betray Jesus that seemingly hastened Jesus' death. Were it not for Judas, the religious officials had planned to wait until after the Passover celebration to kill Jesus because they feared a riot (Mark 14:1–2). But in reality, Judas's betrayal was on God's timetable, because Jesus knew ahead of time about His betrayer (Luke 22:21).

Judas had been among the Twelve when they were paired up to teach and heal (9:1–6). His faults prior to Jesus' betrayal didn't seem much worse than those of the other disciples. So perhaps the best explanation for what makes him decide to betray his master is Luke's short comment that "Satan entered Judas" (22:3 NIV), prompting him to go to the chief priests and strike a deal to turn Jesus over to them (22:3–6).

Luke gives the account of Judas's agreement with the chief priests and officers (22:3–6) just before the Lord's instructions concerning the preparation for the last supper (22:7–13). This order of events is significant, for had Judas known in advance the place where the Passover was to be eaten, he could have arranged for Jesus' arrest there.

📄 **22:7–38**

THE LAST SUPPER

Jesus' instructions for finding a place to celebrate the Passover (22:7–13) are just as cryptic as those for acquiring a donkey to ride into Jerusalem (19:28–35). But Peter and John faithfully obey, and the upper room is secured.

Demystifying Luke

The Passover itself began at the exodus of the Israelite nation from Egypt. The word that Moses brought to Pharaoh from God, "Let My people go. . ." (Exodus 5:1 NIV), was challenged by Pharaoh: "Who is this God, that I should obey Him?" (Exodus 5:2). The plagues were God's answer to this question. But while Pharaoh often agreed to release the people of Israel, he would renege once the pressure was off. The final plague was the smiting of the eldest son of the Egyptians, which resulted in the release of the Israelites. The firstborn sons of the Israelites were spared by means of the first Passover celebration. The Passover animals were slaughtered, and some of the blood was placed on the doorposts. When the death angel saw the blood on the doorposts, he "passed over" the house. This celebration was made an annual feast for the Israelite nation.

Luke writes of Jesus first taking the cup (22:17), then the bread (22:19), and then the cup again (22:20). Current Lord's Supper sacraments normally begin with the bread and follow with the wine. But if Jesus were following a traditional Passover celebration, there would have been four cups during the dinner.

None of the Gospels hint strongly that the Last Supper will eventually become as significant as it is to the church. The symbolism and weight of the event becomes evident in retrospect, but the disciples are not aware at the time. They don't notice that Jesus is instituting a new covenant and fulfilling the old covenant (22:15–16).

Luke's account of this event emphasizes the fact that the Last Supper has two distinct meanings. Verses 15–18 refer to the significance of the Passover for the Lord Jesus. The reference to eating (the bread, presumably) and drinking has its own meaning for Him as Israel's Messiah. The reason why He can say that He has eagerly desired to eat the Passover is revealed in verse 16: He will not eat it again until its fulfillment in the kingdom of God. So, too, for the cup. He will not drink the cup again until the kingdom of God is fulfilled (22:15, 17, 19–20).

Normally, we tend to look at the Passover as being a prototype of the death of Christ on the cross. Jesus looks beyond the cross, to the crown. The joy set before Him is the kingdom, and the suffering of the cross is the way this joy will be realized. Thus, Jesus focuses on the joy of the fulfillment of the Passover and is encouraged and enabled to endure the cross because of it.

In Matthew and Mark's parallel accounts of the Last Supper, Jesus is said to have indicated to His disciples that one of them would betray Him. The disciples are greatly saddened, and one by one each asked if he could be the traitor (Matthew 26:21–25; Mark 14:18–21). Luke's account adds an interesting comment (22:21-24). He passes over the sorrow of the disciples and informs us that the conversation quickly deteriorates into a finger-pointing session, where the disciples seem to look more at one another to find the culprit than to look within themselves. They actually end up in an argument over which of them is the greatest. From a search for the great sinner, the disciples move to a scrap over the greatest success among them.

Jesus responds with the criteria of greatness He expects from His followers (22:24-26). He exhorts His disciples to demonstrate servanthood and promises that their efforts will be rewarded—not only with their inclusion in His kingdom, but also with authority (22:27-30). When Jesus tells His disciples that the greatest must be the servant of all, He is simply reminding them that they must be like Him. He is not asking them to do anything that He is not doing Himself.

The disciples' preoccupation and debate over their own position, prestige, and power is inappropriate for several reasons:

1) This is the way the heathen behave.
2) It is the opposite of the way Jesus has manifested Himself, even though He is the greatest of all.
3) The preoccupation with greatness is untimely, for that which the disciples are seeking will not come in this life but in the next.

At some point during the evening, Jesus singles out Peter and warns him of a specific temptation the disciples will face (22:31). Just as Satan was at work in turning Judas against Jesus, the evil one is also about to attempt to test the other disciples (22:31). Although Peter will be singled out as one who will soon deny his Lord, the "you" in verse 31 (NIV) is plural. Jesus is warning them all. The word picture regarding wheat is this: In the process of getting from the fields into the storehouses, wheat is cut down, trampled, and tossed about. Jesus' followers could expect a similar experience before becoming productive members of the kingdom.

Jesus' reference to Peter (the nickname Jesus gave him, meaning "the rock") as Simon must have hurt, too. Simon was Peter's name before he met the Master. Looking back to this moment from what we know of history, it suggests that Peter would be acting like his old self, and not as a disciple of the Lord when he denied Jesus.

Peter thinks he is ready to withstand any kind of suffering—even death. But Jesus states, in no uncertain terms, that by morning light Peter will already have denied Him three times (22:33-34).

Verses 35-38 raise numerous questions. Jesus had previously told the disciples not to take provisions with them when they went out (9:1-6). Is Jesus changing His mind? Yes and no. The key to proper interpretation is verse 37, a reference to Isaiah 53. The passage in Isaiah, detailing various aspects of an unpopular, suffering Savior rather than a victorious Messiah, was not even considered messianic until after Jesus had died. The Greek word translated as "transgressor" (NIV) or criminal here refers to a rebel, someone defiant of God.

The fact that Jesus is crucified between two criminals does fulfill the prophecy of Isaiah 53:12, but it does so in a kind of symbolic way, so that it also leaves room for a broader, more sweeping fulfillment. Jesus is numbered (perhaps, as has been suggested, allows Himself to be numbered) among transgressors, and the two thieves are definitely that. But it could also be said that since Jesus is now dealt with as a criminal, His disciples are regarded in the same way. Jesus and His disciples are considered transgressors.

Yet Jesus is surely speaking figuratively about purchasing swords. When He says, "That is enough" (22:38 NIV), He probably doesn't mean two swords are enough. Indeed, one sword is too many in the garden during His arrest. And never in the rest of scripture are believers told to use force against their enemies. The only swords they wield are spiritual ones (Ephesians 6:17). So Jesus' comment very likely means they have partaken of quite enough foolish talk because His statement concludes their dialog on greatness, power, and priority.

📄 **22:39–65**

JESUS' ARREST

After the Last Supper in the upper room, Jesus and the disciples go "as usual" to the Mount of Olives (22:39 NIV)—more specifically, to Gethsemane (Matthew 26:36). This was apparently a regular stop for Jesus, and private. Perhaps Judas knew he could lead Jesus' opponents to Gethsemane without the likelihood of encountering Jesus' adoring crowds.

First, though, Jesus asks the disciples to pray and then goes off by Himself to do the same. Like any other human being, He doesn't want to die. But He is fully committed to God's will and carrying out His part of the plan. Luke's account of the agony of our Lord in Gethsemane is considerably shorter than those of Matthew and Mark. Luke, for example, does not set the three disciples (Peter, James, and John) apart from the other eight, even though these three are taken by our Lord, to watch with Him at a closer distance. Neither does Luke focus on Peter, although in the other accounts, Jesus specifically urges Peter to watch and pray. While Matthew and Mark indicate three different times of prayer, with our Lord returning twice to awaken His disciples and urge them to pray, Luke refers to only two. Luke's record of Jesus sweating drops of blood is also unique to this Gospel (22:44). This reference may refer to the physical condition in which a person's stress response causes capillaries to break and blood to mix with his perspiration. Or, it may be a reference to the fact that Jesus is sweating so profusely that it is as if He is bleeding.

Though He is in such great sorrow and anguish that an angel comes to minister to Him, He doesn't ask for the disciples' prayer support. Rather, He asks them twice to pray that they won't fall into temptation (22:40, 46). He knows what is coming and wants them to prepare, but they fall asleep instead. Jesus' prayer, while it has three sessions and takes up a fair amount of time, can be summed up in His surrender to the will of God if the suffering could not be taken way (22:42). Jesus speaks of what is to come as a "cup." In other places in scripture, a cup is used as a visual image of the wrath of God (Habakkuk 2:16; Revelation 14:10). Jesus' agony is due to the cross that looms before Him. He is not in agony because He will be forsaken by men, but because He will be forsaken and smitten by God. Jesus is dreading, suffering in the anticipation of His bearing of the sins of the world and the wrath of God, which they deserved.

Demystifying Luke

Perhaps Luke's interest as a physician motivated him to record that Jesus' "sweat was like drops of blood" (22:44 NIV). Hematidrosis is a very rare condition in which severe stress results in people literally sweating blood. Scripture does not say this was the case for Jesus, but it is a possibility. In either case, Jesus was undergoing unprecedented, supernatural suffering. Luke also noted that the disciples weren't merely sleepy, but that their great fatigue was the result of their sorrow (22:45).

Jesus rouses the disciples and goes out to meet the crowd that has come for Him (Matthew 26:46; Mark 14:42). Luke's account of the arrest is again more concise than other Gospels. He dwells not on what is done to Jesus, but on what Jesus says and does.

1) Jesus rebukes Judas for betraying Him with a kiss (22:48).
2) Jesus orders a cease-fire and is obeyed, by both His own disciples and by the crowd of armed men who have come to arrest Him (22:49–51).
3) Jesus heals the servant's ear, so that all damages are corrected. (Luke again uses his eye for detail to note it was the right ear [22:50–51].)
4) Jesus rebukes the religious leaders for the way in which they deal with Him (22:52–53).

Luke reveals Jesus to be in control of the situation—a willing arrestee for whom they have no need for all their weapons (22:52). They expected a fight, but Jesus does not resist. They find Jesus unshaken. It is these arresting officers who are shaken up. John's account informs us that they actually draw back and trip over themselves when Jesus identifies Himself to them (John 18:6).

The disciples aren't prepared for crisis. They all flee (Matthew 26:56), but Peter follows at what he thinks is a safe distance. When recognized, he quickly denies knowing Jesus. Before long two others have associated Peter with Jesus, and then as he is making his third denial, a rooster crows (22:60). If that isn't bad enough, Luke tells us Jesus turns and looks straight at Peter (22:61). Jesus' prediction (22:34) certainly comes rushing back to Peter, and he can do nothing but leave and weep bitterly (22:62). Luke's account of Peter's denial gives us no explanation for Peter's presence there in the courtyard of the high priest's house. Neither does he give us the reason why Peter denied his Lord when confronted with the fact that he was one of His disciples. Luke simply gives us a straightforward account of Peter's three denials.

Meanwhile, Jesus is being blindfolded, mocked, beaten, and insulted by His guards (22:63–65). Notice that they are not abusing Jesus as though He were a hardened criminal or a violent man who has caused others to suffer and so deserves to suffer as well. They are mocking Jesus as a prophet. They want Him to give them some kind of magical display of His powers. In the process they are fulfilling Jesus' own words, that a prophet is persecuted, not praised, for his work. Thus, Jesus is here identified with the prophets who have gone before Him to Jerusalem, to be rejected and to die.

Take It Home

With faith so seldom challenged these days, how many believers really know how strong their faith is? Are they like Peter, verbally bold and even overconfident, only to stumble at the first real trouble? How do you evaluate your own level of faith? Can you look back at a turbulent time and see that your faith was either shaken and/or grew stronger as a result? Do you think your daily life would be much different if your faith were stronger?

LUKE 22:66–23:56

JESUS' TRIALS AND CRUCIFIXION

The Trials	22:66–23:25
Jesus' Crucifixion	23:26–43
Jesus' Death	23:44–56

Setting Up the Section

After Jesus' betrayal by Judas, arrest in Gethsemane, and denial by Peter, He undergoes a series of trials where He is rejected by both the Jews and the Gentiles. It seems that Pilate tries, but fails, to spare His life.

He is crucified between two thieves and buried in a borrowed tomb. The events surrounding the death of our Lord, as described by Luke, fall into several distinct sections. The first of these is the Via Dolorosa ("Way of Sorrow"), the way to the cross, described in 23:26–32. The second is the actual crucifixion scene, the events surrounding the execution of our Lord, taking place on Calvary, in 23:33–43. The final section, in 23:44–49, is the account of the death of our Lord, along with Luke's description of the impact of these events on some of those who witnessed it—namely, the centurion, the crowd, and the women who had accompanied Jesus from Galilee.

📖 22:66–23:25

THE TRIALS

No time is wasted in passing sentence on Jesus. Only hours after His nighttime arrest, the elders convene. By law, they have to wait until the break of day (22:66). Jesus is brought before the group and drilled as to whether or not He is the Christ.

Other Gospels delve more into the scheming of the religious leaders. The Sanhedrin had to resort to another illegal ploy. Could they somehow trick Jesus into bearing witness against Himself? While the law of that day had its own fifth amendment, which prevented the accusers from forcing a man to testify against himself, could they somehow get Him to acknowledge that He is the Messiah, and even better, that He is the Son of God? If so, then they could find Him guilty of blasphemy, a crime punishable by death?

The official Jewish council that oversaw Jesus' trial was the Sanhedrin, a final court of appeals. Certain members of the seventy-member body were sympathetic to Jesus (23:50–51), but apparently they were either absent or out voted.

Luke is again content to show that Jesus is in control. Jesus' retort (22:67-69) shows that He realizes this trial is little more than a sham. He isn't tricked or coerced into saying what His accusers want to hear; He speaks because His time has come.

Jesus affirms He is the Messiah. You can imagine the Sanhedrin's response when Jesus indirectly confirms He is the Son of Man. This expression, found in Daniel's prophecy (Daniel 7), implied not only humanity, but deity. Will He admit He is the Son of God? Jesus' response is a grudging admission that implies something like, "yes, but not the way you understand messiahship." Nevertheless, it gives the Sanhedrin the grounds it needs to accuse Jesus.

The Jewish officials, of course, consider His words to be blasphemy (although Jesus spoke the truth). No matter how they had mistreated Jesus, disrespecting His human rights, now all they need is the cooperation of the state to kill Him—they could pass a death sentence, but couldn't carry it out.

So the next stop was to present their case before the governor of Judea, Pontius Pilate. Luke's account of the secular trial of Jesus is quite distinct from the other accounts.

- Luke is the only account to include the trial before Herod.
- Luke's account describes Pilate more in terms of his intentions and desires, than in terms of his actions.
- He tells us that Pilate proposes that he will punish Jesus, and then release Him.
- He does not emphasize the external pressures brought to bear on Pilate, as the other Gospels do.
- He emphasizes Jesus' silence.
- He most strongly emphasizes Jesus' innocence.

Luke informs us in verse 2 that members of the Sanhedrin (who apparently all came along to bring charges, see verse 1) press three charges against Jesus, all of which are political (that is, against the state), and none of which are religious. The charges against Jesus are:

1) stirring up unrest and rebellion;
2) opposing taxation by Rome; and
3) claiming to be a king (23:2).

Pilate appears to have been a savvy politician. He passes right over the first two charges. If Jesus were a revolutionary, would not the Romans have known about Him much sooner? Indeed, did not the Romans know of Jesus? Surely they had long ago determined that He was no threat. Revolutionaries there were, but Jesus was not among them. And neither did the Roman IRS have any evidence that Jesus had ever so much as implied that the Jews should not pay their Roman taxes. And, as Jesus had emphasized to His arresters, had He not taught publicly, day after day, so that His teaching was a matter of public record (see 22:52–53)?

Pilate does address the third charge (23:3) asking Jesus only to respond as to whether or not He is the king of the Jews. When he can find no foundation (23:4) he tries to dismiss the charges. After all, even if Jesus claimed to be a king, He had no military backing or political power.

The chief priests and the crowd protest, insisting that Jesus stirs up the people all over Judea by His teaching, starting in Galilee. By doing so, they have disclosed that Jerusalem is simply the last place where Jesus has created some measure of unrest. He is not a Judean, a man of Jerusalem, but a Galilean. Thus Pilate delights in ruling that this case is really not in his jurisdiction. The case must go to Herod the Tetrarch, for he is the one who rules over Galilee (3:1). And so Jesus, along with the religious leaders and the rest of the crowd, are sent, still early in the morning, to bother Herod.

While Pilate seemingly had little interest in Jesus and virtually no previous contact with Him, Herod at least had a fair amount of indirect contact. One of the women who followed Jesus and helped to support Him was Joanna the wife of Chuza, Herod's steward (8:2; 24:10). Also, there was Herod's relationship with John the Baptist. So there were several reasons that Herod would have been informed about Jesus' ministry. Herod is pleased to meet Jesus in person (23:8) and is hoping to see a miracle, or at least interview Jesus. But Jesus does not respond. Herod has Jesus dressed in an elegant robe and returns Him to Pilate after he and his soldiers get tired of mocking Him (23:11). Surprisingly, this experience forges a friendship between Pilate and Herod, who were previously enemies (23:12).

Why does Luke include this incident with Herod while no other Gospel writer does? Perhaps to show that everyone rejected Jesus as the Messiah, including Herod. It was necessary for Rome and the Gentiles to share in the rejection and the crucifixion of Christ so that all people, not just the Jews, might be guilty of His innocent blood.

It seems, not only from verse 13 but also from the parallel accounts, that Pilate takes Jesus aside after He is brought back from His trial before Herod, and that he attempts to satisfy himself concerning Jesus' guilt or innocence. When he comes out, Pilate calls the chief priests and rulers of the people (for it is they who are pressing him for a guilty verdict) and reiterates that he is unconvinced of any criminal charges that merit the case presented against Jesus, reminding them that by his actions, Herod had also acknowledged the innocence of Jesus.

Demystifying Luke

In verse 18 the name of Barabbas appears. The editors of the NIV and the NASB have chosen to omit verse 17 because it is not included in the oldest and most reliable manuscripts. The content of the verse though—the custom of releasing a prisoner—is clearly mentioned in the parallel accounts (Matthew 27:15–26; Mark 15:6–15; Luke 23:18–25; John 18:39–40). The custom may have come about as a kind of goodwill gesture on Pilate's part.

With Jesus again in Pilate's jurisdiction, Pilate tries three more times to convince the crowd to release Jesus (23:18–22). Yet they even insist on releasing Barabbas, a convicted murderer, rather than Jesus, a man of peace. And even after Pilate attempts to satisfy them by having Jesus beaten, they still insist on His crucifixion (23:23–25).

JESUS' CRUCIFIXION

There are two major incidents described in Luke's Gospel, both of which occur on the way to Calvary. The first is the commandeering of Simon of Cyrene. The second is Jesus' response to the wailing women. These two incidents are both prophetic of the unpleasant things to come for the nation of Israel, and specifically for those who lived in Jerusalem.

Normally, convicted criminals carried their own crosses (the horizontal piece) to the execution site, but Simon of Cyrene is commandeered by the Roman soldiers to carry the cross for Jesus (23:26). Presumably, the beatings and other demands of the evening have been too physically strenuous for Jesus. Simon was an innocent bystander, so far as the rejection and crucifixion of Christ was concerned. He was a man from a faraway place—Cyrene, a city in Africa (see Acts 2:10; 6:9), and he was not in Jerusalem but was heading there from the country. He was as removed from the rejection of Jesus as was possible.

Jesus' words to the women of Jerusalem—to weep for themselves and their children rather than Him—places the sorrow on them as He tells them what to expect (23:27–31). The future destruction of Jerusalem, which caused Jesus to weep as He entered that city (19:41–44), is the same destruction over which the women of Jerusalem are now told to weep. These women should not mourn so much over Jesus' death (after all, it would be the cause of their salvation), but they should mourn over that destruction that will take such a terrible toll on them and on their children.

Jesus' presence among humankind had been a remarkable, though generally unrecognized, blessing. His words in verse 31 say, in essence, "If the very Son of God is in your city, and the Roman army deals with Me this way, what do you think your destiny will be in My absence?" While crucifixion was not a Jewish means of executing men, nor was it all that common at the time of our Lord's death, crucifixion would be the rule of the day when the Romans came to sack the city of Jerusalem. It is said that thousands were crucified, at least, and that there was a shortage of crosses and of wood to build them due to the demand.

Critical Observation

Luke's account is unique, making contributions omitted in the other Gospel accounts. He included three incidents which are not reported elsewhere in the Gospels:

1) the words of Jesus to the women of Jerusalem (23:27–31),

2) the conversion of the thief on the cross (23:38–43), and

3) the words of our Lord, asking God to forgive His tormentors (23:34).

The place called the Skull (23:33) is the meaning of *Calvary* (Latin), or *Golgotha* (a Greek transliteration of an Aramaic word). Crucifixions were gory and gruesome, yet Luke spares us many of those details. He says simply that Jesus is crucified along with criminals. Matthew and John show how Jesus' death fulfilled Old Testament scripture; Luke remains focused on the love and salvation of the Messiah.

- Even as Jesus is being nailed to a cross, and people are gambling for His clothes, He prays for their forgiveness (23:34).
- And while hanging on the cross, when one of the thieves has an abrupt change of heart, Jesus still responds (23:43).

Demystifying Luke

The belief and salvation of the thief is recorded only in Luke's Gospel, and was pivotal to the tone of Jesus' crucifixion. Prior to that point Jesus receives only scoffing and other verbal and physical abuse; afterward such things are no longer mentioned, and Jesus' death takes on a somber and supernatural dignity.

23:44–56

JESUS' DEATH

The sixth hour is noon, by Jewish timekeeping. So the darkness must be eerie as the sun stops shining for three hours in the middle of the day (23:44–45)—an appropriate setting for the Savior of the world to, at last, commit His spirit into the hands of His heavenly Father (23:46). Meanwhile, the curtain in the temple that veiled the Most Holy Place and Ark of the Covenant is torn in half. With the death of Jesus, people will henceforth be able to approach God boldly, without requirement of animal sacrifice or priestly intervention. Jesus forever fulfills both essential roles: sacrifice and priest (Hebrews 4:14–16).

The response of the onlookers to Jesus' death is quite a contrast to what was recorded during His trial and during the first stages of His crucifixion. His death prompts a confession of faith from the Roman official in charge, declaring Jesus' innocence (23:47). Luke's record of this declaration is a thread in the theme of innocence that he weaves through the trial and crucifixion account.

Even the crowd's response becomes more subdued. People leave in sorrow and/or contrition. And Jesus' female followers simply stand and watch (23:48–49).

It is a member of the Sanhedrin who makes the official request to tend to Jesus' body. Joseph of Arimathea (with the help of Nicodemus [John 19:39]) goes to Pilate, takes Jesus' body, prepares it with spices (75 pounds) and wrappings, and places it in Joseph's brand-new tomb (23:50–53; John 19:38–42). This was done in the final hours before sunset when the Sabbath began and such a task would not be allowed.

Joseph and Nicodemus were both, to a great degree, outsiders. What they did seemed to be because of their position and authority. What they did, as far as we know, they did apart from any involvement on the part of the disciples of our Lord or the women who had long been following along with Him. While the disciples of John the Baptist claimed the body of John and buried it (Mark 6:29), the disciples of Jesus did not do so.

The women who are concerned for Jesus want to anoint His body, but the best they can do is gather their spices and wait until the Sabbath is over (23:54–56).

Critical Observation

The sequence of events in Jesus' crucifixion is not always clear, and Luke leaves out a number of phenomena that the other Gospels include, so that we cannot tell for certain the exact order of the events. Here is a general idea, however, of how the events appeared, keeping in mind the accounts of all the Gospel writers:

- The victims were nailed to their crosses, which were raised and fixed in position.

- Either prior to this or shortly after, drugged wine was offered to deaden the pain.

- The clothing of Jesus was gambled for and divided among the four soldiers.

- Railing accusations and mocking occurred throughout the ordeal—the crowd somehow seems to file or pass by the cross.

- Jesus cried out, "Father, forgive them. . ." (Luke 23:34 NIV).

- The criminals joined in reviling Christ.

- The thief on the cross came to faith in Jesus as his Messiah (Luke 23:40–43).

- Darkness falls over the scene, from the sixth hour (noon) till the ninth hour (3:00 p.m.).

- Jesus cried out, "my God, my God, why have you forsaken me?" (Matthew 27:46 NIV; Mark 15:34 NIV).

- Jesus said, "I am thirsty" (John 19:28–29 NIV) and drank a sip of vinegar.

- Jesus said, "It is finished" (John 19:30 NIV).

- Jesus bowed His head and said, "Father, into your hands. . ." (Luke 23:46 NIV) and died.

- Immediately, the curtain of the temple tore in two, top to bottom.

- An earthquake and the raising of dead saints occur (Matthew 27:51–54).

- The legs of the other two were broken, but Jesus' legs were not broken, since He was already dead (John 19:31–37).

- A soldier pierced Jesus' side with a spear—blood and water gushed out (John 19:34).

- A centurion (and the other soldiers who witnessed it) recognized He was the Son of God (Matthew 27:54; Mark 15:39) or the righteous/innocent one (Luke 23:47).

- The crowds left, beating their breasts, while the Galilean followers stayed on, watching from a distance.

Demystifying Luke

When Luke wrote that it was the day of preparation (23:54), he was referring to the Sabbath laws. Since there was no work to be done on the Sabbath (from Friday evening until Saturday evening), which included no cooking, preparations had to be made on Friday for the family's meals on Friday evening and Saturday (the Sabbath). The same "no work" laws would have kept the women from tending to Jesus' body on Saturday, so Sunday morning was their next opportunity.

Luke gives no clue as to the women's state of mind during their wait, but it must have been a sorrowful time indeed. Just a week before, Jesus had ridden into Jerusalem to the acclaim of the crowds. He had been teaching daily in the temple. The suddenness of His Thursday night arrest and Friday afternoon death and burial, coupled with their inability to do anything on the Sabbath, was surely cause for intense grief and perhaps even hopelessness. But what none of them yet realized was that the story of Jesus was far from over.

Take It Home

It can be disheartening to see that, after Jesus invested so much of His time in His apostles, His final hours were spent alone. His old friends seemed to have betrayed, denied, and deserted Him. Yet at the same time, new disciples (Joseph of Arimathea and Nicodemus) had a burst of faith and courage that enabled them to go public and tend to His body and burial. If you are a long-time follower of Jesus, what can you learn from this account? What can you learn if you are a new believer?

LUKE 24:1–53

RESURRECTION AND SECOND CHANCES

The Empty Tomb	24:1–12
Cleopas and His Friend	24:13–35
A Final Training Period	24:36–53

Setting Up the Section

After the bleakness and despair of Jesus' horrid crucifixion, His followers have an assortment of amazing epiphanies. The women discover an empty tomb and angelic messengers announcing His resurrection. Two disciples on the road have a heart-burning conversation before they realize their fellow traveler is Jesus Himself. And finally the apostles get to see Jesus and hear His explanation for everything that had happened. Consequently, even the absence of Jesus' physical presence would not deter their worship and praise of God.

THE EMPTY TOMB

The women who had wanted to anoint Jesus' body on Friday have not been able to, but they have marked the location of the tomb where He was laid (23:55). Perhaps they even noticed that someone had already anointed His body (since seventy-five pounds of spices had been used [John 19:39]), but they want to see to it themselves.

Even at this point, the apostles aren't involved. Surely the women could have used help carrying their load of spices or protection for travel in the dim morning light (24:1), but they travel alone for their discomfiting task.

When they arrive, they see the stone has been rolled away (24:2). They enter the tomb and hardly have time to wonder what has happened before two angels address them. The angels' clothing is fiercely radiant, probably allowing the women to see clearly that Jesus' body is not there. So that it cannot be said that the women merely forgot the burial place of Jesus and went to the wrong tomb, Luke (along with the other Gospel writers) reports that the angels inform the women that they have come to the right place, seeking Jesus, but that He is not there (24:5–7; Matthew 28:5–6; Mark 16:6). Matthew tells us that one angel invited the women to see the place where He once lay (Matthew 28:6).

The women are looking for the living among the dead (24:5). The angels confirm that Jesus' body isn't just gone; He has risen (24:6). To further explain, the angels remind the women of Jesus' own words (24:6–7; 9:22), and the women begin to remember and comprehend what Jesus had taught them.

Critical Observation

Luke doesn't mention it, but Judas had killed himself by this time (Matthew 27:1–10; Luke will briefly describe Judas' suicide in Acts 1:18–19). He begins referring to the apostles as the Eleven (24:9, 33), although other biblical writers continue to refer to them as the Twelve.

The women return to tell the apostles, but the Eleven don't believe them. Still, Peter decides to check out their story (along with John [John 20:1–9]), and runs to the tomb. He sees the open tomb and wrappings for the body, but registers no understanding or belief that something miraculous has happened (24:9–12).

CLEOPAS AND HIS FRIEND

Two more disciples are discouraged (24:17) as they walk the seven miles from Jerusalem to Emmaus, discussing the events of Jesus' death. We do not know the exact location of the small village of Emmaus, only its distance from Jerusalem. If they did not live in Emmaus, they may have been staying there, in the suburbs as it were, for the Passover celebration. The huge influx of people may have necessitated finding accommodations outside the city.

One of these disciples is named Cleopas (24:18); the other is not named. By virtue of the length of this account, it seems that Luke places a great deal of importance on this incident. It takes up much of his account of our Lord's post-resurrection appearances.

Along the way Jesus joins them, although they don't recognize Him (24:15–17). This might only mean that Jesus appears to the men in His resurrected body, but it seems to mean that He appears to them in a body that is not immediately recognizable. This could mean, for example, that the nail scars were not apparent, so all the telltale indications of His identity would have been concealed.

Jesus asks what they are talking about, and they tell Him what little they know (24:17–24). It was, they said, the third day since He had died. This could be a reference to Jesus' words that He would rise again on the third day. What was more, some of the women, they told Jesus, had gone out to the tomb and found it empty. The women further claimed to have seen angels, but alas they did not see Jesus. The very things that seemed to point to the resurrection of Jesus had no impact on these two men at all.

Jesus gently scolds them for not comprehending what the prophets had written in light of all that had happened (24:25–26). They had a partial understanding, like many of the Israelites of their day, but perhaps they chose to overlook the prophecies about the suffering of the Messiah while dwelling on the portions declaring His victory and glory. So Jesus teaches them what was said in all the prophecies (24:27).

When they get to Emmaus, Jesus gives them the opportunity to let Him walk away. But they insist that He stay with them (24:28–29). For one thing, it is late. But perhaps they are also interested in all He has been telling them. They sit down to eat, and as Jesus gives thanks and breaks bread, they recognize Him (24:31). At that instant, He disappears.

In a sense this breaking of bread with these two men was a prototype of heaven and of the joys that await the Christian. At the Last Supper, Jesus spoke of the kingdom in terms of a banquet meal (22:24–30), at which time He would serve His followers (12:37). Jesus said that He would not eat the Passover again until it was fulfilled in the kingdom of God (22:16). Jesus disappears because that great day is yet ahead when they will fellowship at His table in the kingdom. But this meal made the joy and anticipation of that occasion even greater.

They get up at once, driven by a burning in their hearts (24:32), and return to Jerusalem to tell the Eleven. By that time, Jesus has also appeared to Peter (24:34; 1 Corinthians 15:5), so they begin swapping their joyful stories.

📄 **24:36–53**

A FINAL TRAINING PERIOD

In his account of the post-resurrection appearances of Christ, Luke's emphasis is on what takes place in Jerusalem, not so much on what happens in Galilee (as, for example, Matthew recorded in 28:16-20). There are many appearances, some of which are described in one or more Gospels, and others of which may be described by another. There were probably a number of appearances that were not even mentioned.

While the disciples are discussing their experiences, Jesus appears again. Jesus' first words to this group are of peace (24:36). This is not the disciples' response, however. They are startled, Luke tells us (24:37). Why are they not overjoyed? Why are they frightened and upset? The use of "startled" (NIV) suggests that the disciples are caught off guard, as though they never expected to see Jesus. They think He is a ghost (24:36–37).

It is easier for the disciples to believe in a ghostly Jesus than in a Jesus who is literally and physically present. The issue really comes down to belief or unbelief. The disciples thought they really believed. They say that they believe (24:34). But their response seems to communicate something else.

The thrust of verses 36–43 is Jesus' provision of physical evidence for His resurrection. The first evidence is the Lord, standing before them. He is not, as they supposed, a ghost. He encourages them to touch Him, and to see that He has flesh and bones (24:39). He also encourages them to look at His hands and His feet (24:39). The inference is clear that both His hands and His feet bare the nail prints that He had from the cross. In this sense, at least, His body is like the body He had before His death. Finally, Jesus eats some of the fish that they are eating, the final proof that His body is, indeed, a real one (24:41–43).

As Jesus reasons with the startled group, He opens their minds to allow them to understand what the biblical prophecies had meant (24:44–45). Paul will later reaffirm that it is only through God's revelation that anyone can properly interpret and understand the truths of scripture (1 Corinthians 2:6–16; 2 Corinthians 3:14–18).

Demystifying Luke

This final section of Luke (24:24–53) is compressed. Luke later tells us that forty days passed between Jesus' resurrection and His ascension (Acts 1:3). The teachings in verses 45–49 were likely taught and reinforced throughout that period.

Jesus reminds them of the prophecies about Himself:
1) the rejection, suffering, death, and resurrection (24:46);
2) the proclamation of the gospel to all nations (24:47); and
3) the promise of the Holy Spirit (24:48–49).

While Jesus makes it clear that His death and resurrection are for all nations (24:47), it will later take a lot of discussion and debate (as well as divine revelation) before the early church fully understands that Gentile believers are as entitled to salvation as Jewish ones. The universality of the gospel—the fact that the Messiah would die for the sins of all who would believe, Jew or Gentile—was one of the greatest irritations for the Jewish religious leadership, especially for those who did not see themselves as sinners. Yet even the Abrahamic covenant, the great promise upon which Judaism was based, revealed this very truth: "And I will bless those who bless you, and the one who curses you I will curse. And in you all the families of the earth will be blessed" (Genesis 12:3 NASB).

In the light of the fact that the salvation that the Messiah came to bring was for all nations, the Great Commission comes as no new revelation, but as an outflow of the work of Christ on the cross of Calvary and of the Old Testament prophecies that foretold of the salvation of men of every nation. Notice that Luke (both here and in Acts 1:8) records the Great Commission, not so much as a command but as a promise, a certainty (24:47–48).

As one final miraculous assurance that Jesus has been sent from God, He is taken up into heaven as they all watch (24:50–53). He leaves them with a blessing and they worship Him. In addition, they "stayed continually at the temple" (24:53 NIV).

Luke seems to end his Gospel rather abruptly. But his "ending" isn't intended to be the final word. He continues the story right at this point in the book of Acts.

Take it Home

Christians today can fall into the very same trap into which the first-century disciples fell. We read and study the scriptures through the grid of our own sin, desires, ambitions, and preferences. We arrive at our own idea of what God should be like and what His kingdom should be, and then we are tempted to rearrange the scriptures to suit our ideas. How often we do this in those areas of tension, where two seemingly contradictory things are somehow linked. We would be wise to be like the Old Testament prophets, who heard the Word of God but couldn't always fathom its meaning based on their life experiences. Sometimes when we don't understand, we have to hold two truths in tension, seeking and praying to understand their interrelationship. We have to trust that even if we, in this life, can't see exactly what God has for us in the future, we can still trust Him to reveal Himself in His own time.

THE GOSPEL OF
JOHN

INTRODUCTION TO
JOHN

While the Gospels of Matthew, Mark, and Luke are identified together as the *synoptic* Gospels because of their similarities, the Gospel of John stands apart in style and in content. John's style is simple in vocabulary, yet profound and even sometimes poetic. As for content, he records events that the synoptic Gospels don't. Jesus' teaching also has a different focus. In the synoptic Gospels, Jesus' teaching focuses on the kingdom of God, but in John His teaching centers more on His own identity and how His presence manifests God the Father.

DISTINCTIVES

John's Gospel does not record Jesus' parables or some of the well-known events recorded in the other Gospels—such as His baptism, temptation, and transfiguration. It does, however, include the accounts of eight miracles performed by Jesus, only three of which appear in the other Gospels. While the other Gospels describe works of Jesus without much explanation, John's Gospel, providing fewer events, includes more exchange about the people involved and the significance of each event to those people.

AUTHOR

The author of this Gospel does not identify himself by name, though he is referred to as "the disciple that Jesus loved." Through the years, a variety of possible authors have been proposed, yet the apostle John, of the original twelve disciples, still seems the most likely candidate.

John was identified in the New Testament as the son of Zebedee and Salome, and as the younger brother of James. Jesus called James and John the "Sons of Thunder" (Mark 3:17). John was working as a fisherman when Jesus called him as a disciple.

PURPOSE

John states his purpose for writing in the Gospel's closing:

Jesus did many other miraculous signs in the presence of his disciples, which are not recorded in this book. But these are written that you may believe that Jesus is the Christ, the Son of God, and that by believing you may have life in his name (John 20:30–31 NIV).

The central theme of this Gospel is Jesus' revelation of God the Father and the connection that revelation enables between humanity and God. This Gospel is a call to faith as well as an encouragement to those continuing in their faith. Some compare it to a first-century tract written to explain Jesus' identity and to inspire others to have faith in Him.

HISTORICAL CONTEXT

There is some disagreement as to when John's Gospel was written, but most scholars date it in the late first century.

John probably wrote the Gospel while he was ministering in Ephesus, an important coastal city on the western shore of modern Turkey. Before John, first-century leaders such as Paul, Timothy, and the ministry couple Priscilla and Aquila influenced Ephesus.

While the early Christian movement had a presence in the area, it was not without conflict. The famous Temple of Diana and the trade from the manufacture of idols associated with the temple were part of the fuel for the conflict. By the time John was ministering in Ephesus, there was also opposition from the Jews. The first-century Christian church began as a predominantly Jewish movement, but by the late first century, those ties had been broken. In fact, John may have been dealing with opposition from the Jews reminiscent of the opposition that his Gospel describes Jesus facing.

THEMES

John's dominant theme is Jesus' identity as the Messiah, Son of God, the revelation of the Father. He also thematically points out the foolishness of the Jewish leaders who rejected Jesus as the Messiah. Several other themes run throughout the Gospel:
- **Eternal life.** In John's Gospel, eternal life is equated with knowing God, which happens through knowing Jesus.
- **The Holy Spirit.** Jesus' work will continue in and through His followers by the work of the Spirit who will guide, direct, and mediate the presence of the Father.

CONTRIBUTION TO THE BIBLE

Along with this Gospel, John wrote three short letters included in the Christian New Testament, identified as 1, 2, and 3 John. Many also believe he wrote the book of Revelation. The Gospel of John is often the first book a faith seeker reads in the Bible. John 3:16 stands as a hallmark of the love of God, often the one verse people of all backgrounds are familiar with.

STRUCTURE

The commentary for this book is laid out by chapters for ease of use, but here is a look at the broader structure of this book of the Bible:

Prologue	1:1–18
Jesus' Ministry—The Seven Signs	1:19–12:50
Jesus' Farewell Address, Trial, Death, and Resurrection	13:1–20:31
Epilogue	21:1–25

THE PROLOGUE OR INTRODUCTION   1:1–18

The Deity of Christ   1:1–5
John: The Forerunner of Christ   1:6–8
The Light of Christ   1:9–13
The Incarnate Christ   1:14–18

THE WITNESSES   1:19–51

The Witness of John the Baptist   1:19–28
The Second Witness of John the Baptist   1:29–34
The First Disciples   1:35–51

THE PUBLIC MINISTRY OF JESUS   2:1–25

The First Sign   2:1–11
Scriptural Faith vs. Superficial Faith   2:12–25

A MEETING AT NIGHT   3:1–21

Nicodemus   3:1–21
The Final Witness of John the Baptist   3:22–36

A MEETING BY THE WELL   4:1–54

The Woman at the Well   4:1–26
The Harvest   4:27–42
Knowing Christ   4:43–54

THE POSITION OF JESUS   5:1–47

The Authority of Jesus   5:1–18
Jesus Claims to Be God   5:16–24
The Power and Authority of Jesus   5:25–29
The Witnesses of Jesus' Deity   5:30–47

REVEALING HIMSELF — 6:1–71

The Awesome Power of Jesus — 6:1–15
The People of Glory — 6:16–29
The Bread of Life — 6:30–40
Rejection and Revelation — 6:41–71

CHALLENGES TO RESPOND — 7:1–8:11

The Response of Jesus' Family — 7:1–13
Spiritual Insight — 7:14–24
Ignorance in Wisdom's Clothing — 7:25–36
Come and Drink — 7:37–52
A Woman Caught in Adultery — 7:53–8:11

FROM PRESENTATION TO CONDEMNATION — 8:12–59

The Light of the World — 8:12–20
The First Condemnation of Israel — 8:21–30
Genuine Faith — 8:31–32
The Corruption of Man — 8:33–36
Man's Only Security — 8:37–47
Spiritual Ignorance — 8:48–59

THE BLIND MAN — 9:1–41

What the Blind Man Saw — 9:1–41

JESUS CONFRONTS THE LEADERSHIP — 10:1–42

Woe to the Shepherds — 10:1–21
The Deity of Jesus — 10:22–42

THE PRIVATE MINISTRY OF JESUS — 11:1–57

A Faith That Is Larger than Life — 11:1–44
The Plan of Men—the Plan of God — 11:45–57

THE FAITHLESS AND THE FAITHFUL   12:1–50

The Priority of Worship   12:1–8
The Beginning of the End   12:9–26
The Power of the Cross   12:27–36
The Unbelief of Israel   12:37–50

FINAL WORDS   13:1–38

Love in Action   13:1–17
A Traitor in the Camp   13:18–30
The Distinguishing Mark of the Church   13:31–38

HOPE FOR THE DISCOURAGED   14:1–31

Hope for the Hopeless   14:1–3
Clarity for the Confused   14:4–31

FINAL INSTRUCTIONS   15:1–27

Abide in Jesus   15:1–11
Abide in Love   15:12–17
The Cost of Abiding   15:18–27

A HELPER FOR DIFFICULT DAYS   16:1–33

A Final Word on Persecution   16:1–4
Better Days Are Yet to Come   16:5–15
The Transforming Work of the Spirit   16:16–33

JESUS' PRAYER   17:1–26

Jesus Prays for Himself   17:1–5
Jesus Prays for His Disciples   17:6–19
Jesus Prays for All Believers   17:20–26

JESUS' TRIALS   18:1–39

The Sovereign Control of Jesus   18:1–11
Humanity's Corruption and Jesus' Innocence   18:12–27
What Is Truth?   18:28–39

JESUS' DEATH   19:1–42

Behold, the Man   19:1–16
The Culmination of History   19:17–42

JESUS CONQUERS DEATH   20:1–31

The Empty Tomb   20:1–18
Jesus and the Disciples   20:19–31

EPILOGUE   21:1–25

Fishing Instructions   21:1–14
Breakfast by the Sea   21:15–25

JOHN 1:1-18

THE PROLOGUE OR INTRODUCTION TO THE GOSPEL OF JOHN

The Deity of Christ   1:1–5
John: The Forerunner of Christ   1:6–8
The Light of Christ   1:9–13
The Incarnate Christ   1:14–18

Setting Up the Section

This first chapter of John is a summary of the message of the entire Gospel—Jesus has come as the light of the world, and some reject and others accept. The first eighteen verses of chapter one offer an outline of his letter. Each topic that John will show us about Christ is introduced in these first verses.

1. The Deity of Christ (1:1–5)

2. The Forerunner of Christ (1:6–8)

3. The Rejection of Christ (1:9–11)

4. The Acceptance of Christ (1:12–13)

5. The Incarnation of Christ (1:14–18)

These topics represent the foundation of Christianity.

📄 1:1–5

THE DEITY OF CHRIST

As we study the Gospel of John we find its purpose is to present Jesus as God's Son so that we might believe in Him and have eternal life. In fact, John gives us the two-fold purpose of his Gospel in 20:30-31:

1) That you might believe that Jesus is the Christ (Messiah), the Son of God
2) That believing in Him you might have life in His name

Throughout this Gospel, John shows us Jesus as the self-revelation of God and the various responses of the people around Him to that revelation. Some reject this truth and others accept it.

These first five verses reveal five truths about the deity of Christ:

1) *The Eternality of Christ (1:1).* John's first words draw the attention of the reader to the opening lines of Genesis, where Moses writes, "In the beginning God" (Genesis 1:1 NIV). Another way to say this is that before time began the Word was there.

Critical Observation

Why does John call Jesus the "Word" (Greek: *Logos*)? One reason could be because this would make a point to both Jews and Greeks.

- **For the Jewish mind** this described the LORD God because the LORD (*Yahweh*) was a God who spoke. Each day of creation begins with, "Then God said . . ." God's power was manifested through His spoken word.

- **For the Greeks**, all of the little gods that they worshiped were just a part of the one big god of reason and philosophy. The name of this power source in Greek religion is also the Logos ("the Word")—the power source that created everything and the power source that sustains everything.

2) *Jesus Is Distinct from God (1:1).* When John says that "the Word was with God" (NIV), it means more than one person in the room with another person. The Greek word used here carries the idea of being intimately related or facing each other. John is saying that Christ was distinct from the Father, and yet, in union with Him. This was a stumbling block to the Jews of Jesus' day. They believed in one God. Then Christ comes and declares that He is God, yet distinct from God the Father. This is the foundation of the teaching known as the Trinity, that there is one God, but He exists as three distinct "persons"—Father, Son, and Spirit. John presents Jesus the Son as fully God, but distinct from the person of the Father.

3) *Jesus Is God (1:1).* John is not saying that Jesus is simply divine, as if He is an extension of God. He is saying that Jesus is God in bodily form, and He is God completely. This is why Jesus tells the disciples in John 14:9, "Anyone who has seen me has seen the Father" (NIV).

4) *Jesus Is Creator of All Things (1:2-3).* This is both a negative and a positive statement. All things came into being by Jesus, which means nothing came into existence without Him.

5) *Jesus Is the Source of Spiritual Life (1:4-5).* Life and light are reoccurring themes in John. The concept of *life* here applies to the spiritual life of a person. John refers to Christ as the source of life more than fifty times in this Gospel. In addition, Jesus is the source of light. Some Bible translations say the darkness couldn't *understand* the light. Others say the darkness couldn't overpower the light. The Greek word can mean either of these things. It is possible that the author is making a play on words and that both meanings are intended.

JOHN: THE FORERUNNER OF CHRIST

This passage introduces not only John the Baptist, but also a complex aspect of early Christianity—the transition from the Old Testament to the New Testament. Why did the Gospel writer introduce John the Baptist at this early point? Because his message is critical in understanding Jesus as the Messiah.

John the Baptist was the connection to the Old Testament to point people to Christ. He was the last Old Testament prophet and the first New Testament evangelist. In verse 7, we get a clear and simple description of his message—he came as a *witness*. As it does still today, this word has a connotation of a person who gives testimony in court so that people might be convinced of the truth.

The Gospel writer adds one last comment about John the Baptist—that he was not the light, but came to bear witness to the light. This is important because the Jews were looking for a Messiah. They had not heard from God through a prophet in over four hundred years. Many wondered if John was the Messiah himself. If the messenger was misunderstood in this way, then the message that he preached could be lost (Acts 19:1–7).

THE LIGHT OF CHRIST

The author draws a contrast between John the Baptist and Jesus in verse 9. Jesus is the true light that gives light to all mankind. Does this mean that Jesus placed an understanding of Himself in every person? No. It is the idea that Christ came and shined His light upon all people. This forced humanity to make a decision about who He was.

This is a key theme in John's Gospel—that Jesus' light forces people to come to grips with their sin. John uses the imagery of light more than twenty times to refer to Jesus. He continues to draw a distinction between the world in darkness and the light of Jesus.

Verse 10 describes Jesus as the creator of the world. He shined His light upon the world, and they did not know Him. Jesus came to His own, the Jews, yet they—particularly the religious leaders—did not receive Him (1:11). With key exceptions, Jesus was not recognized by those who had creation as a witness or by those who had scripture as a witness. But verses 12–13 reveal the hope of those who do recognize and make themselves a part with Christ—they are given the right to be called children of God. (See Romans 8 for Paul's teaching on this adoption into God's family.)

Take It Home

As a Christian, you are part of God's family. You are brought into fellowship with God in which:

- You are a son and not a slave.
- You are valued and not discriminated against.
- You are accepted and not rejected.

These things come to those who believe in His name. It does not matter that people did not see Jesus, for Jesus came to this dark place to take on mankind's sin so that God would save mankind.

📄 **1:14–18**

THE INCARNATE CHRIST

"The Word became flesh" (1:14 NIV). This is what we call the incarnation—God becoming human. Jesus was not a man who became divine—He was divinity that took on humanity. This belief of Jesus taking on humanity is central to Christianity.

The word translated as *dwelling* or *living* (1:14) means "to pitch a tent" or "take up residence." This is an image referring back to the Old Testament when God was believed to reside in the tabernacle, and then in the temple. Jesus lived on earth for thirty-three years as the presence of God on earth.

The *glory* of God (1:14) does not refer to a shining light or phenomenon. It is simply the sum of all of His attributes. Jesus revealed the grace and truth of God on earth in His nature and His work. That is what the disciples saw.

John the Baptist (1:15), as the witness of Jesus, is the link between the Old Testament and the New Testament. By mentioning John the Baptist, someone who was still well known when this Gospel was written in the mid-to-late first century, the Gospel writer includes a credible witness in identifying Jesus as the Messiah. John's words describing Jesus, communicate a paradox—Jesus came after him, yet existed before him.

There are a variety of interpretations of the phrase "fullness of his grace" in verse 16 (NIV). It could refer to Jesus' abundance of grace, or the replenishing nature of His grace, or a number of other possibilities. Whatever the exact meaning of that phrase, the grace we have received in Jesus is enough and does give good things to us over and over again. And while that grace does contrast with the Law of Moses (1:17) both reveal God's nature to us.

Critical Observation

The Old Testament law anticipated the grace of a future sacrifice. Ancient people came to God by faith just as we do. What did they have their faith in? It was not the Law, but in what the Law pointed them to. The Law showed them that God would provide a sacrifice that would take the guilt of their sin. So, the Old Testament worshiper trusted in the future grace that would come—the Messiah. When Jesus came, He was the fulfillment of the hope that was only understood in part in the Old Testament.

"No one has ever seen God" (1:18 NIV). While the Old Testament does describe times when God was revealed to people by appearing as a man or through some representative, God did not ever fully show Himself to people, for His holiness would consume them. Yet, Jesus Christ has revealed God to us. He is God put on display.

The description of Jesus in verse 18 focuses on the intimate relationship between Jesus and the Father. To be at the side of the Father means that Jesus is uniquely related to the Father. God the Father and God the Son share an intimate relationship with each other, as a result of being one (Hebrews 1:1–2).

Demystifying John

This next section begins a different writing style for John. The first eighteen verses of this chapter were primarily doctrinal statements concerning the deity and humanity of Jesus Christ. We now move to the actual narrative of the book. John 1:19–12:50 is often referred to as a collection of signs because it includes seven miracles that reveal Jesus' revelation of God the Father. Rather than looking at statements to evaluate their meaning, we look at conversations and events to determine their significance.

Remember that this Gospel is not as much a chronological history of Jesus as it is a photo album. Each story is like a snapshot. These stories are a collection of events in the life of Christ that prove that He is the manifestation of God the Father.

JOHN 1:19-51

THE WITNESSES

The Witness of John the Baptist   1:19–28
The Second Witness of John the Baptist   1:29–34
The First Disciples   1:35–51

Setting Up the Section

This first account begins with John the Baptist and the inquisition of the religious establishment. It introduces the first of many question-and-answer times with the Jewish leadership.

📖 **1:19–28**

THE WITNESS OF JOHN THE BAPTIST

There were rumors that John was the Messiah himself. That's why it was essential to these religious leaders to explore his identity. John was baptizing and ministering to the people, so these men were justified in their need to confirm or deny his work as being from God.

Demystifying John

John records quite a few dialogues between Jesus and the Jewish religious leaders. While he often refers to these leaders simply as the Jews, they are made up of several groups. Understanding who they are can help us understand the significance of the questions they ask or the way that they respond.

- **Jews:** This term appears more than seventy times in the Gospel of John. In many cases it does not refer to the Jewish people as a whole (Jesus and His disciples were also Jews!), but to the religious leaders who opposed Jesus. That is why some translations render the word as "Jewish leaders" in certain contexts.

- **Priests:** The priests oversaw the temple worship. They were commissioned to determine whether or not a person's sacrifice was proper. They were in charge of all worship.

- **Levites:** The Levites, in general, were the ones in charge of caring for the temple, as well as keeping order in the worship. A certain family of the Levites—the descendants of Aaron, Moses' brother—served as priests.

- **Pharisees:** A group or sect of religious leaders within Judaism who devoted themselves to keeping the Law, especially its oral interpretations and applications.

In this Gospel, these names appear often, and the interplay between the groups is significant to the story. Though there are exceptions, typically the various religious groups were somewhat antagonistic toward each other. Yet, we see them work together in their opposition to Jesus.

When the priests and Levites ask John the Baptist who he is, he knows what they are really asking. So he responds immediately that he is not the Christ (1:20).

The inquiry as to whether he is the Old Testament prophet Elijah (1:21) relates to a prophecy in Malachi 3:1 and 4:1–6, of the coming day in which the enemy of Israel would be destroyed by God. Before this great day of the Lord, God said that Elijah would come and restore the hearts of the people. John assures them he is not the Old Testament prophet.

The next question, whether John is "the Prophet" (1:21 NIV), may refer to the "prophet like [Moses]" of Deuteronomy 18:15 (NIV). Again John answers, "No." When asked for his identity, John gives them a significant description from Isaiah 40:3: "the voice of one calling in the desert, 'Make straight the way for the Lord'" (1:23 NIV). He is saying that he is the fulfillment of this prophecy. God had called him to prepare the hearts of Israel for the coming of the Messiah:

1) By calling people to repentance
2) By baptizing those who repented

Critical Observation

Throughout history, before a great move of God, the people were to consecrate themselves (cleansing and setting themselves apart from sin) so they would be prepared. For John the Baptist, the cleansing was accomplished through repentance. The setting apart was accomplished through baptism.

Those questioning John either did not understand his answer or did not believe him, for this next question shows little regard for the powerful answer he has just given. The delegation begins a second line of questioning concerning the authority under which John practices his baptisms (1:24–25). Baptizing was not the role of just anyone.

John's answer to this question is important (1:26). John's water baptism is less significant than the baptism of the Spirit. John's baptism is not the act of salvation, but rather the preparation for it. Notice John states that the Messiah is already present.

John said he was not fit to untie Jesus' sandals (1:27). The household servant who untied someone's sandals was the lowest of the lowest slave. So John is saying that he was not even good enough to be the lowest servant to this man.

The Bethany most commonly mentioned in the Gospels lies a short distance southeast of Jerusalem, on the road to Jericho. The Bethany mentioned here (1:28) is a region located on the other side of the Jordan.

THE SECOND WITNESS OF JOHN THE BAPTIST

This section includes John's second testimony—the witness that Jesus is the Son of God.

Jesus comes on the scene the day after John is questioned by the religious leaders (1:29). If we were to harmonize this chronology with the synoptic Gospels (Matthew, Mark, Luke), Jesus would probably be coming back from the wilderness after being tempted. John has already baptized Jesus, and so he has already had one encounter with Him.

John makes the mighty declaration that Jesus is "the Lamb of God, who takes away the sin of the world!" (1:29 NIV). John's original hearers would have taken this phrase as a reference to the prophecy of Isaiah. Isaiah 53:4–9 describes the Messiah who would sacrifice Himself willingly, like a lamb at slaughter.

Critical Observation

John uses the singular form of the word *sin* rather than the plural. He's talking about the root of sin as a whole, not just the individual sins committed one at a time. By taking care of the root of sin universally, he then takes care of the fruit of sin, or individual sins.

John the Baptist continues his description of Jesus by tying together a previous sermon that he preached about the coming Messiah (1:30). John had already preached that the Messiah would be greater because the Messiah existed before John. In that first-century culture, the older person had more status. To acquire age was to acquire wisdom, which was the prize of life. John identifies Jesus as the Messiah, but John is the older man of the two. Yet Jesus existed before John—He existed as God.

Demystifying John

John's Gospel is noted for its irony. People miss the obvious point of conversations with Jesus. Words are used with ironic double meanings. In John the Baptist's case, he presents Jesus as the one who existed before John, even though Jesus is younger than John. These kinds of twists run throughout the Gospel.

John describes his role in preparing the way for Jesus. He admits that he did not at first recognize Him (1:31). It is not that he did not know Jesus at all, but rather, he could not come to the full realization of Jesus' messiahship or His role on earth. Nevertheless, John's role was to baptize so that Israel might be ready for the coming of the Messiah—to call the Israelites back to God so that they would be ready for the Messiah.

How did John know that Jesus was really the Messiah? He was given a sign by God, and that sign was revealed at Jesus' baptism—the Spirit came down like a dove and rested on Jesus (1:32–34).

THE FIRST DISCIPLES

This passage reveals five witnesses that testify to the nature and work of Jesus Christ.

- John the Baptist. John sees Jesus coming again and tells his disciples that He is the Lamb of God (1:36). The disciples do not need anything more than that designation for them to understand who Jesus is. They understand this to mean that this is the one who takes away the sins of the world. John's words were enough to convince them to follow Jesus (1:37).
- Andrew. Verse 40 reveals that Andrew is one of the two disciples described in verses 35–39. At the time that this Gospel was written, Peter was the more prominent disciple, so Andrew is identified as the brother of Peter. For the sake of the non-Jewish reader, the Gospel writer defines the word *rabbi* (1:38)—master or teacher. The word originally came from a root word meaning "a great man," but came to be used of a respected teacher. By calling Jesus "Rabbi" they are showing their respect to Him. In asking where He is staying, they imply a desire to, in essence, set up an appointment to learn from Him.

Demystifying John

Verse 39 mentions it being the tenth hour when Jesus spent time with Andrew and the other disciple. Both Romans and Jews tended to count hours from sunrise, so this would make it about four o'clock in the afternoon. Some scholars, however, think it was 10:00 a.m., counting ten hours from midnight.

Andrew's witness is immediate (1:41)—he has found the Messiah. Notice that John translates *Messiah* as "Christ" for his Greek readers. Both *Messiah* (Hebrew) and *Christ* (Greek) mean "anointed one" or God's chosen instrument. By the first century the term *Messiah* had come to refer specifically to the Savior from King David's line who would deliver God's people.

Andrew brings his brother Simon to meet Jesus, but Jesus knows him already, identifying him by name, then giving him the nickname *Cephas*, an Aramaic word that John translates into Greek for his readers as Peter (*petros*). Both *Cephas* and *Peter* mean a "rock" or "stone." Jesus is laying claim to Simon. He speaks about his role in Jesus' kingdom. Simon will be a key player for Jesus in the next three years of ministry.

- Philip. In verse 43, Jesus calls Philip. The focus of this Gospel is not the calling of the apostles, but the divine nature of Jesus, so these interactions are summaries. Philip was from the same region as Andrew and Peter. In turn, Philip told Nathanael.

Take It Home

Philip's response to Nathanael is the response that we should all have when we share Jesus with someone—come and see for yourself. We need to show the nature of who Jesus is and trust God for the results.

- Nathanael. Nathanael does not think that Jesus is the Messiah (1:46), so he meets Jesus with questions. When Jesus reveals what no ordinary human could have known (1:47–48), this supernatural insight moves Nathanael to confess two things:
  1) Jesus is the Son of God; the one to whom God gave His Spirit.
  2) Jesus is the King of Israel, therefore the ruler of Israel.
  Nathanael probably does not understand the full implications of his declaration (1:49). He believes that this was the anointed one who will sit on the throne of David. Nathanael sees Jesus as more than a great teacher; he sees Him as Israel's king to be worshiped.
- Jesus. In verses 50–51, Jesus makes a declaration about Himself. Jesus' description of angels ascending and descending on the Son of Man is a reference to Jacob's famous dream in Genesis 28. Jacob dreamed that a ladder appeared from heaven to earth with angels climbing up and down the ladder. In essence, Jesus was saying that He is that ladder, the connection between mankind and God. More than eighty times in this Gospel, Jesus refers to Himself as the Son of Man as He does here (1:51).

Critical Observation

Verse 51 begins with the words, "I tell you the truth" (NIV), or as some translations say, "Verily, verily." In the Greek, it is the word *amen* repeated twice. This is a word that carries the idea of an absolute and binding truth that is not to be contradicted. This is why we often finish our prayers with the same word. Jesus begins statements this same way at least twenty-five times in the book of John.

JOHN 2:1–25

THE PUBLIC MINISTRY OF JESUS

The First Sign	2:1–11
Scriptural Faith vs. Superficial Faith	2:12–25

Setting Up the Section

Chapter 1 focused on the words of testimony about Jesus. Now Jesus' actual works witness to the truth that He is the Messiah.

- **Seven miracles—all of which show the glory of God dwelling in Jesus' body**

- **Seven "I Am" statements—which are Jesus' declaration of Himself**

- **Four interviews—in which Jesus discusses with people about Himself**

- **Various discourses—in which Jesus explains the gospel to individuals**

All of this is given to provide a testimony that Jesus Christ is the self-revelation of God.

📖 2:1–11

THE FIRST SIGN

The miracle of Jesus changing the water to wine in this section is the first of seven signs that John offers as proof of Jesus' identity as the Son of God.

Verse 1 begins on the third day of Jesus' journey. This verse draws our attention back to John 1:43, in which Jesus is making His way to Galilee. The idea is that it probably took two days to get to Galilee, and on the day after He arrives, He goes to a wedding.

Mary, Jesus' mother, was invited to this wedding. Jesus probably arrives with His disciples, and they are allowed to attend as well.

Critical Observation

Weddings in first-century Judea were big affairs. Generally they lasted about a week, even longer if the family was wealthy. Every night there was a party, and every night they would parade the couple around town in their wedding clothes. Usually, in the middle of the week, the couple would actually have the ceremony and then spend the rest of the week with the family before they could be alone.

A wedding was an important part of life, for it was the time when the family members of the groom would establish themselves by the type of party that they would throw. If people had a bad time at the wedding—if they did not get enough food to eat or wine to drink—it would reflect poorly on the family. Poorly enough for even the bride's family to think, *What kind of family did we just release our daughter into?*

Running out of wine was a critical situation (2:3) at a first-century wedding. Notice that Mary alerts Jesus to the problem. This might mean that the family was related to Mary, so she was "in the know" on a problem like this.

Demystifying John

Some have claimed that the wine in Jesus' day was not fermented, but there is no evidence to support that claim. All wine in that day became fermented by nature of the fact that there was no refrigeration in an intense climate. You could not stop the fermenting process. Yet wine was often diluted with water and used as a purifying agent, since water was often contaminated and unhealthy to drink. The scriptures caution against drinking to the point of being drunk.

Jesus' nature is revealed in His interaction with His mother (2:3-4). His response that His time has not come appears harsh, but it is not. Jesus also calls His mother "woman" (2:4 NIV). In that day this was the equivalent of saying "lady", or "dear lady." It was a respectful term, yet a distant term. It is a word that one would use to refer to someone who is not a relative, but yet is close and deserves respect.

Many believe that Joseph was dead by this point in Jesus' life. This seems to be supported by the fact that he is not mentioned after Jesus' childhood and the fact that Jesus commends Mary into John's care at his death. If Joseph had already passed away, Jesus, as the firstborn, would be responsible for His mother. This lends some insight into why she would come to Jesus with this problem. Mary, knowing who Jesus is, understands that He will take care of the problem in His time, so she instructs the servants to obey Him (2:5).

Stone water pots were used for the custom of purification (2:6). The law required several types of cleansing, including the cleansing of the hands and the feet before a meal. That is probably what these pots were used for.

Jesus wants the water pots full of water, which is no small task. They will hold, when He is done, 180 to 240 gallons of wine. Filling the water pots required significant effort going to the well and back.

In the first century, the headwaiter was something of a party coordinator. This was necessary because the entire town showed up for a wedding. The servants testified to this particular headwaiter that they have indeed put water into the pots. Then he verifies the quality of wine in the same pots (2:10).

What is the significance of this miracle? John tells us it reveals Jesus' glory. Remember that the purpose of the Gospel of John is to show that Jesus is the self-revelation of God. What Jesus does in the miracle is to display the glory of God in Himself. Note that it is the disciples whose faith is strengthened by seeing this miracle (2:11).

Take It Home

The disciples believed by faith in chapter 1, and then they saw the truth for themselves in chapter 2.

That is the process that we all go through. We all start by faith, without much knowledge. All we know is that at one point we were blind and now we see. We then spend the rest of our spiritual journey seeing Jesus for who He really is and having our faith strengthened as we grow in knowledge and understanding of Him.

2:12–25

SCRIPTURAL FAITH VS. SUPERFICIAL FAITH

In this section, John contrasts the faith of the disciples with the lack of faith of the Jewish leaders and the shallow faith of the crowds. This contrast provides a theological foundation to help us understand the rest of the Gospel.

Critical Observation

There are seven miracles, or signs, that Jesus performs between John 2 and John 11 that show His power and identity.

1. Changing water into wine (2:1–11)
2. Official's son healed (4:43–54)
3. Disabled man healed by the pool (5:1–15)
4. Feeding five thousand men plus women and children (6:1–15)
5. Walking on the water (6:16–21)
6. Healing a man born blind (9:1–12)
7. Lazarus raised after death (11:1–44)

Verse 12 offers the detail that Jesus is going to Capernaum. He will quite often return to this base of operation throughout His ministry in Galilee.

Verse 13 begins the account of Jesus in the temple during the Passover. This was a time set aside for the Jewish nation to remember the deliverance from Egypt that God provided its ancestors (Exodus 12). In this situation it seems that the temple has been turned into a place for merchandising. However, this kind of merchandising was tied into the sacrificial system. Typically the Levites offered an opportunity for worshipers who had traveled to Jerusalem to buy their animals for sacrificing right there at the temple. The money changers were there to convert foreign currency into the currency of the temple so that traveling worshipers could give the proper offering (2:14). This service was intended to be convenient for the worshipers so that they could be free to celebrate and worship. Unfortunately, this temple business took over the courtyard. They all lost the focus of the Passover in their attempt to consolidate and streamline. It is this loss of focus that Jesus rails against. Why does He make a whip (2:15)? Because He has to move sheep out of the temple, and the whip is the best tool to move them quickly.

Note the responses of the people to Jesus' actions. The disciples' minds go to Psalm 69:9 (2:17), a psalm in which David was hounded unjustly because of his love for the temple. The disciples are progressively connecting Jesus with the scriptures. The Jews (and keep in mind that John typically uses this term to refer to Jesus' Jewish opposition), on the other hand, challenged Jesus (2:18) to show them His credentials of authority to create such an uproar. Unfortunately, they missed the obvious—Jesus Himself is the sign of God, not simply the miracles He performs.

Jesus' response refers to tearing down the temple (2:19). There are a couple of Greek words for "temple." One word usually refers to the temple grounds or larger courtyard area (*hieron*) while the other refers to the temple building itself (*naos*). Jesus uses the latter here. This makes an important connection because Jesus is the place God is now dwelling on earth. The religious leaders miss the point of Jesus' comment (2:20–21).

The essence of verses 23–25 is that there are others who believed in the name of Jesus on the basis of His signs, "but Jesus would not *entrust* himself to them" (1:24 NIV, emphasis added). When the text says that He does not entrust Himself, the idea is that He does not connect Himself to these people like He does the disciples because He knows their hearts.

JOHN 3:1–36

A MEETING AT NIGHT

Nicodemus   3:1–21
The Final Witness of John the Baptist   3:22–36

Setting Up the Section

This passage of scripture includes some of the most popular verses in the Christian world. John 3 is the most quoted chapter from the New Testament, and holds within it one of the first verses ever memorized by many American Sunday school children, John 3:16.

This text is popular not only because it sets forth for us the great love of God for humanity, but also because it lays out, in very direct terms, the gospel message. Therefore, it is a treasured chapter in the scriptures for its concise teaching of the nature of humanity, the need for regeneration, and the nature of the Messiah and His great love and work for humanity. We find here a very clear presentation of the gospel and the essentials of salvation and faith.

NICODEMUS

We are told two things about Nicodemus (3:1):

1) He is a Pharisee, a Jewish sect devoted to keeping the Law of Moses.
2) He is a ruler of the Jews, a member of the seventy-member Jewish ruling council called the Sanhedrin.

Nicodemus' first statement (3:2) reveals who he and others think that Jesus is:

- He is from God.
- He is a teacher.
- God is with Jesus on the basis of the signs that He has performed.

His statement also implies a question: Is there more that I should know about who you are?

Jesus begins His reply in verse 3 with the famous, "Verily, verily" (KJV), or the more modern, "I tell you the truth" (NIV). He does this as well in verses 5 and 11. In Greek, the word used here is *amen*, which means "this is the binding truth."

Basically, Jesus says Nicodemus will be unable to understand who He is and the true nature of His life unless he is radically transformed—born again (3:3).

When Nicodemus fails to understand, he responds to the idea of rebirth literally (3:4). Nicodemus has a physical understanding of the kingdom of God rather than a spiritual one. Notice in verse 3, Jesus says that one cannot see (perceive) the kingdom of God unless he is born again, and in verse 5, Jesus says that one cannot enter (experience) the kingdom of God unless he is born of water and Spirit.

What does this mean to be born of water and Spirit? In order to understand we must look from Nicodemus's point of view. While John the Baptist had baptized in water to prepare for redemption, Christian baptism (as a symbol of redemption through Christ) is not a custom yet. Jesus chastises Nicodemus for not understanding (3:10), so Jesus' reference is to something Nicodemus would have heard. In this case it is an Old Testament passage that Nicodemus would be very familiar with—Ezekiel 36, specifically verses 25-27.

In this passage, Ezekiel describes what needs to happen in order for Israel to partake of the kingdom of God—to be washed clean in the water of God and to have God's Spirit placed within. Jesus is telling Nicodemus that he needs to have the birth of water and Spirit—the same birth mentioned in Ezekiel 36. Nicodemus needs to understand that Jesus is not talking about a physical rebirth, but a spiritual one (3:6).

Demystifying John

Jesus' illustration of the wind in verse 8 means, in essence, you must have faith, then understanding will come. Even if you do not know what causes the wind, it does not stop you from believing in it. (Remember this is before our contemporary understanding of meteorology, so there was not the understanding of wind and weather that we have today.)

Jesus' point to Nicodemus in verse 10 is that the truth has been in the scriptures all along. Yet Nicodemus may have spent his life teaching that adherence to the Law of God was the condition to enter the kingdom of God. That was certainly the impression given by the Pharisees of his day.

Nicodemus's failure is a lack of wisdom, not of explanation. It is a failure to believe (3:11–12). Jesus is the one who came from heaven as the revelation of God (3:13). Jesus is God explained. What Nicodemus needs to do if he is going to understand these things is come to grips with Jesus Christ.

The event Jesus refers to in the life of Moses is recorded in Numbers 21:4–9 (3:14–15). A bronze snake on a pole was the means God used to give life to the children of Israel when they were bitten in a plague of snakes. If they looked to the serpent Moses held high, they survived the plague. In the same way, Jesus must be lifted up—on the cross. There He will die and take on humanity's punishment for its sins. Nicodemus is being challenged to turn to Jesus for new birth, just as the ancient Israelites were commanded to turn to the bronze snake for new life.

The word *believe* as used here by Jesus (3:15) means to place trust and faith in something. In this context, it means that your entire relationship with God is resting on this one thing, Jesus Christ.

Verses 16–21 are Jesus' instructions to Nicodemus, explaining in detail the nature of the Messiah so that Nicodemus could understand who the object of his faith should be. In the famous John 3:16, Jesus is explaining to Nicodemus the true nature of God toward the world, the fact that God is love, and that His love extends past Israel to all the people in the world.

Critical Observation

To someone who believed that the world was pagan and deserving of God's judgment, Jesus' proposal that God loves the whole world would have been a surprising thought. Jesus is saying that God did not choose the Jews so that by nature of Judaism they would be saved. God chose the Jews so that through that race the Messiah would come and save people all over the world, Jews included. This was a revolutionary thought for a first-century Jewish Pharisee to take in.

The traditional translation "begotten" used in some versions of John 3:16, is probably better translated as "one of a kind" or "unique." Jesus is the one who is from God, and therefore shares the nature of God. His glory is not just a part of God; He shares in the full nature of God.

There are two types of believing. One type is to mentally understand something. The other type is a belief in something so much that you place all of your hope and trust in that which you believe. Here Jesus means the latter, that all who place their faith in the work of Jesus on the cross will have eternal life.

Jesus next deals with judgment. As a Pharisee, Nicodemus believes that God will pour out His wrath on the world and restore Israel to her position of glory. Jesus' mission is one of salvation, not judgment (3:17). At first this seems a contradiction to verses like John 9:39, in which Jesus pronounces His judgment. But these are different kinds of judgment. The type of judgment that Jesus talks about in 9:39 is the final judgment in which the wicked will be cast away forever, and the righteous will be established in the kingdom of God. Jesus did not come the first time for that judgment. That will be part of His second coming. And that is the kind of judgment He mentions in verse 18.

When He says those who do not believe are judged already (3:18), He is saying that they stood condemned before God prior to Christ, and now they just add to their judgment by rejecting Christ.

Also John doesn't only write that judgment comes from not believing in Jesus, but from not believing in His *name* (3:18). The name of someone in first-century Judaism represented his or her character or nature. To not believe in the name of Jesus is to deny His character or nature.

Verses 19–21 provide the basis for the judgment of which Jesus spoke. This judgment is described in metaphorical terms—light and darkness. The light that enters the world is the coming of God in the person of Jesus Christ. That humanity loved darkness means that humanity preferred to live without the knowledge of God. Why? Because of a fundamentally evil nature.

Notice the contrast in verse 21. The ones who practice the truth actually walk toward the light with no fear at all. *Practicing the truth* comes from a Jewish phrase that means to act faithfully. It is the idea of living out the very standard of God.

Jesus is explaining that those who have been born again do not run away from the accountability of the light. They run toward it. There are two contrasts that Jesus is pointing out about the nature of man in these verses.

1) The person who loves the darkness practices evil and the one who loves the light practices righteousness.

2) The one who loves the darkness shuns the light out of fear of exposure, shame, and conviction; and the one who loves the light comes to the light, not on the merit of his works, but on the works that God has done through him.

Take It Home

The truths given to Nicodemus are important for each of us:

1) A person needs to be born again if he is to have eternal life. A well-lived life is not good enough.

2) Salvation happens when a person looks to the cross of Jesus Christ.

3) A person will never understand God, the things of God, or even the scriptures unless he comes to grips with Jesus Christ first.

Therefore it's no use to only use human logic and human wisdom to convince someone that God exists. We must offer the testimony of Jesus.

THE FINAL WITNESS OF JOHN THE BAPTIST

This section includes more testimony from John the Baptist, confirming for us that Jesus is God and that He is the only way to salvation.

Jesus and His disciples come into Judea (3:22), yet if we look back to the preceding chapter, it's clear that they were already in Jerusalem, which is in Judea. Probably then, they went into the outlying areas of Judea where John the Baptist is also ministering (3:23).

Jesus is doing two things:

1) Spending time with His disciples
2) Baptizing or at least overseeing the baptisms (4:1–2)

The mention of John the Baptist gives us a time frame—he is not yet in prison (3:24; Matthew 14:3–5). This means that this account happens early in the ministry of Jesus. All the other Gospels go from the temptation of Jesus to the imprisonment of John, skipping this account. But this Gospel writer wants us to see the overlap of the ministries.

A discussion is brewing on the part of John's disciples and a Jew or a group of Jews (3:25). (Some early manuscripts have the word *Jew* in the plural, and others refer to one Jewish person.) The issue of this discussion is Jewish purification, the custom of ritual cleansing. In short, any time a person became ceremonially unclean for any reason—such as sickness or making contact with something unclean—that person was to cleanse with water. This act symbolized purity in devotion to God, and the cleansing of all defilement from the world. In some cases, the person just cleaned a part of the body, and in other cases he or she washed entirely.

This topic takes on added meaning when you put it in the context of a key component of John the Baptist's ministry—baptism with water. Somewhere in the discussion, the disciples of John are alerted to the fact that Jesus is also baptizing people—many people. So they alert John (3:26).

John's response makes the point that it is the sovereign hand of God that makes ministry happen. If people come, it is because God brought them, and if people go to Jesus it is because God sent them to Him. John's disciples are taking too much credit for what God does.

In all the Gospels, John the Baptist is presented as a man who is very clear about his role in God's kingdom (3:27). His own testimony about Jesus can be found in John 1:29–31 (also see Matthew 3:11–15). In verse 29, John explains his role as a best man in a wedding. Being best man gives him no rights to the bride. The wedding doesn't center around him. His role as best man is to make sure the wedding happens smoothly and the bride is safely placed into the hand of the groom.

John the Baptist feels joy and excitement as he sees the bride (the believers in Christ) being delivered into the hands of the bridegroom (Jesus). Thus, his perspective is that of the two of them, only Jesus should become greater (3:30).

John the Baptist offers five reasons that Jesus must gain emphasis and he must step back:
1) Jesus came from heaven, and therefore is above everyone on the earth (3:31).
2) Jesus speaks from a firsthand knowledge of the kingdom of God (3:32).
3) Jesus says and does all that God would say and do on earth because He is God (3:33).
4) Jesus speaks the words of God (3:34).
5) Jesus is the sovereign ruler of the world and all that is in it (3:35).

John's point to his disciples is that Jesus is God the Father revealed; therefore, the central religious question is, who is the object of your faith (3:36)? If Jesus is rejected as the focus of a person's faith, then that person has to face the consequences of sin—the eternal wrath of God. This wrath does not imply a sudden burst of anger but simply the reaction of God's righteousness to humanity's unrighteousness.

JOHN 4: 1–54

A MEETING BY THE WELL

The Woman at the Well   4:1–26
The Harvest   4:27–42
Knowing Christ   4:43–54

Setting Up the Section

The Gospel writer John is continuing to show us that Jesus is the revelation of God the Father, and in this text, he uses Christ's conversation with a Samaritan woman.

📄 **4:1–26**

THE WOMAN AT THE WELL

Verse 1 connects us to the previous chapter, in which we are told that more people are coming to Jesus and His disciples to be baptized than to John the Baptist for baptism. This piques the interest of the Pharisees who consistently opposes Jesus (4:1–2). As Jesus becomes aware of the Pharisees' interest, He moves out of Judea to avoid an untimely confrontation.

John writes that Jesus has to pass through Samaria (4:4). On a map of Israel, you find Judea on the bottom and Galilee on the top. Sandwiched in between is Samaria. The Jews and the Samaritans had an extreme prejudice toward each other, dating back as far as 450 BC. They only had dealings as a last resort, and, if time and resources allowed, would probably go out of their way to minimize contact with each other. Jesus' purpose in going through the region has to do with His mission—it is essential to meeting the woman who would be at the well.

Demystifying John

There were several key historical events that contributed to the animosity between the Jews and the Samaritans.

- In 720 BC, Assyria took over the northern kingdom and replaced most of the Jews with people from other lands. The nationalities mingled and the Samaritan people were born. The Jews were very particular about intermarrying and, therefore, looked down on the Samaritans who even in their first generation were only half-Jewish.

- In 450 BC, when Jerusalem was being rebuilt, the Samaritans wanted to help, but the Jews refused to let them. This contributed to the animosity.

- Manasseh, a Jewish man (not the king by the same name), built a temple on Mt. Gerizim because that is the place that Moses proclaimed the blessings of the covenant to the people. The Samaritans worshiped at this temple, which greatly offended the Jews who worshiped in Jerusalem.

- In addition, the Samaritans only followed the first five books of the Old Testament and rejected the rest of the Old Testament scriptures.

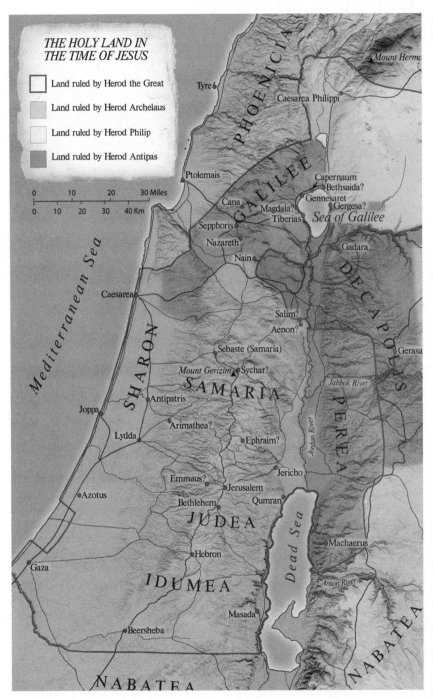

THE HOLY LAND IN
THE TIME OF JESUS

Land ruled by Herod the Great

Land ruled by Herod Archelaus

Land ruled by Herod Philip

Land ruled by Herod Antipas

0   10   20   30 Miles

0   10   20   30   40 Km

Mount Hermo

PHOENICIA

Tyre

Caesarea Philippi

Ptolemais

GALILEE

Capernaum
Bethsaida?
Gennesaret
Cana
Magdala?   Gergesa?
Sepphoris   Tiberias   Sea of Galilee
Nazareth

Mediterranean Sea

Nain

Gadara

DECAPOLIS

Caesarea

Salim?
Aenon?

Sebaste (Samaria)
Gerasa

SHARON

Mount Gerizim   Sychar?

Jabbok River

SAMARIA

Antipatris

Joppa   PEREA

Arimathea?

Jordan River

Lydda   Ephraim?

Jericho

Emmaus?

Azotus   Jerusalem

Bethlehem   Qumran

JUDEA

Dead Sea

Machaerus

Hebron

IDUMEA   Arnon River

Gaza

Masada

Beersheba

NABATEA

NABATEA

The property on which Jesus stops is not only significant because it had a well; it also had historical significance. It is a piece of property that Jacob, an important ancestor of the Jewish nation (1 Kings 18:31), bought and then gave to his son, Joseph (4:5–6). The Samaritans felt that they had the same heritage as the Jews (who reject them), so they would feel as connected to this property and its history as the Jews would. Jesus stops at the well at the sixth hour, which probably means about 12 noon (4:6; see 1:39).

The fact that the Bible mentions only this woman at the well is a noteworthy detail (4:7). Going to the well was typically a task women did as a group.

Jesus' request for a drink from her is a break in tradition for several reasons. In that day and time,

- Men did not talk with women in public.
- Rabbis did not talk to women.
- Jews did not talk with Samaritans (the woman even gave voice to this custom [4:9]).

In John's added explanation, the phrase "have no dealings with" (4:9 NASB) meant that Jews would never even touch a utensil of a Samaritan, for in doing so they would become unclean.

With his next statement, Jesus turns the tables (4:10). At the beginning of this conversation Jesus is thirsty, and the woman has the source to quench His thirst. Now Jesus turns it to the fact that she is thirsty, and He has the source to quench her thirst. The Greek words translated "living water" refer to a well that is fed by an underground spring; therefore it always produces fresh water.

The woman first responds with what is obvious to her—Jesus doesn't have anything with which to draw the water. To her this is foolishness (4:11–12). She, like Nicodemus in chapter 3, is missing a spiritual truth and responding to a physical impossibility (3:4).

Jesus draws a contrast between earthly water and spiritual water. The word "well" (4:14 NASB) again refers to a spring-fed well with a continual source.

It would seem from the woman's response that she is motivated by convenience (4:15). Would living water keep her from having to walk out to the well each day?

Jesus then starts to deal with her heart, asking questions that will delve into her lifestyle and reveal His power (4:16–19).

The woman's question about where people should worship seems to be on a different track from the conversation (4:20). The Samaritans worshiped on Mt. Gerizim, and the Jews worshiped in Jerusalem. Jesus responds to her question with three truths (4:21–24):

1) He states that worship as she understands it will be rendered obsolete.
2) He states that salvation springs forth out of Judaism. Since the Jews include the writings of the prophets, they have all the promises there—including those of the Messiah.
3) He explains in detail the nature of true worship. The point of this statement (4:23–24) is that true worship is not based on location but on the condition of the worshiper's heart.

When the woman refers to the Messiah—the first reference in John's Gospel—Jesus actually declares Himself to be that Messiah (4:26). It is a significant twist that the first person Jesus declares His messiahship to is a Samaritan, a woman, and a social outcast.

THE HARVEST

The way the Greek manuscript is worded at the beginning of 4:27 makes the point that the disciples walked into the conversation as Jesus is declaring Himself to be the Messiah (4:26). Knowing that makes it surprising that they choose to comment on Jesus' talking with a woman.

In some translations, verse 28 says that when the woman runs to town to spread the news, she goes first to the men. If so, this would be because women in this culture could not hold any position of authority. The men, who had more power within that society, could evaluate and determine if Jesus was the Messiah.

The misunderstanding that occurs between Jesus and the disciples regarding food is that same misunderstanding that occurs throughout the Gospel of John—the things of the earth versus the things of heaven (4:31–33). In verse 34, Jesus moves the disciples from the physical world to the spiritual world by describing His devotion to the will of God and how that devotion is what drives Him in all that He does.

Demystifying John

The exact four months that Jesus refers to in verse 35 is not clear, but it is clear that the time for the harvest of souls is at hand. In verse 36, Jesus is continuing the metaphor of the harvest time. In that day, when it was harvest time, the man who sowed the seed would hire reapers. It was the reaper's job to harvest the fruit. When a reaper completed his section, he was paid. Jesus is saying that we do not need to wait for the spiritual harvest time—it is here!

In verse 37, Jesus gives a key principle in understanding the work of God: In the work of the kingdom, there will be some who sow and others who reap, and the work of God is dependent upon each of these factors. Then, in verse 38, Jesus gives the disciples their commission. This will be the first of many times that Jesus explains to the disciples their purpose. Jesus tells them that they will be reaping a crop they have not worked for. In a specific sense, they have done nothing in Samaria, but more generally, they are building on the works of others—Moses, John the Baptist, and obviously, Jesus.

It is significant that the townspeople believe the word of a woman—a woman who is probably a social outcast (4:39–42). Yet it is equally significant that as the people spend time with Jesus, they recognize the truth of who He is in a way that His own townspeople hadn't (4:41–42).

KNOWING CHRIST

Jesus is finishing the trip He started at the beginning of this chapter (4:43; see 4:3). He was leaving Judea because it is not time for the confrontation to begin there between the Pharisees and Himself. While verse 44 can seem out of context, it foreshadows the fact that Jesus is headed home, specifically to the site of His first miracle, and rejection is waiting there.

At first it seems that the Galileans believe in Jesus (4:45), but their belief was based on the miracles that Jesus does rather than who Jesus is. Then the royal official approaches Jesus and begs Him to come and heal his son (4:46–47). If you compare the request of the centurion in Matthew 8:5–13 to this man's request, you can see the difference between a request based on a knowledge of who Jesus is and one that is not. The centurion based his request on Jesus' authority and the authority of God. This official seems to only know Jesus' reputation as a miracle-worker.

When Jesus responds with somewhat of a rebuke in verse 48, He is responding to the fact that these people are looking for Jesus to do His tricks, His signs and wonders. They will not believe in Him based upon His Word. Look at the contrast in verse 42—the Samaritans believed based upon His Word.

In verse 49, the royal official reveals the limitations he believes Jesus faces. He asks Jesus to come before his child dies because he believes that after death there is nothing Jesus can do. Yet when Jesus declares the child healed (without being present with the child), the man believes.

The synchronized details that John includes—the child being healed at the moment Jesus spoke—reveals that it was the word of Jesus that healed the boy. Jesus did not have to conjure up spirits, make a potion, or speak a magic spell. Jesus' very words were the power to save this boy. This man suddenly does not look at the miracle, but at Jesus, and believes. The miracle serves as a vehicle to show that Jesus is the revelation of God.

This healing is the second of the seven signs that John offers in this section as proof of Jesus' identity as the Son of God.

Take It Home

The account of the woman at the well teaches us that God uses many different people, despite our prejudices, and many different means to prepare the hearts of others. It is our job to be faithful to the call and the task that He has for us. The good news is for everyone.

The account of the royal official leaves us asking, who do we see Jesus as? Is our faith placed in what He can do for us (some kind of divine room service), or in whom we believe Him to be? This Gospel writer wants us to see the Man behind the miracle, the Savior of the world. Have we come to grips with Him, as these people did?

JOHN 5:1-47

THE POSITION OF JESUS

The Authority of Jesus	5:1–15
Jesus Claims to Be God	5:16–24
The Power and Authority of Jesus	5:25–29
The Witnesses of Jesus' Deity	5:30–47

Setting Up the Section

The struggle that we experience individually as we seek to surrender ourselves to God's will is similar to what plagued Jesus' relationship with the religious leaders of His day. As He exercised His authority as God, the religious leaders became increasingly angry—not wanting to believe Him to be God or to have authority over them—and desired to kill Him. They did not want a new leader to work outside of their system. They didn't want a new way of doing things. Therefore, when Jesus required them to submit to Him, they rejected Him. This conflict became the source of the anger that built in the Pharisees and caused them to seek to kill Jesus.

📖 **5:1-15**

THE AUTHORITY OF JESUS

In the previous chapter, Jesus traveled from the southern region, Judea, northward to Galilee. Here He travels south again, back down to Jerusalem.

John does not mention the particular feast that brings Jesus back to Jerusalem (5:1), but it is important to note that Jesus went to these festivals, such as Passover. The festivals were given by God to the Jews to celebrate the various aspects of God's work on behalf of Israel. They were required under the Jewish law.

Jerusalem was a city with a wall around it. There were multiple gates through which a person could enter the city, such as the Sheep Gate (5:2). As the name implies, it was the gate through which the shepherds brought their sheep in and out to graze. The pool near the gate had five entrances and was probably spring fed, which means that it would bubble up every time the fresh water came in. This bubbling is what the people would wait for, hoping to be healed.

Verse 4, in some translations, is marked with parentheses or an asterisk, or footnoted, or may not even appear. The verse, an explanation, does not appear in some of the oldest manuscripts of the New Testament that we have access to. It is probably a footnote added later to explain how the people of that day interpreted the bubbling up of the water.

When Jesus asks questions to open a dialogue with a man waiting to be healed (5:5-6), we learn about the man through his answers (5:7):

1) He has no friends there to assist him.

2) He is disabled in such a way that he can't move well.

With three simple commands Jesus heals the man (5:8-9): Get up, take up your bedding (probably a mat made of straw that could be rolled up), and walk. Notice that the man said nothing of record. He does not argue with Jesus; he just jumps up, rolls up his bed, and walks. Why? Because Jesus spoke with the ultimate authority of God.

At the end of verse 9, John offers what becomes a sticking point for the rest of Jesus' ministry—Jesus heals this man on the Sabbath.

Critical Observation

The Old Testament had forbidden work on the Sabbath. The rabbis divided work into thirty-nine classes, including picking something up and taking it from one place to another (unless it was an act of mercy, like moving a paralytic). Therefore, on the Sabbath, a Jew had to be very careful not to transgress any of these thirty-nine classes of work.

It's obvious from the response of the religious leaders that they have a greater concern for their rules than they do a miracle from God (5:10–13). This is because they could not fathom that anything good could come outside their laws. Their system was the system that the Messiah would come through, and anything outside of that system was surely evil.

Jesus' later words to the healed man make it appear as if this man's condition was a result of some sin (5:14). Jesus addresses the man's behavior. We get no further background explanation, but it is interesting to the note the man's response once Jesus confronts him (5:15).

This healing is the third of the seven signs that John offers in this section as proof of Jesus' identity as the Son of God.

5:16–24

JESUS CLAIMS TO BE GOD

When the healed man identifies Jesus as the man who has made him well, the conflict is set between Jesus and the religious establishment (5:15–16). The core of this conflict was who had the authority—Jesus the Messiah, or the Pharisees, the interpreters of the Jewish religious system.

Note two things in Jesus' initial response to the religious leaders (5:17):

1) God does not stop working on the Sabbath, so Jesus won't. The emphasis of the Sabbath when God established it (Genesis 2:1–3) was not that God stopped working all together. He rested from the work of creation.

2) Jesus is claiming an exclusive relationship with God ("My Father" [NIV]).

Both elements of Jesus' response declare that He is God. Jesus did not bow to the Pharisees authority; He establishes His authority and calls for them to submit to Him. And they understand His meaning, thus begin to plot murder (5:18).

Jesus begins His reply in verse 19 with the famous "Verily, verily" (KJV), or the more modern, "I tell you the truth" (NIV). He does this as well in verses 24–25. In Greek, the word used is *amen*, which means "this is the binding truth." Then Jesus goes on to explain emphatically that He is God because He:

- Implements God's will (5:19–20)

- Exhibits God's power (5:21)

- Judges with the same authority (5:22)

- Receives equal honor (5:23)

All these things together leave no doubt that Jesus claimed to be one with God. In verse 24, He lays down the gauntlet before the religious establishment—only those who believe in Him will escape judgment.

📄 5:25–29

THE POWER AND AUTHORITY OF JESUS

Verses 25–29 expound upon Jesus' declaration in verses 21–22. He is the source of life, and if you reject that life, you will be judged by Him. This passage shows Jesus' power to raise the dead.

Jesus opens verse 25, affirming the truth of what He is about to say, and that what He is about to say will happen very soon. He is telling the Jewish leaders that they are at the precipice of the time when the dead will live—salvation.

Demystifying John

If we understand what *dead* means, then we can understand just what condition man is in before He is saved. A dead person is insensitive to life. Stick a pin in that person, and he or she will not feel it. In a spiritual sense, to be dead is to be insensitive to the things of God. It means that person has no desire to be a part of God, has no ability to ever get to God, and has no senses to react or respond to God. As far as any true spirituality, a person is unable to respond because he or she is a spiritual corpse.

Verse 26 tells us why the Son of God is able to give this life: Because the Son is life. Jesus also has been given the authority to execute judgment (5:27).

Notice that when Jesus is referred to as the giver of life in verse 25, He is called the Son of God. When Jesus is referred to as the judge of all of mankind, He is referred to as the Son of Man (5:27). This concept of the Son of Man is not a new one to the Pharisees. They knew from their study of the Old Testament that the Son of Man would be the judge of the earth, and would come to have authority over the earth.

Verses 28 and 29 describe a different kind of resurrection. At this judgment, there will be two groups of people there: those who are going to heaven and those that are going to hell. And the determination of where a person will be going is his or her works. This does not imply that salvation comes through works, but it is evidence that real faith is seen through works, because faith leads to good works.

THE WITNESSES OF JESUS' DEITY

Jesus just finished, in verse 29, His declaration that as God, He will be the judge of all mankind. Coming out of this statement, Jesus reiterates one of the key principles of this entire discourse, the key point His argument with the Jews is based upon: Jesus and the Father are one (5:30).

The idea behind verses 31–32 is that the tremendous burden of proving the claims of Jesus is not placed solely in His testimony but upon the testimonies of others. In this first-century culture, a testimony alone is no testimony. According to Deuteronomy 17:6 and 19:15, every testimony needed at least two or three witnesses to confirm that it was the truth.

In verses 33–39, Jesus offers four testimonies to confirm His deity:

1) John the Baptist pointed Jesus out to the Jewish religious leaders as the Messiah. He declared Jesus the Lamb of God (5:33; see 1:19–34). Jesus talks about John the Baptist in the past tense, so he is probably already in prison or perhaps already killed (Mark 6:17–29). The word that the Gospel writer uses for "light" in talking about the great preacher and prophet (5:35) does not mean that he was the source of light, but that he was a lamp that shed light.

2) Jesus' own work testifies of His deity (5:36). No one could do the miracles that Jesus did. Only God can do these miracles. Jesus says this in the context of healing a man who was lame for thirty-eight years (5:1–9).

3) God the Father testifies to the deity of Jesus Christ (5:37). God gave His witness at Jesus' baptism (Matthew 3:16–17). The way to hear the witness of God is to believe in the Son, and if you fail to believe in the Son, you do not receive the witness of the Father.

4) The scriptures certainly bear witness of the Messiah. Some translations of the Bible open verse 39 as a command for the Jewish leadership to search the scriptures. Others open verse 39 as an observation that these men do search the scriptures. With either interpretation the end result is the same—these men knew the scriptures but came to the wrong conclusion about who Jesus is.

In verses 40–44, Jesus explains Himself. The fact that He points out their error in not believing who He is has nothing to do with winning their approval. Since Jesus has God's approval, the fact that the religious leaders disapprove of Him is what condemns them.

There were others rising up in Jesus' day, claiming to be the Messiah (5:43–44). Some of them won a lot of recognition, even religious acclaim. Some fit more of the popular idea that the Messiah would come to fight a political battle rather than a spiritual one. The fact that the leaders don't recognize the real thing, from the scriptures they had based their lives on, is their condemnation (5:45–47). Some examples of the writings of Moses that point toward the Messiah are Genesis 3:15 (the descendant of Adam that will defeat the serpent), Numbers 24:17 (the star that will rise out of Israel, Jacob's descendants), and Deuteronomy 18:15–18 (the prophet that God will raise up).

JOHN 6:1-71
REVEALING HIMSELF

The Awesome Power of Jesus   6:1–15
The People of Glory   6:16–29
The Bread of Life   6:30–40
Rejection and Revelation   6:41–71

Setting Up the Section

Chapter 6 continues within the ministry of Jesus in Galilee, and it provides the same basic structure as chapter 5. In chapter 5 we see Jesus performing a miracle and using that miracle to proclaim His deity as Lord of the Sabbath. In chapter 6 we see Jesus performing a miracle and then using that miracle as a platform to proclaim His deity as the Bread of life.

📄 6:1–15

THE AWESOME POWER OF JESUS

Chapter 6 begins with John referencing previous events before Jesus goes on His way (6:1). What does John mean when he says "after this" (NIV)? If you look at John 5:1, you will observe that Jesus went to Jerusalem, and it is there that He healed a man and had His first confrontation with the religious leaders. Then, if you look at 6:1, you will notice that He is crossing to the other side of the Sea of Galilee. Somewhere between verses 5:47 and 6:1 Jesus went to Galilee. Remember, the purpose of John is not to give a chronological history of Jesus' life, but rather to give us snapshots of the deity of Jesus Christ.

Of the many months spent in Galilee, John focuses on this particular account, which is in the later portion of Jesus' ministry in Galilee. Therefore, between verses 5:47 and 6:1 there is approximately six months to one year that has passed. For more of the Galilean ministry, read Matthew 4:12–15:20.

John 7:1 tells us why Jesus moved into Galilee—because the Jewish leaders in Judea wanted to kill Him. Because it is not time for Him to die, He avoids Judea and spends some time concentrating on Galilee.

Verse 2 introduces us to the multitudes that are pursuing Jesus—approximately fifteen thousand people. They are following Jesus because of His miraculous healings.

Jesus goes to the mountain (6:3) to be alone with the disciples and instruct them. If we compare this scripture to Mark 6, we discover that the disciples just returned from their first ministry assignment, and Jesus wants to debrief them from that experience.

Critical Observation

Verse 10 states that there were five thousand men. That count does not include women, children, and servants. If you add in a conservative guess of those groups left out, there could be at least fifteen thousand people, and some even estimate there were as many as twenty thousand.

Jesus poses the dilemma of feeding the crowds to Philip (6:5–6), who was from that area and would know most about the resources that were available. Of course verse 6 reveals that Jesus already knows what He intended to do. The denarius (6:7 NASB) used in Philip's calculations was equivalent to one day's wage.

The barley loaf that is part of the solution that Andrew offers is not equivalent to a contemporary loaf of bread. It would have been more like a muffin. That's why the boy had five. The fish were probably pickled fish that were spread on top of the cakes. This was a common meal in that day. The main part of the meal was the bread, and the fish served as a topping. This meal reveals to us that this boy is probably poor, since barley loaves were the meal of the poor at this time.

In the Greek there are two different words that some versions of the English Bible translate as "men." One word typically means mankind in general, and the other typically means men as a gender. Verse 10 first refers to people in general, but the count included in the verse is for actual men who were present.

In Mark's account of this story, Jesus asks that the people sit in groups of fifty and one hundred (Mark 6:39–40). Notice the dedication of the disciples in that they have no idea how Jesus will feed the people, yet they followed His directions in organizing them.

In the Jewish catechism, the children are taught that if you do not thank God for your food, it is equal to stealing from God, for food is a gift from God. Thus we see Jesus' prayer of thanks in verse 11. A typical Jewish thanks for a meal would have been something like this: Blessed are you, O Lord our God, King of the universe, who brings forth bread from the earth.

Jesus then bypasses the natural order of things, and transforms five muffins and two fish into thousands of portions. Verses 12–13 paint the picture of each disciple with a basket full of miraculous leftovers. Jesus uses the need of these people to teach the disciples a lesson—that He is greater than any need.

The people's response to the miracle (6:14) is a reference to Deuteronomy 18:15–18, the promise to bless the children of Israel with a prophet like Moses who will speak the words of God. These people believe that Jesus is that prophet.

The point that they failed to see was that Jesus wasn't going to be their king until they repented. If they had fully understood the passage in Deuteronomy, they would have realized that they should have fallen before Him in sorrow and repentance. But instead they are telling Jesus what He must do. The people fail to really listen to Jesus' words; they want Jesus on their own terms.

This miracle of feeding the crowd is the fourth of the seven signs that John offers in this section as proof of Jesus' identity as the Son of God.

Philip's reaction to Jesus' question likely mirrors what our reaction would have been in the same situation. When God tests us, our first instinct is to calculate the feasibility of a solution and try to determine ourselves if it will work or not. But God's solution is most often only seen by faith.

📄 **6:16–29**

THE PEOPLE OF GLORY

In this passage, Jesus deals with the multitudes: those who want the theology of glory and not the theology of the cross. He has just miraculously fed close to fifteen thousand people then escapes before they forcefully claim Him as their king.

"Evening" in verse 16 (NIV) probably refers to late afternoon, just before sunset. The disciples had a five to seven-mile journey ahead of them to Capernaum.

The Sea of Galilee is six hundred feet below sea level, in a cup-like depression among the hills. When the sun sets, the air cools; and as the cooler air from the west rushes down over the hillside, the resulting wind churns the lake. Since the disciples are rowing toward Capernaum, they are heading into the wind; consequently, they would make little progress in the storm (6:18).

The disciples are about halfway across the lake by the time they see Jesus approaching (6:19). Other accounts of this story reveal that they think Jesus is a ghost.

Once they realized it is Jesus and He gets in the boat, they instantly reached Capernaum. The Gospel writer moves on without drawing any conclusions, but it is clear that the disciples have just witnessed two miracles (including the feeding of the large crowd) that reveal Jesus as the Master of the earth.

This miracle of Jesus walking on the water is the fifth of the seven signs that John offers in this section as proof of Jesus' identity as the Son of God.

Verses 22–25 reveal that the crowds are watching Jesus closely. They realize only one boat started across the sea, and Jesus wasn't on it. So how did He get to the other side?

Jesus begins His charge in verse 26 with the famous, "Verily, verily" (KJV), or the more modern, "I tell you the truth" (NIV). He does the same as well in verses 32, 47, and 53. In Greek, the word used here is *amen*, which means "this is the binding truth."

Jesus' charge is that their pursuit is not because they saw signs, but because their bellies were filled (6:26). The people looked at the miracle, and stopped there. They failed to recognize what that miracle meant. There was something much more significant than just the feeding of the crowd: Here was the Messiah putting Himself on display for all to fall before Him in repentance and worship. These people are coming to Jesus to have their needs met, not to be redeemed.

In that day, many people could not read, so when the king wanted people to understand that a decree was his, he would place his seal on it. The seal was the recognizable stamp that allowed people to know that something was approved by the king. Jesus says that the Father has placed His seal, His mark of approval, upon Him as the sole dispenser of eternal life.

Jesus is saying, "Do not trivialize My coming as simply a source of food. God sent Me to dispense life" (6:27).

The people respond by focusing their attention on work (6:28). They have no idea that salvation is a gift of God, given by grace and mercy, acquired by faith. The multitudes ask for a work to do to be saved, and Jesus responds with faith in Himself (6:29).

📄 6:30–40

THE BREAD OF LIFE

Jesus is in the middle of a conversation with the multitudes. He has just told them that they must look to the food that gives eternal life, not just to the food that feeds the body. They ask what they must do to get this food, and Jesus has told them that they must place all of their trust in Him. It is at this point that this passage begins.

Verses 30–33 can be broken down into two thoughts: first, the demand of the people to have Jesus prove His claim, and then the response of Jesus to that demand.

The people are asking for a sign before they will place their trust in Jesus. Their fathers ate manna in the wilderness (Exodus 16:1–5), how could Jesus top that? Note that asking for a sign is evidence of their lack of faith. Asking for a sign is an act of pride that makes God subject to the people, not the other way around.

Jesus responds that the people have made four errors in their understanding of the Old Testament, and it has affected their understanding of Him, as well as their understanding of salvation (6:32–33).

1) Moses didn't give the bread, God did. In the same way, it is God who gives them the true bread from heaven. Both are gifts from God, not the miracles of mere humans.
2) Jesus is not just interested in satisfying bellies, but in satisfying the souls.
3) Manna is physical, not spiritual. All manna really did was paint a picture of what the true eternal manna (sustenance) is going to be like.
4) Manna was only for Israel, the true bread is for the world. Spiritual bread is not exclusive to a particular group; it is for everyone.

Again, a demand—give us this bread (6:34)—and Jesus' response. In calling Himself the Bread of life, Jesus is saying people must partake of His nature and His life in order to have the hunger of the soul satisfied. It is important that people understand the key role that Jesus plays in connecting humankind to God.

Jesus made seven "I am" statements, starting with John 6:35.

- "I am the bread of life" (6:35 NIV).
- "I am the light of the world" (8:12 NIV; 9:5 NIV).
- "I am the [door or] gate" (10:7 NIV).
- "I am the good shepherd" (10:11, 14 NIV).
- "I am the resurrection and the life" (11:25 NIV).
- "I am the way and the truth and the life" (14:6 NIV).
- "I am the true vine" (15:1 NIV).

In verse 36, Jesus shifts gears a little and begins confronting the people on their fundamental problem—they do not truly believe in Him (6:36). There is more to it than simply seeing Jesus as a prophet or as an earthly king or as a great man. He wants us to see Him as God in the flesh and realize that our life amounts to nothing apart from Him.

In verses 37–39, Jesus explains the nature of salvation. The role of the Father is to turn on the light of understanding in humanity. The role of the Son is not to cast out or drive away those that come. Jesus is going to protect and preserve those who have come to Him.

Demystifying John

This issue of Jesus rejecting the Jews was a common question in the time that John wrote this Gospel, so it is historically significant that he included this teaching of Jesus. The foundation for why Jesus rejects his Jewish opposition is here in John 6:37. He would never cast away a true child of God, only those who were not given to Him by the Father.

Many people were confused in the latter first century as to how Christianity and Judaism fit together. The problem was not Judaism itself, but a dependence on the Law to be saved instead of faith in Christ's work on the cross.

In verse 38, Jesus wants the people to hear that it is His role to do what the Father wants—He is not an independent leader. Jesus has come down from heaven to do the Father's will, and what is the Father's will? To keep hold of those given to Him and to raise them up on the last day (6:39). The last day is simply the final judgment when the righteous will enter the kingdom, and the unrighteous will go to eternity in hell. This would hold great meaning to a first-century Jewish listener. The Jews longed for the day of resurrection. It is such a key part of Jewish theology that even today a devoted Jew would not have his body cremated for in doing so he might hinder the process of this resurrection.

In verse 40, Jesus reiterates the message of verses 38–39.

The words used here to describe looking to Jesus, depict the same kind of looking a person does at a table full of food at Thanksgiving; as you look, you want to have some of the food. To believe, in this context, means to no longer rely on yourself and your own way of thinking, but to trust in and rely on the mind, will, and way of Jesus Christ. It is acting on what you see in Jesus.

Notice the promise for those who do this: Jesus will raise them up on the last day and guarantees eternal life to those who trust in Him for salvation and life.

As for His Jewish listeners, Jesus just reworked their theology. They thought that they were going to be raised up on the last day by being obedient Jews. But Jesus just said that they must abandon all that they hold sacred and simply trust in Him for salvation.

📄 **6:41–71**

REJECTION AND REVELATION

In verse 41 the Gospel writer moves from Jesus' conversation with the multitudes to a conversation with the religious leaders. This shift gives us the theological content of what happened.

Critical Observation

Remember that John moves from one situation to another by simply focusing on what Jesus said and the various responses to Him. As a result, this Gospel often combines the dialogue of various accounts that all teach the same thing. John gives us a theological account rather than a strict chronological account of the ministry of Jesus Christ.

Jesus' Jewish opposition has a problem with one aspect of His teaching. It is the claim of deity. The Jews grumble because Jesus' claim puts Him on par with God—the ultimate arrogant and criminal blasphemy. These men think that they know Jesus—the Son of a Galilean carpenter (6:42). They know His mom and His dad, and they know where He came from. They refuse to accept that He is from God, and therefore, they refuse to go through Him to get to God.

Jesus simply tells these men that grumbling will get them nowhere—what they need is the hand of God. Notice that Jesus states that He is the source of the resurrection from the dead (6:43–44).

Jesus offers the Jewish opposition a description as to how God draws people to Himself, and by doing so, offers an indictment. He refers to an Old Testament teaching found in both Isaiah and Jeremiah, and implied in many other passages. The quoted material in verse 45 is just a rephrasing of a passage in Isaiah, claiming God's restoration of His people (Isaiah 54:13–14). The simple reality is that God teaches His people, allowing them to understand the message of Christ, and He instructs them as to what is truth and what is not.

The point of God's teaching is in verse 46. No man has ever seen God except Jesus. He came from God as the explanation of God. He is the revelation that we need to understand.

Verses 47–48 provide the foundational point that Jesus wants the religious leaders to hear—if they will believe in Him, they will have eternal life. Next, He exposes the error of their thinking by referring back to the manna. In essence He says, if you reduce God to just an earthly God and His provision to just physical provision, you have nothing. Then in verse 50, Jesus contrasts the benefits: Manna prolongs the death process, but the bread out of heaven gives life. Verse 51 summarizes the heart of the issue at stake. They are to look to Jesus Himself as the spiritual Bread.

Verse 52 says that the Jews are arguing with each other. This could mean they are angry at the statements Jesus made, and so they are standing around shouting about it. Perhaps more likely though, they are divided in their opinions as John has noted on other occasions. Note the progression—in verse 41 the people are complaining, but by verse 52 they are angry.

Jesus responds to these men by first explaining the sacrifice of His body. Notice that in verse 53, He adds that they must not only eat His flesh but also drink His blood, or there is no life. This would have been even more troublesome for Jesus' listeners. To the Jews, drinking blood was a major offense; they were forbidden to ever drink blood.

Jesus offers three benefits that come when a person looks to Him for salvation.

1) Eternal life (6:54–55)
2) Unity with Jesus (6:56–57)
3) Abundant life (6:58)

The use of the word *disciple* in verse 60 is a reference to all the people that are following Jesus at this point. In saying that Jesus' teaching was hard, they are implying it is difficult to accept (6:60).

When Jesus asks them if His words offended them (6:61) or made them stumble, He is using a word that describes an old-fashioned trap for an animal—a box held up by a stick with bait attached. Over time, this word developed the connotation of anything that trips someone up.

Jesus' question about ascending to heaven (6:62) means, in essence, if you saw Me going back to heaven, then would you believe that I came from heaven?

In verse 63, He deals with the problem that the multitudes had concerning their need and His provision of that need. In the middle of verse 63 the central issue of true discipleship surfaces again: The words of Christ are the dividing line between life and death.

After asking His questions, Jesus identifies the problem (6:64)—unbelief. Salvation is not a question of intelligence; it is a question of faith. In this text we are indirectly introduced to Judas. John adds this insight of Jesus because he wants us to see that not even Judas is beyond the knowledge of Jesus. Jesus is fully aware of the unbelief of the people and fully aware of the nature of Judas.

Verse 65 is the theology behind Jesus' statement—it takes a work of God for a person to believe.

There are two aspects to Peter's answer to Jesus (6:66–69)—faith and faithfulness. Speaking for the group, Peter declares that they do not stumble over Jesus' claims. Rather, they believe Jesus' claims. That is the faith, but notice also the faithfulness. It is at the beginning of Peter's statement. Peter says they will stay with Jesus. They are committed to His teaching, to going where He goes. His words do not make them run away from Jesus, instead, they make them run to Jesus.

Notice Jesus' response to Peter's statement (6:70–71). He chose the disciples. The multitudes came on their own accord but the disciples were called. And He chose one who would betray

Him. Judas's presence is a part of the plan of God. Jesus purposely picked one who would betray Him.

Take It Home

John's Gospel makes it clear that faith and faithfulness are the core foundations of true discipleship. Believing and sticking are the marks of the Christian life. We have also seen that the mark of a false disciple is one who accepts the person of Jesus, and is willing to accept the miracles of Jesus, but rejects the words of Jesus. They refuse to live by what Jesus taught. What kind of disciple are you?

JOHN 7:1–8:11

CHALLENGES TO RESPOND

The Response of Jesus' Family	7:1–13
Spiritual Insight	7:14–24
Ignorance in Wisdom's Clothing	7:25–36
Come and Drink	7:37–52
A Woman Caught in Adultery	7:53–8:11

Setting Up the Section

From chapter 7 of the Gospel of John, the focus is more on the reaction of the people to Jesus. A theme from this point on will be people's inability to understand who Jesus is.

Another theme that runs throughout this Gospel is Jesus' divine timetable. John will show that Jesus' will only happens at God's appointed time.

THE RESPONSE OF JESUS' FAMILY

Verse 1 gives us the reason that Jesus trained His disciples in Galilee rather than Jerusalem. If Jesus were to perform a public ministry in Judea, it would create such a stir that His death would likely be carried out before the appointed time. Therefore, Jesus stayed in Galilee.

The feast mentioned in verse 2, the Feast of Tabernacles ("dwellings") or Booths, had a two-fold purpose: It celebrated the harvest that God provided for that year, and it looked back to the provision that God gave Israel while her people were living in tents in the desert. It looked to the present as well as to the past. During the celebration, all the Jewish males were to come to Jerusalem, set up tents, and celebrate. The tents symbolized the tents that the Israelites lived in during their wandering (described in the book of Numbers).

Verse 3 mentions Jesus' brothers, of which He has four. It is in the setting of the feast that Jesus' brothers make a request of Him: They want Jesus to get out of the villages and go to the city where the leaders and the people can see what He does and listen to His claims. This request, though, does not come from their faith (7:5). They are saying, *if* what you are doing really proves you are from God, then go and have it verified.

Jesus gives the reasons He will not go in verses 6–9:

1) It's not the right timing. Revealing Himself in Jerusalem precipitates His trial and death. It's not yet time for that.

2) Those He would teach would resent Him for revealing the sin in their lives. While His brothers would be free to go, His visit would have greater ramifications.

In the end, Jesus does go to Jerusalem, but in secret (7:10–13). As He had described, people were looking for Him, so His appearance in the open would go unnoticed. While there is discussion about His identity, it is a somewhat taboo subject amid the resentment that is building in the religious leaders.

Critical Observation

Jesus' interaction in Jerusalem reveals a typical scenario played out every time He seeks to teach in the temple.

1) Jesus teaches.

2) The religious leaders react.

3) Jesus confronts them.

4) The people react.

5) Jesus confronts again.

6) The leaders remain even more committed to killing Him.

📖 7:14–24

SPIRITUAL INSIGHT

After Jesus points out the importance of timing to His brothers (7:6–8), John is very specific that He arrives at the temple in the midst of the feast, perhaps Wednesday or Thursday of the week. There would have probably been a full audience, since people were already in the midst of celebrating.

John doesn't focus on the content of Jesus' sermon, but rather the response that people have to His teaching. The point of this passage is that Jesus does come in and teach, not before the religious leaders, but before all the people.

Notice that the religious leaders are astonished at the way Jesus handles the text of scripture, yet point out that His teaching is not grounded in the systems of the day (7:15). In that day, all true learned men had a teacher, and that teacher authenticated them. This way they could wash out self-proclaimed prophets and false teachers.

Jesus responds both to their comments on His teaching and their comments on Him as a teacher (7:16–17). He tells them that His teaching is indeed based on someone else (implying God Himself) but that a person must have full and complete faith in God before he can ever assess whether Jesus' teaching is from God or not.

These people raise the question of Jesus' teaching, and Jesus in return raises the question about their ability to hear and understand. In essence, Jesus says, "You are not in any position to evaluate what I say because you don't want to do the will of God." Jesus then moves from their attack on His teaching to their attack on the teacher (7:18). One of the primary differences between Jesus and all the false messiahs is who received the glory from the teaching. Jesus says that if He seeks the glory of God, then He must be pure and righteous.

Next, Jesus exposes the impure motives of His accusers—they want to kill Him. How can they proclaim themselves followers of the Law if they are intent on murder (7:19; see Exodus 20:13)?

The crowds do not believe such a thing could be true about their leaders. A demon must be the source of Jesus' seemingly insane behavior (7:20). But Jesus reveals the problem with the religious leaders. He refers back to something that was recorded in John 5 (7:21–23). Jesus healed a man, and then told the man to arise and take up his mat. It was illegal, according to Jewish laws, to carry anything on the Sabbath, and therefore, by Jesus telling this man to carry his mat, Jesus was going against the man-made laws of the Sabbath.

In His response, Jesus also refers to circumcision, a practice that God had instituted through Abraham (Genesis 17:10–12). The Law stated that a male is to be circumcised on the eighth day; Jesus points out to the leaders that they will circumcise a child even if the eighth day falls on the Sabbath. The leaders did not consider it wrong to do work on the Sabbath if it was in obedience to God's Law. Therefore, to them it was not against the Sabbath to circumcise, but completely consistent with the Sabbath.

In verse 23, Jesus highlights the fact that the leaders would regularly break their Sabbath laws in order to keep the Law of Moses. Yet Jesus performs one work, and they hated Him for it. What Christ is doing is completely consistent with what Moses taught. The problem, then, is not that Jesus is out of line with Moses, but that the leaders do not really understand the Law of Moses.

Jesus goes one step further in exposing their problem (7:24). They have been judging according to appearances. Jesus' work for the man in John 5 was a symbol of the work of God in the lives of every believer. But because these leaders were caught up in their own legalistic standards, they were not able to evaluate or understand Jesus at all. Their judgment was based on appearances, not the heart behind the laws of God.

📄 7:25–36

IGNORANCE IN WISDOM'S CLOTHING

Verse 25 introduces the reaction of the residents of Jerusalem. This reaction not only confirms the fact that the leaders want to kill Jesus, but it also illustrates the ignorance of the people regarding Jesus. The fact that the Jewish leaders are allowing Jesus to speak publicly causes the people to wonder if the leaders know that Jesus really is the Messiah (7:26). But they rule out that idea based on their misunderstanding of Old Testament prophecy (7:27).

There was a prevalent misinterpretation of Malachi 3:1, and portions of Isaiah 53, that the Messiah would appear out of nowhere. This created a belief that no man will know where the Messiah will come from. Their logic is this: Since they know Jesus is from Nazareth He cannot possibly be the Messiah.

Jesus' shouted response (7:28–29) opens with a possibly sarcastic phrase, almost equivalent to, "So you know Me, do you?" The point of His response is that He comes not from Nazareth, but from God. He is not a self-proclaimed prophet, but a sent one. The implication then is that these people do not know the God whom Jesus really comes from.

As throughout this section of John's Gospel, Jesus' words bring about anger for some and belief for others (7:30–31). The religious leaders are ready to take definite action against Him (7:32). Jesus' response (7:33–34), in its most basic meaning, is that He will return to heaven, and they will not be able to follow. Yet even that simple message is misunderstood. Jesus' listeners thought He was literally going away somewhere (7:35–36). They want to know if Jesus is saying He is going to the outcast Jews that lived among the Greeks. The idea of this passage is not that these Jews were simply scattered in Greece, but to indicate that they were scattered among Greek-speaking people—the Gentiles.

📄 7:37–52

COME AND DRINK

On this last day of the feast, Jesus gives Israel the call of faith that the entire Old Testament was longing for. This moment in Israel's history is a defining one. For on a very strategic day, Jesus will offer Israel the salvation that was promised since creation and anticipated through all of Israel's history.

The last day of the Feast of Tabernacles was the high point of this celebration of God's provision for the Israelites during their forty years of desert wandering. On the last day of the feast, a golden chalice was filled with water from the pool of Siloam and was carried in a procession by the High Priest back to the temple. As the procession approached the Water Gate, the door in the temple wall that gave access to the water hole, three blasts from the shofar—a special trumpet—was sounded.

The water was offered to God at the time of the morning sacrifice, along with the daily drink offering, wine. The wine and the water were poured into their own special bowls, and then poured out on the altar. The Feast of Tabernacles was related in Jewish thought both to the Lord's provision of water in the desert and to the Lord's pouring out of the Spirit in the last days. Pouring at the feast refers symbolically to the Messianic age in which a stream from the sacred rock would flow over the whole earth.

It is on this day that Jesus proclaims Himself the source of water for thirsty people (7:37–38). The scriptures have already declared that the result of believing in Him is, from the depth of your being, flowing rivers of living water. This is reminiscent of the living water Jesus spoke about with the Samaritan woman at the well in John 4.

The outpouring of the Holy Spirit will not be in its full form until Jesus returns to heaven. That is why John adds an interpretation for the reader (7:39). The coming of the Spirit is a theme that will emerge again in John, as Jesus tells the disciples that when He goes, the Holy Spirit will come (14:16).

At this point, the people divided into several veins of thought:

1) Some thought that Jesus was the fulfillment of Deuteronomy 18:15 (7:40). Many Jews in that day interpreted this verse to mean a great prophet that would arise to come alongside of the Messiah—a prophet in the magnitude of Moses, or any of the great men of God. These Jews were placing Jesus in that category of great leaders of Israel.

2) Others referred to Jesus as the Christ (7:41) or Messiah. There were some who believed in His claims and declared that they believed in Him.

3) Still others ruled Him out as Messiah on the basis that He came from Galilee rather than from Bethlehem as was prophesied (7:41–42). They have no idea that Jesus was born in Bethlehem, therefore, they are mistaken. Had they asked, or researched, they would have discovered that Jesus was from the city of David, and the line of David, and therefore, qualified as the Messiah.

There is division among the people (7:43–44) and a conflict among the leadership. The guards failed to seize Jesus because they are so awed by His words. In response to this, the Pharisees pointed out that while some of the people may have fallen for Jesus out of ignorance of the law, the religious leaders know better (7:47–49).

Then Nicodemus speaks up (7:50–51). This is the Pharisee who had come to Jesus secretly, saying, "Rabbi, we know you are a teacher who has come from God. For no one could perform the miraculous signs you are doing if God were not with him" (3:2 NIV). Nicodemus was one who was willing to consider that Jesus was from God, unlike many of his peers. He offers a point of reason—they are wrong in the way that they are dealing with Jesus. By law they should at least hear Jesus and attempt to validate His claim.

The Pharisees rebuff Nicodemus, but not without mockingly asking if he is motivated to validate Jesus because he is from the same place, Galilee (7:52).

A WOMAN CAUGHT IN ADULTERY

Some Bible translations do not include John 7:53–8:11. It was not originally part of this section of John's Gospel. While it was not a part of the earlier manuscripts of John, it is unlikely that it is totally fiction. It is probably an added snapshot of Jesus' ministry, inserted later from oral tradition. While the language of the story does set it apart from the rest of this Gospel, the event is completely in line with Jesus' character and ministry.

What has led up to this moment? The Pharisees have become increasingly angered at Jesus. He has repeatedly confronted them. Since they can't arrest Him, or get the people to stop believing, they decided to trap Him with a situation in which there is no right answer. This is an effort to get Him to contradict the Law of Moses.

The Mount of Olives, where the people came to hear Jesus teach (8:1), was one of His places to pray, and He is there often from this point on in John's Gospel. It is not unusual that Jesus sits down to teach (8:2). This was typical for a Jewish rabbi—he sat and the people stood.

It is both the scribes and the Pharisees who come to Jesus with the adulteress woman. While it was common to bring religious questions to a rabbi to answer, in this case, the ulterior motive was to trap Jesus (8:3–6).

Critical Observation

The scribes studied and copied the Old Testament Law. Because of their familiarity with it, they are sometimes called lawyers or teachers of the Law. This familiarity also made them experts on the application of the Law—religious and ethical practices. Since this was a culture that centered around the law, the scribes held an essential role. If anyone had a question concerning some practical outworking or technical subtlety, he would consult a scribe.

The Old Testament law taught that those who commit adultery should be killed because their action attacks the very heart of the family and society (Leviticus 20:10). However, adultery was so common in Jesus' day that often this law was ignored. The people of the day did not agree with the practice of killing for adultery, and the Roman authorities banned the practice by the Jews.

Thus, when the religious leaders bring a woman caught red-handed in adultery, Jesus is being asked to choose between the Law of Moses and the legal and accepted practice of the day. If He suggests they stone the woman, He is breaking Roman law. If He chooses mercy, He breaks Moses' Law. Because these men do not understand the plan of God, they can't understand how justice and mercy can become reconciled.

The Bible does not reveal what Jesus writes in the ground (8:6). When He does respond, His answer is based on Deuteronomy 13:9 and 17:7, which instructed those who had witnessed a crime to be the first to inflict the punishment for that crime. Since the religious leaders are the ones who caught this woman, they are the ones who should actually make the first move. Therefore, Jesus is upholding the law entirely.

Jesus' response also places the execution of this woman on the shoulders of those who brought her. There is the implication that you cannot accuse someone of something that you yourself have done, or are guilty of. The question is not whether or not the Law of Moses should stand in this case, but whether or not these men are qualified to be this woman's judge. Their hearts are not bent on the glory of God, but rather on causing Jesus' downfall. Their own hypocrisy disqualifies them.

While Jesus does write in the dirt again, verse 9 makes it clear that the religious leaders leave because they heard Jesus' statement, not because they read what He wrote. Notice the order in which they leave: The older ones left first. The retreat continues until only Jesus and the woman are left. Finally, she moves from being the object of an evil plot to the object of God's mercy. In showing mercy (8:10–11), Jesus addresses both her position and her practice.

- The positional statement: I do not condemn you.
- The practical statement: From now on sin no more.

Her position might be forgiven, but she must now practice righteousness.

Take It Home

We are to live with the same instruction Jesus gave the adulteress woman—this is the life of the Christian. We are forgiven. And as a result we walk in righteousness. Christ's death on the cross did two things: It forgave human sin—literally all of the wrongs that were committed against God—and second, it conquered the power of sin in a person's heart. That is the power of the cross, the place where God's mercy and God's justice meet.

JOHN 8:12-59

The Light of the World	8:12–20
The First Condemnation of Israel	8:21–30
Genuine Faith	8:31–32
The Corruption of Man	8:33–36
Man's Only Security	8:37–47
Spiritual Ignorance	8:48–59

Setting Up the Section

For eight chapters John has been detailing the claims of Jesus Christ. Jesus has given sufficient evidence that He is the Messiah. He has declared Himself the object of the Passover, the object of the Feast of Tabernacles, the source of light, the source of life, the source of eternal life, and the only way to heaven. Jesus has backed up His claims with the miracles that the scriptures said would accompany the Messiah.

How have the Jews responded? The crowds have seemed motivated to follow Jesus as long as He fed them and healed them. Unfortunately, in the following chapters, what has started as a hope that Jesus is the Messiah, will, by the end of chapter 8, turn to an attempt to murder Jesus.

At this point, Jesus changes from a public presentation of Himself to a public condemnation of Israel. This is a turning point in the Gospel of John. Israel is being chastised for her rejection of the Messiah.

8:12–20

THE LIGHT OF THE WORLD

Jesus is in the court of the treasury when He makes His next claim (8:12, 20). That treasury is located in one of the outer courts of the temple. It is actually located in the court of women, the innermost place women could go into the temple. It's also where people brought their money to give as offerings.

John's mention of this detail—Jesus in the treasury—is a good example of the kinds of details that give this Gospel an eyewitness kind of authenticity.

To fully understand the power of Jesus' claim to be the light of the world (8:12), look back at a prophecy of the Old Testament prophet Malachi (Malachi 4:2) that concerns the spiritual healing that God will provide through the sun (rather than Son) of righteousness. Throughout the Old Testament, light is a metaphor for God's presence and work and of the future Messiah:

- The glory of God's presence was represented by light (Exodus 13:20–22).
- The protection of God was represented by light (Exodus 14:19–20).
- The psalms described God as light and salvation (Psalm 27:1).

- God's Word, His truth, is described as a light (Psalm 119:105; Proverbs 6:23)
- God's light is His revelation (Ezekiel 1:4–8) and salvation (Habakkuk 3:3–4).
- The light of God's face was His people's strength and victory (Psalm 44:3).

There are many other examples, but in short, the coming of the Messiah was light to a dark world.

To the darkness of	Jesus is the light of
falsehood	truth
ignorance	wisdom
impurity	holiness
sorrow	joy
death	life

Jesus is laying claim that He is the promised sun of righteousness. And He adds a consequence for those that respond to His claim: Those who follow Him will not walk in darkness (8:12). This is a parallel to God's presence with the Israelites on their journey out of Egypt described in the Old Testament—a pillar of fire to guide them by night (Exodus 13:20–22).

Jesus' claim is one that this crowd would have understood because of its familiarity with Isaiah's great prophecy of the coming of the Messiah: Those in darkness will see a great light (Isaiah 9:2–7). Jesus is telling the people that Isaiah's prophecy is fulfilled in Him. In order to receive the blessings promised in this prophecy, they must follow Him.

In light of the Pharisees' challenge (8:13), Jesus reveals the basis for His claim.

1) His origin. His witness is true because He came from heaven and speaks with divine approval. Unfortunately, these people still see Him as someone from Galilee. They don't understand His true origin (8:14).

2) His ability to judge. The point here is not that Jesus will never judge, but rather, that Jesus does not use the same superficial standard for judging that these people are using (8:15). Jesus says that His judgment will not be based on human wisdom because He is God (8:16).

3) Divine testimony. Since Jewish law requires two witnesses to confirm any testimony, Jesus is saying He has two witnesses: Jesus and God, His Father, because they are one. This should satisfy the demand of the Law (8:17–18). Again, the people look at Jesus' response from a small, human perspective—where is His father (8:19)? They are proving that they have no idea who Jesus is. Therefore, Jesus places His finger on the problem by saying, "You do not know me" (NIV). Their inability to recognize Jesus testifies that they really do not know God Himself.

Jesus' statements would have been outrageous to those who did not believe in Him. The conflict for these religious leaders is building, yet God's timing is still in effect (8:20).

THE FIRST CONDEMNATION OF ISRAEL

The tenor of Jesus' ministry changes as He begins to pronounce the judgment that the people of Israel will face for rejecting their Messiah. They cannot go where He is going because of their lack of faith in Him (8:21).

The Jews, which in John's Gospel refers to the Jewish leadership, miss this solemn warning. They suggest that He might be talking about suicide (8:22). In rabbinical teaching, anyone who committed suicide would be placed in the darkest part of Hades forever. Their response, then, is filled with an arrogant undertone. The only place that Jesus could go that they would not find Him would be the recesses of Hades, so He must be talking about killing Himself. They miss the point of Jesus' statement entirely.

Jesus' response to these leaders turns the tables. In essence He says, "I am not the one who is going to go to the pit; actually, you are from that pit" (8:23). These leaders thought that their religious practices had enabled them to transcend the world, but in all reality, they were engulfed in the world's system.

Next Jesus addresses their unbelief (8:24): They will die in their sins unless they believe in Him. If they fail to believe, they will not only be sinners by nature, but they will also be sinners by choice, which will seal their fate.

Jesus defines belief very specifically—faith in Himself (8:24). In response, these leaders give Jesus an opportunity to clarify Himself (8:25).

Critical Observation

Verse 26 is the turning point at which Jesus switches from His public ministry to Israel to a public condemnation of Israel's leaders. Jesus says His judgment comes from God and, therefore, is true. He reveals the stark reality of their situation.

In verse 27, John tells us that these leaders miss the point that Jesus was sent from God. Therefore, Jesus introduces a function of the cross: to reveal who Jesus is (8:28). In verse 29, He drives the same point home, which has been a contention all along with the religious leadership—Jesus will always do that which pleases God. Many of the people believe in Jesus because of His words (8:30), but the conflict with the religious leaders continues on.

GENUINE FAITH

Jesus defines genuine faith as that which holds to His teaching (8:31–32). To "hold to" (8:31 NIV), in this context, means to "remain" or "continue" for the long term. It conveys the idea that a person will not fall away. True discipleship means living Jesus' teaching so continuously that it becomes part of the believer's life, a permanent influence and stimulus in every area of life. Jesus is not saying you must prove by staying the course that you have good enough faith. He is saying that as you continue in His teaching, then it becomes obvious that you are one of His true disciples.

8:33–36

THE CORRUPTION OF MAN

Jesus has just defined true faith as that which abides or continues in His teaching. His listeners respond by touting their heritage—we are descendants of Abraham, why would we need to be set free by Your truth (8:33)? They believed that because they were Jewish, they were inwardly free, even though they were outwardly in bondage as a nation. They misunderstood that when God called the Jews as His people, He was not calling them to a salvation meant exclusively for them, but rather to be the people that His salvation would come through.

Jesus begins His reply in verse 34 with the famous, "Verily, verily" (KJV), or the more modern, "I tell you the truth" (NIV). He does the same as well in verses 51 and 58. In Greek, the word used here is *amen*, which means "this is the binding truth."

Jesus outlines the seriousness of humanity's problem with sin in verses 34–36. Simply, it is that sin affects every aspect of our being. In other words, the whole person is corrupted by sin. We may not have allowed sin to run its full course in our lives, but sin is slavery whether it runs its full course or not. Jesus describes to His listeners that not only does a person sin by action, but actually, they are sinners in the very depth of who they are. They are enslaved to that sin.

Building on that slavery image, Jesus sets up a contrast between a slave and a son (8:35). The son has a permanent place; the slave is only kept as long as he or she is useful. There is a prophetic undertone to this statement. Jesus has been warning them that they will be rejected if they don't believe in Him.

The only one who can set a slave free would be the rightful heir of the family. Only the father or the firstborn son can do this (8:36). That means Jesus can set humanity free from the enslavement of sin. What an offer. Only the heir of the house is allowed to set a slave free, and only Jesus can set any of us free from our sin.

8:37–47

MAN'S ONLY SECURITY

In verse 33, the Jewish leaders make the claim that they are not slaves to sin if for no other reason than because they are Abraham's descendants. In verses 34–36, Jesus clarifies that all humanity is corrupted by sin. In verses 37–41, He then questions the notion that these leaders are true spiritual descendants of Abraham. Physical lineage does not denote spiritual lineage.

In a physical sense, the Jews who oppose Jesus are the descendants of Abraham. Yet that is not enough to make them a part of the family of God. If they are truly children of Abraham, they would not be seeking to kill the Messiah. They are outwardly conformed to the law, but inwardly their hearts are bent on murder (8:37). They have not given Jesus' teaching permanent residence in their lives, as Jesus talked about in verse 31.

Jesus' next statement is a cutting one—those who oppose Him speak a different language than He does and have a different father. While the Jewish leaders maintain their family ties with Abraham (8:39), Jesus points to Abraham's works of faith (Hebrews 11:8–12, 17–19). These Jews who oppose Jesus are self-righteous workers who find their security not in God's promises and His power to fulfill those promises, but in their own works.

Notice the progression of the statement made by Jesus in verse 40. They want to murder a man who has told them the truth about their situation, God's truth. They are rejecting God's revelation. Abraham loved the truth and did not run from it. Abraham sought to serve God, and sought to follow the truth, not do away with it. Thus, they are not the spiritual children of Abraham (8:41).

In response, they claim not to be illegitimate children—God is their Father if for no other reason than because of their Jewish heritage. Jesus' point remains: If God were truly their Father, then they would love Jesus because He came from the Father. How could you be of God if you hate the Messiah (8:42)?

In telling them that they are unable to hear Him, Jesus is addressing a fatal flaw (8:43). The problem is His communication is not the obstacle; it is their ability to understand Jesus that is the issue. Because they cannot hear Jesus, they fail to grasp the true meaning of His words. This logic leads them to a startling conclusion in verse 44: Their system, their beliefs, and their hearts are grounded in evil. Satan's desires are murdering and lying, and these have become the desires of these Jewish leaders. Jesus speaks the truth (8:45) and they don't recognize it. They are content with a lie. They want to kill Him, and find no problem with that. Jesus is clear both about who they are and who He is (8:46–47).

📖 8:48–59

SPIRITUAL IGNORANCE

Jesus continues in His dialogue with the religious leaders. He has been clear with these men about who He is, and what He came to do. In addition, He has been clear about their spiritual condition and their need to trust in Him as the Messiah.

In verses 42–47, Jesus had confronted the leader, saying that their inability to recognize Him as God's Son revealed the fact that, spiritually, they were not God's children. Though they were Jews by heritage, their faith did not prove them to be the spiritual sons of Abraham.

In response to Jesus' bold claims, the Jewish leaders pose a question that reflects how they feel about Jesus. They ask Jesus how they can come to any conclusion other than that He is both a Samaritan and possessed by a demon (8:48). While there are other places in the Gospels where Jesus is accused of working under the power of Satan, this is the only place where He is accused of being a Samaritan.

Critical Observation

To fully understand the accusation posed by the Jewish leadership in verse 48, examine the feelings of the Jews toward the Samaritans. The Jews believed that the Samaritans were, first of all, traitors to Israel. It was the Samaritans' forefathers—Jews of the northern kingdom of Israel—who, during the early stages of the captivity under Nebuchadnezzar, married outside of the Jewish nation, and therefore their offspring were not fully Jewish. These descendants took on the customs and religious practices of the nations that they married into and so practiced a corrupt version of Judaism. The Jews of the southern kingdom rejected these mixed marriages and the mixed culture that they produced.

Keep in mind that Jesus has just criticized these men at a tender spot—their heritage as the descendants of Abraham. For them to attack Jesus' heritage is to respond in kind. In calling Jesus a Samaritan, these leaders are accusing Him of betraying Judaism in the same way they believed the Samaritans had.

Jesus does not respond to the accusation that He is a Samaritan (8:49). Jesus loved the Samaritans (John 4). He does, however, flatly deny that He is possessed. Jesus is concerned with honoring God (8:50). He doesn't respond to attacks that have nothing to do with that role.

Then Jesus returns the conversation to the purpose of His time on earth—all who keep His word will not "see death" (8:51 NIV). The word *see* in this verse means "to look with understanding" or "to experience." Jesus is saying that when you place your faith in Him, you will not experience eternal separation from God. Therefore, physical death is nothing but the journey from this life into eternity with God forever, skipping the horrors of separation from God's mercy and grace.

The response Jesus receives to this statement is based on a physical understanding of death. These Jewish leaders miss the spiritual truth of what Jesus is saying (8:52–53). In taking offense, they merely wonder, *Who does He think He is?*

Jesus' answer to their query angers them even more. He tells these men first that He is not out to honor Himself by offering eternal life. His goal is not to demean Abraham but to honor God the Father (8:54–55). Abraham was overjoyed at the promise of the Messiah, yet these men stand in the Messiah's presence and reject Him. But when Jesus points this out (8:55), the Jews' response once again diminishes His statement to a simple physical fact: Jesus isn't old enough to have known Abraham (8:57).

For these argumentative religious leaders, though, Jesus' claim in verse 58 is unmistakable. Jesus calls Himself *I am*. That is the personal name of God used in the Old Testament when God spoke to Moses (Exodus 3:14). Jesus is saying, "I am God."

Leviticus 24:16 states that anyone who claims to be God, and thus blasphemes God, should be stoned. This is why, in verse 59, the men pick up stones with intent to execute Jesus.

JOHN 9:1–41
THE BLIND MAN

What the Blind Man Saw   9:1–41

Setting Up the Section

Chapter 9 is a key chapter in the Gospel of John because it serves two purposes. First, it serves as a theological summary of the entire Gospel of John. Second, it is a transition between Jesus' public ministry to Israel and His public condemnation of Israel. Because the leaders reject Jesus as God and the Messiah, Jesus will condemn them. Because they failed to honor Jesus as Lord and Messiah, they will suffer the consequences.

In this section of John's Gospel, made up of seven signs or miracles, the healing of the man born blind is the sixth sign.

9:1–41

WHAT THE BLIND MAN SAW

Some believed that any physical infirmity was a result of a sin committed by that person or someone related to that person. This may have been based on a misunderstanding of verses like Exodus 34:7. Thus, the disciples ask who is at fault for the man's blindness (9:1–2).

Jesus gives the simple answer that no one sinned (9:3). The reason for this man's blindness is that God's power will be put on display in this man's life. Verse 4 is a call to make the most of the time that God has given. Jesus uses a workday illustration to make His point. There is an appointed amount of work that God has planned for Jesus, and Jesus must complete that work while He is here on earth (John 17:4).

In verse 5, Jesus tells the disciples His purpose—He is the light of the world, the revelation of God on earth. He is showing the glory of God to everyone.

The way that Jesus heals this man—the mud on his eyes and the command to wash in the pool (9:6–9)—contains several possible allusions to the Old Testament. It is clearly reminiscent of the Old Testament prophet Elijah healing a man named Naaman of leprosy by having him wash in the Jordan River (2 Kings 5:1–14). Some also connect the word *Siloam* to the river called Shiloah in the Old Testament. Isaiah 8:6 speaks metaphorically of Israel rejecting "the gently flowing waters of Shiloah" ([NIV] meaning God's sustenance) and allying itself with the king of Syria. Another possible allusion is to Genesis 49:10, "the scepter will not depart from Judah. . .until Shiloh comes" (NASB), a passage interpreted by the rabbis with reference to the Messiah. Whether these allusions are present or not, by interpreting the word Siloam as "sent" John links the pool of Siloam to the Messiah—the one "sent" by God (3:16; 4:34: 5:23, 37; 7:28; 8:26, etc.)

Naturally, the people want to see who it was who caused such a miracle, but because the man never saw Jesus he cannot point Him out to them, though He calls Him by name. This is the second time in John that Jesus is accused of transgressing the Sabbath. In chapter 5, He healed a man on the Sabbath, and the leaders were more upset about Jesus' breaking the Sabbath than they were awed at the miracle. In this case, Jesus could be accused of breaking three Sabbath rules:

- He had healed a man.
- He had made a mud pack.
- He had anointed a man.

There are three interrogations performed by the Pharisees to get to the bottom of the incident.

1) 9:13-17. The Pharisees question the man. Their questions center around the process Jesus used to perform the healing, concerned more about the rules than God's glory.

2) 9:18-23. The Jewish leaders then interview the parents. They could discredit the miracle if the man had not been born blind. Unfortunately for them, the parents, out of fear, only confirm their son was born blind, and then defer any other questions to him. They were afraid of disagreeing with the Pharisees and being excommunicated, or cut off from the synagogue. If they were cut off, they would not be able to work, they would be kicked out of their home, forced to live as outsiders, and not be welcomed into heaven when they died.

3) 9:24-34. The leaders again call this man to be questioned. They cannot deny the fact that he was blind from birth; therefore, the only thing left is to attack the character of Jesus. If Jesus is a sinner, then it does not matter what miracle He performs—it is all evil. The one thing this man will not relinquish, though, is that he was blind and now he sees (9:25).

The man's answer—asking if they want to be disciples of Jesus—could be a sarcastic response (9:27). It was probably obvious that their interest was not motivated by a desire to be Jesus' disciples.

Next, the Jewish leader elevate themselves by claiming they are disciples of Moses (9:28-29). When they refer to God speaking to Moses, they are referring to Moses' special connection with God. The idea of Moses and God conversing together conveys God's approval and blessing. This reveals how much the leaders reject everything that Jesus has said. Jesus has said over and over that He is from heaven and that He and God are one.

The healed man's response reveals a spiritual common sense that is lacking in the religious leaders. What the man finds remarkable is not that Jesus healed him, but the unbelief of the officials (9:30). Jesus just performed an amazing miracle, and yet they refuse to admit that Jesus is God.

The man's logic works this way (9:31-33):

1) We know that God does not hear sinners.
2) God hears those that do His will.
3) To heal someone blind from birth must be a miracle of God.
4) Since it is a miracle of God, the person who performed this miracle must have been obeying God. God heard Him.
5) Therefore, if Jesus were not from God, God wouldn't have empowered Him to work this miracle.

Responding in anger, the leaders curse the man and throw him out of the synagogue (9:34-35). Because of that, Jesus seeks the man out and asks him if he believes in the Son of Man. The word *believe* means trust, and the title *Son of Man* refers to Jesus being the Messiah, the revelation of God on earth (Daniel 7:13–14). Keep in mind that when the man asks who the Son of Man is, he has never actually seen Jesus. His eyes had been covered with mud, and then he was taken to the water where he received his eyesight.

Critical Observation

Notice the progression of the man's increasing faith in Jesus:

"The *man they call Jesus* made some mud and put it on my eyes" (9:11 NIV, emphasis added).

"He is a *prophet*" (9:17 NIV, emphasis added).

"If this man were not *from God,* he could do nothing" (9:33 NIV, emphasis added).

"Then the man said, 'Lord, I believe,' and he worshiped him" (9:38 NIV, emphasis added).

When Jesus speaks about judgment, He is not referring to the final judgment of the world, but rather the judgment that causes a decision to be made—to accept or to reject.

Jesus uses the illustration of sight. If you don't know you are blind, you have a problem. It's the same with spiritual sight. The Jewish leaders are spiritually blind, but are unaware of it (9:40–41).

Take It Home

Jesus' words are a warning for all who believe they see the truth. The Jewish leaders were convinced that they were right, that they could see the truth, but they missed what God was doing through Jesus. The only way to be free is to fall before Jesus and exchange all that you are for all that He is. When you admit you are blind, then you will receive sight.

JOHN 10:1–42

JESUS CONFRONTS THE LEADERSHIP

Woe to the Shepherds   10:1–21
The Deity of Jesus   10:22–42

Setting Up the Section

Jesus is continuing to answer the question that was asked by the Pharisees in 9:40. They wanted to know if they are blind, and they are. And because they are blind, chapter 10 goes on to explain, they are not the true shepherds of Israel. Instead, they are false shepherds that harm the sheep.

Verse 22 marks the end of a very important part of the life of Jesus. In the last part of

this chapter, Jesus will end His public ministry to the leaders of Israel, and begin His private ministry to the disciples.

Though this is the last in a series of confrontations between Jesus and the leaders of Israel, the same theme emerges: The leaders question Jesus, and Jesus declares that He is God. The dialogue will cover the same ground covered in the past several chapters, yet the religious leaders remain unconvinced.

📄 10:1–21

WOE TO THE SHEPHERDS

Jesus begins His allegory with the famous, "Verily, verily" (KJV), or the more modern, "I tell you the truth" (NIV). He does the same as well in verse 7. In Greek, the word used here is *amen*, which means "this is the binding truth."

Critical Observation

Jesus' illustration (10:1–5) centers on first-century sheepfolds. The sheepfolds of Jesus' culture were large enclosures, open to the sky, but walled around with reeds, stone, or brick to protect against robbers, wolves, and other beasts.

The shepherd entered the sheepfold through a large door, though sometimes animals and robbers clambered over the walls elsewhere in order to prey upon the sheep.

At the doors of the large sheepfolds, some large enough to hold thousands of sheep, a porter, or doorkeeper, remained on guard. This doorkeeper would only admit those who have the right to enter. All those who climb into the sheepfold some way other than by the door are robbers or attackers.

The King James Version refers to Jesus' teaching here as a "parable" (10:6), but a better translation of the Greek word would be "illustration" or "analogy." Jesus expands on this illustration (10:7–9) by calling Himself the door to the sheepfold. Anyone who wants to be a part of the kingdom of God must go through Him. When He refers to all who came before Him as criminals, He is not teaching that Moses and the prophets were among that group. He is referring instead to the more recent history—the teachers and leaders who are in power at the time.

In verse 10, Jesus continues to explain the true heart of the leaders of Israel and compares them with Himself. Jesus uses the picture of thieves at the sheepfold to communicate that if a teacher is pulling his followers away from faith in Christ, that teacher is destroying them. This is aggressive language for Jesus to use in a direct confrontation with the leaders questioning Him.

In contrast to death and destruction, Jesus brings life, abundant life. When a person comes to the door of Christ for salvation, he or she is given a life that is full, complete, and not lacking anything.

Jesus continues to compare Himself with the religious leaders of the day (10:11–13). He is the shepherd; they are the hired help. In calling Himself the shepherd, Jesus claims Himself not only the path to salvation (the door or gate) but also the provision of salvation.

There is a bond between the sheep and the shepherd (10:14–15). Included in this bond between Jesus and His sheep is the bond between Jesus and His Father. Both relationships are secure. The true shepherd cares for the sheep in such a way that He gives His all. That is the depth of the relationship between Jesus and the sheep.

In verse 16, Jesus speaks of the Gentiles as the other sheep outside of Israel that He will redeem. He will bring those to the fold, and they will become one with the Jewish believers. They will have one single flock, with one single shepherd. That is what His sacrifice will bring.

The death of Jesus is not something that Jesus is forced to do (10:17–19). It is not something that Satan does to Jesus—it is something that Jesus does on His own initiative. It is the power and authority of Jesus that causes Him to give His life, and it is the very authority of God that Jesus possesses that causes Him to rise from the dead.

The reactions Jesus receives are not unusual (10:19–21):

- Rejection—He has a demon and is insane.
- Consideration—How can He be a demon or insane if He heals the blind?

Throughout Jesus' ministry, He meets with these reactions. Some reject Him outright. Others look at what He does and wonder if He is for real.

📄 10:22–42

THE DEITY OF JESUS

Some time has passed between verses 21 and 22, probably a couple of months. It is winter, and the Feast of Dedication is happening. Jesus is walking around the portico of Solomon. This was one of the only fully enclosed places in the temple, and therefore, in the winter months this is where you would find many of the rabbis and religious leaders, as well as most of the people.

Demystifying John

The Feast of Dedication is also called Hanukkah. This feast is not a feast required in the Law of Moses. It was one added later in Israel's history during the four hundred-year period between the events recorded in the Old Testament and the events recorded in the New Testament.

In 167 BC, the Syrian king Antiochus Epiphanes overran Jerusalem and polluted the temple, setting up a pagan altar to displace the altar of Israel's God. Eventually a leader emerged, Judas Maccabeus, who developed an army, and led the Jews in what we today would call guerilla warfare. They recaptured the temple and spent eight days rededicating it to God. It was decreed that a similar eight-day feast of dedication should be held every year. Hanukkah begins on the twenty-fifth day of the Jewish month of Kislev, a date that varies throughout December on our calendar.

It is during this Feast of Dedication that the Jews press in on Jesus in the temple and ask Him to reveal once and for all if He is the Christ (10:24). *Christ* is a title rather than a name.

It's the Greek equivalent of the Hebrew *Messiah*. Both words mean "anointed one."

Keep in mind that the Jews want a champion leader like Judas Maccabeus to conquer Rome for them. If Jesus is that man, He should speak now. If not, He should be killed—that is the pressure behind this question.

When Jesus says that He has already answered them (10:25), He is not referring to a specific statement, but rather to the works that were done in the Father's name. Those works were witnesses to Jesus' role as Messiah. But the religious leaders failed to believe. In verse 26, Jesus begins to explain why they did not believe—because they were not sheep of His flock. Jesus has continued to tell them through His miracles and His claims that He is the Messiah, but they cannot hear because they are not of the sheep of God.

Take It Home

While verses 28–29 continue Jesus' explanation of the distinction of those who are God's sheep, they also teach us about Jesus' role as our shepherd. Not only does He know the sheep, but He protects the sheep. He gives them eternal life. The reason that we have eternal life is that we have the life of Christ within us, and therefore, we become partakers of that perfect eternal life that preserves us. We are protected in the hand of God.

Notice that in verses 28–29, Jesus refers to His hand and to God's hand interchangeably. This is one more subtle illustration of a truth given directly in verse 30—Jesus is fully God.

The Jewish leaders have challenged Jesus to define Himself again for them. Jesus does and declares Himself as God. For the Jewish opposition, Jesus' claim is blasphemy. They respond by preparing to stone Him (10:31) for the second time (the religious law required that anyone who claims to be God be stoned to death). To these first-century Jews, God did not dwell in human bodies or in idol forms. You could not get close to Him or you would die. From that perspective then, how could Jesus, who is human and bound to this earth, actually be God?

When the leaders threatened to stone Jesus previously (8:13-59), Jesus disappeared. This time He remains and asks them a question. Jesus had manifested the works of God on earth (as prophesied in Isaiah 61:1). Of these works of God, Jesus wants to know, which ones render Him deserving of death (10:32)?

In response to the accusations of blasphemy (10:33), Jesus refers these men to Psalm 82:6. In Psalm 82, God called out to the unjust rulers. He had appointed them as "gods," His sons, His representatives on earth. The title *gods*, in this context, implies authority or ruler (10:34). Jesus makes an argument from the lesser to the greater (10:35-38). If these men could be called sons of God, and without performing any great works of God, could He not rightly be called the Son of God, having manifested God's works? All that Jesus has done has been the work of the Father. No one could have done what Jesus did.

Since they remain unconvinced, He leaves, waiting for the right timing (10:39). This time He travels beyond the Jordan (10:40).

From here on out in the Gospel of John, Jesus will focus on teaching His disciples and preparing the way for His death, resurrection, and the future church. The people to whom Jesus ministered, who in turn came to believe in Him, are in sharp contrast to the leaders who failed to believe. This serves as the point of transition. The leadership of Israel rejected, but the people in the villages believed the preached word of John the Baptist and the works of God manifested in the life of Jesus. All the people needed to do was hear the message, and they believed (10:41–42).

JOHN 11:1–57

THE PRIVATE MINISTRY OF JESUS

A Faith That Is Larger Than Life   11:1–44
The Plan of Men—the Plan of God   11:45–57

Setting Up the Section

The issue here is faith. As a group of people struggle with death, the ultimate conqueror, will they believe that Jesus is even more powerful than death? The disciples believe that Jesus is going to die when He goes back to Judea. The sisters of Lazarus believe that death has conquered their brother. It seems it has not yet occurred to anyone that Jesus' power is greater than death.

📄 **11:1–44**

A FAITH THAT IS LARGER THAN LIFE

Not much has been said about Lazarus until this miracle. In fact, more people know Mary and Martha, so John's Gospel gives them as a point of reference to know who their brother is (11:1). Mary's anointing of Jesus' feet (12:1–8) must have been a well-known story by the time this Gospel was written because John references it here (11:2) even though the story hasn't appeared in this narrative yet.

Lazarus is noted as someone Jesus loves (11:3). This term of endearment, of course, signifies a close relationship. Jesus had healed others He had never met; surely He would come and heal this man who means so much to Him.

Critical Observation

Verse 4 is key to this account. Jesus declared that Lazarus' sickness would not result in death. Lazarus will die, but his death will not be final. This sickness will provide the occasion for God to be revealed through the power of Jesus raising Lazarus from the dead.

This issue of the mutual glory of Jesus and the Father is one of the sore spots for the Jewish religious leaders. They believe they honor the Father, and yet, at the same time, they are dishonoring Jesus. Jesus has been telling them that there is mutual glory shared between the two, and therefore, if you dishonor Jesus you dishonor God.

Notice the tension in verses 5–6. Jesus has a deep affection for Lazarus and his sisters, yet He waits two days to respond to them. Why does He wait? It is clear to us now that Jesus waits so that Lazarus will be dead when He arrives, and Jesus can then raise him from the dead.

The last time that Jesus had been in Judea, the religious leaders tried to kill Him (11:8). This is why the disciples are hesitant to return. Jesus responds to their fear with the image of the safety of daylight (11:9–10). In that culture there were no street lamps or lightbulbs, so for the most part, work stopped at sundown. A person working at night would not be able to see well and would stumble around accomplishing nothing. If that same person works in the daylight, he does not stumble because he can see. In other words, as long as the disciples are in the presence of the light, nothing will get in the way of their mission.

When Jesus describes Lazarus as asleep, the disciples miss His point (11:11–16). Lazarus is actually dead, not asleep, and they are charged with a divine mission, not just a mandate to escape danger. Thomas's almost fatalistic comment in verse 16 reveals that their eyes still were not open to the bigger issues going on around them.

The four days (11:17) Lazarus's body was in the tomb was sufficient to confirm that he was dead. As was the custom of the day, relatives and neighbors would have come to care for the family in this time of grief. In addition, at most funerals, the family would hire a funeral band to play sad music, and professional mourners. This would have been a large gathering of people, all centered on the grieving family members to mourn with them (11:18–19).

While perhaps not obvious at first, Martha's comments reflect a lack of faith. While she is sure that Jesus *could have* done something about Lazarus, now that he is dead, she is just as sure that Jesus can do nothing about the situation. Her interpretation of Lazarus's potential resurrection is the final judgment resurrection (11:20–24).

Critical Observation

In verse 25, we see the lesson of the story. Jesus is changing the focus of the conversation from the eventual resurrection of the dead to the fact that He is the one with the power and authority over death. Jesus is the source of resurrection and life (11:25–26).

In response to Jesus' claim, Martha's statement of faith models the ideal response. In the midst of all the rejection Jesus received from the religious leaders, Martha sees Jesus for who He is, and believes (11:27).

It seems that Martha makes the attempt to be discreet when she alerts Mary that Jesus has come, yet those watching follow on her heels. Mary's words to Jesus echo those of her sister's in verse 21 (11:28–32).

Amid Martha and Mary's grief, and the looming question of whether Jesus had waited too long to do anything about the situation, Jesus is deeply moved (11:33) or deeply agitated. At first it appears that Jesus is weeping with them, as the Jews interpret His actions (11:35–36). However, there are several elements of this situation that would have been disturbing, for instance the limited faith of His close friends. The word "troubled" (11:33 NIV) could communicate that kind of idea. Why would Jesus be upset at their grief? Perhaps because they were acting as if there is no hope. They reduced the power of Jesus to His earthly presence instead of trusting Him as the Son of God.

The crowd refers back to the miracle Jesus performed in chapter 9. If He had healed a blind man, couldn't He have saved Lazarus?

Lazarus's tomb was typical for that time—a cave carved into rock with a stone to block the entrance (11:38). These tombs were often large enough for people to move around inside, since it was common for more than one body to be buried there. This grave was similar to the one Jesus would soon be raised from.

As Jesus stands before the grave, calling for the stone to be moved, Martha struggles to look beyond her circumstance to see the glory of God as Jesus promised (11:39–40). In this context, the glory of God does not refer to a grand light show. It simply refers to an authentic display of who God is. As throughout the Gospel of John, Jesus is that display of God's glory.

Jesus' prayer of thanks reaffirms the claim that He has made throughout this section of John's Gospel—that He has been sent from heaven and is the physical manifestation of the Father (11:41–43).

The grave clothes on Lazarus were typical for that culture. Embalming was not a part of Jewish burial customs. The body was typically washed, dressed, and wrapped in linen, but was not put into a coffin. Instead it was carried into the tomb and left in a prepared place, perhaps a carved shelf or shallow grave. Spices and perfumes were placed in the grave clothes and in the tomb to mitigate the odor of decay. A separate piece of cloth covered the head.

When Lazarus is raised, the fact that his body is restored after four days of decay is a part of the miracle.

11:45–57

THE PLAN OF MEN—THE PLAN OF GOD

When Jesus calls Lazarus from the grave, the responses are divided (11:45–47). The leaders do not see Lazarus's resurrection as a sign that Jesus is the Messiah. Instead, they see it as competition. The council they convene is made up of both the Pharisees and the chief priests. Most of the chief priests were from the party of the Sadducees. Typically, the Pharisees and the Sadducees did not get along, yet, in this case, they were united in one purpose—opposing Jesus.

Demystifying John

The Sanhedrin was the highest Jewish authority, sometimes referred to as the high council. It was composed of seventy-one members, one high priest (Caiaphas, in this case) presiding over seventy men. Most of the members were Sadducees, but there was a minority of Pharisees.

Typically, the Sanhedrin sat in semicircular rows so that its members could see each other. Clerks sat at either end. Students, often disciples of the scribes, also attended. While the trial of Jesus involved some irregularities in the procedure of this ruling body, it was typically a group known for a high interest in fairness and justice.

It is obvious from this text that miracles alone will not convert the human heart. The leaders do not deny the miracles of Jesus. In this case, they are not as upset by Jesus' miracle as they are about the numbers of people believing in Him. If Jesus is allowed to go unchecked, then more will believe that He is the Messiah, and the status quo will be threatened. If the Jews begin to see Him as a king, then Rome could become involved (11:48).

Notice these things about their response:

1) They still call Jesus a man (11:47), even in light of His miracles.
2) Their fears are exaggerated (11:48). Jesus' followers were often divided. Particularly when He taught about the cost of discipleship, many fell away.
3) They come to illogical conclusions (11:48). Jesus' mission is not to be king in the earthly sense. They seem to have forgotten, even as religious men, that God is more powerful than Rome. They should fear His displeasure more than Rome's.

Caiaphas is the high priest. In fact he served for eighteen years (AD 18–36) as an appointment of Rome. Notice his words in verses 49–50. He is saying, in essence, that it would be in the best interest of the religious establishment if Jesus is used as a scapegoat. There is no real ground under Roman law that Jesus should be executed, yet Caiaphas seems to feel His death would keep some perceived peace with Rome.

Under Roman law, the Jews were allowed to govern themselves, but they were not given the authority to execute anyone. So, if the goal is to execute Jesus, these men are faced with a dilemma because Jesus never broke the Roman law.

John says that Caiaphas does not make his statement about Jesus' death on his own initiative (11:51). Caiaphas thinks he is speaking of the destruction the leaders are plotting, but his statement is more meaningful in light of the sacrifice Jesus will make to provide eternal life for so many (11:52). Jesus' death is going to bring the lost and scattered souls from every tribe and every nation together into one body. Caiaphas has no idea that what he thinks he has devised is really the plan of God. He seeks destruction, but God has planned life.

With the commitment the leadership has made to end Jesus' life (11:53), the stakes have changed, and Jesus withdraws (11:54). It was the previous Passover mentioned in John's Gospel at which Jesus, on the Sabbath, healed the man who had been lame for thirty-eight years. He then declared Himself God, with full rights to break the man-made Sabbath laws (John 5). The conflict that surrounded that Passover has only grown over time.

Take It Home

God is sovereign over the plans and motives of people. In this case, God has a plan for the evil heart of the leaders. God uses both good and evil, and God even uses the things that do not make sense to us.

Therefore, if someone has wounded or inconvenienced us, or even falsely accused us, we can still have faith in God, and believe that even in the worst of times He is in control. Jesus' sense of timing throughout His ministry speaks of the kind of faith that rests in God's timetable rather than fear of the power of people and their opinions.

JOHN 12:1-50

THE FAITHLESS AND THE FAITHFUL

The Priority of Worship   12:1–8
The Beginning of the End   12:9–26
The Power of the Cross   12:27–36
The Unbelief of Israel   12:37–50

Setting Up the Section

In the previous chapter Jesus raised Lazarus from the dead, revealing Himself to be the resurrection and the life. This miracle created a lot of attention for Jesus, which increased the anxiety of the religious leaders over Jesus' ministry.

This passage begins with a contrast of a faithful heart, Mary, and a deceitful heart, Judas.

📄 **12:1–8**

THE PRIORITY OF WORSHIP

Jesus is in Bethany at a dinner with Lazarus and his family (12:1). If you read the same accounts of this story in the other Gospels, you will find that Jesus is in the house of Simon the Leper, and He is there with the disciples (Matthew 26:6–13; Mark 14:3–9). It is six days before the Passover (12:1), the beginning of Jesus' final week before His death and resurrection.

A distinction of John's account is his focus on the feet of Jesus. The other Gospels describe Jesus' body being anointed. John may have focused his account this way because in chapter 13, foot washing will become a major teaching point of Jesus.

Mary pours about twelve ounces of a valuable perfume (nard) on Jesus' feet (12:3). It was not uncommon for a special guest in that day to be anointed with a perfume when he arrived. The region was hot and dusty, and the people did not have showers in which to clean up.

People were typically dirty and a little smelly. When a special guest would arrive, sometimes they were greeted with a douse of perfume to help the smell.

In anointing Jesus, Mary broke several customs of the day:

- She approached Jesus at the table. In that day men and women dined at different tables.
- She let her hair down in public. Women did not let their hair down in front of men. That was a sign of intimacy, only to be shared between husband and wife.
- She wiped His feet with her hair. Not only did a woman not let her hair down in public, but she certainly would not have touched a man with her hair.

Mary was placing all that she had at the feet of Jesus. She was humbling herself in front of Him, and presenting everything to Him out of a heart of love and devotion. She was literally foreshadowing Romans 12:1, presenting herself as a living sacrifice. Her act was one of devotion. It also foreshadowed Jesus' death. In a sense, Mary was anointing Jesus for His death and burial (Matthew 26:12; Mark 14:8).

In this passage, Mary's actions stand in contrast to the actions of Judas. When John adds the detail that Judas will later betray Jesus, he isn't saying that Judas was already intending to betray Jesus. His Gospel was written years after the fact, and Judas's betrayal was common knowledge. John's addition of detail here adds weight to Judas's comments. Judas is upset that this perfume is wasted on Jesus (12:4). His question (12:5) reflects two key areas of defect in him: what little regard he has for Jesus, and his sinister heart. Judas was the one in control of the finances, and because he was greedy, he would steal from the money box. If the perfume had been sold, he could have gotten access to the cash (12:6).

In defending Mary's actions to Judas (12:7-8), Jesus is making the point that Judas needs to get his priorities straight. Nothing is to be more important than the glory of God. Nothing is to take center stage more than the worship of God.

📖 12:9-26

THE BEGINNING OF THE END

When people hear that Jesus is in Bethany, they come to see Him (12:9). However, the crowd is interested in the miracles Jesus performs, not necessarily worshiping the Messiah. It is because of these crowds that the chief priests decide to not only plot Jesus' death, but Lazarus's death as well. Lazarus's presence gives testimony to Jesus (12:10-11). A movement is continuing to form around Jesus that threatens the current religious leaders.

The next day, when the crowd gathers to meet Jesus as He enters Jerusalem (12:12), the people do two things:

1) They bring palm branches. Greeting a hero with palm branches was a custom of that day. It symbolized honor for a leader, national pride, and a conquering warrior. By laying down palm branches they reveal that they see Jesus as a political Messiah sent to reestablish Israel as a nation. They are worshiping Jesus with the right words but with the wrong motives.

2) They call out, "Hosanna!" This comes from Psalm 118, and it was a common scripture that was quoted during this time of the year. Psalm 118 originally was used to describe a Jew making his way to Jerusalem for worship. Because many Jews were making their way to Jerusalem for the Passover, this psalm would be sung along the way. Also, in many Jewish

writings of the time, there was a messianic connection to this psalm, signifying that this verse is talking about the coming of the Messiah. Because of this teaching, these people are standing in the street, proclaiming their allegiance to Jesus, whom they are hoping is their Messiah and will conquer Rome.

This misunderstanding of Jesus' role prompts some fear in the religious leaders. They see the people of their nation beginning to center around Jesus as their national hero, and they think for sure that Rome will intervene and further take away their independence.

Jesus' entrance into Jerusalem (12:14–15) fulfills the Old Testament prophecy of Zechariah 9:9. In John's account, the details are left out, yet he still confirms that Jesus fulfills it. The quotation here is not an exact quotation.

Demystifying John

In Zechariah 9:9–11, God promised that a king would come to Israel and three things would happen:

1) The wars in Israel would end.

2) Peace would be proclaimed.

3) Because of the blood of the covenant, prisoners would be released.

The context of this passage is victory in Israel. This victory is being proclaimed by Jesus, but it is being accomplished not by a war, but by Jesus' death. That is the significance of the donkey, in that day a sign of someone coming in peace. Jesus accepted their praise, but He also showed the people that He was not out to conqueror Rome but to conquer sin. While they have their eyes on politics, Jesus has His eyes on their souls.

It is not until Jesus ascends into heaven that the disciples are able to look back and understand that the scriptures declared He would ride in on a donkey as the Messiah, and that the kingdom that He would destroy would be the kingdom of sin. At the point of Jesus' acclaimed entry into Jerusalem, they miss the paradox of life in death, of greatness in humility, of hope in suffering.

Verses 17 and 18 tell us that the people who are with Jesus are enthralled by His display of power, but not focused on identity. In John 11:57, the leaders directed anyone who saw Jesus to report His location so He could be arrested. In chapter 12, the people obviously ignore that order (12:19).

Verses 20–22 preview what is to come. The "Greeks" John mentions are probably "god-fearers"—Gentiles who worshiped the God of Israel but had not fully converted to Judaism. They have come to worship during the Passover. These Gentiles serve to signify that Jesus is the Savior of the whole world. And so with the blindness of Israel being confirmed by the plot of the leaders and the ignorance of the people, John offers a picture of salvation offered to the Gentiles.

Jesus' response to the inquiry of these Gentiles is that the time has come for Him to be glorified (12:23–28). For the Jewish listeners around Him, Jesus' words might be mistaken for a statement that it is time for Him to take Rome, which, of course, is not what Jesus has in mind.

The illustration of the kernel of wheat that is useless until it dies and produces a harvest (12:24) reveals that Jesus' glorification will happen through His death. Verse 25 describes the result of His death upon the lives of His true followers. This truth is critical to Christian discipleship: Those who have contempt for themselves will be the ones who live eternally, but those who have a high regard for themselves will lose their lives.

Jesus begins His illustration in verse 24 with the famous, "Verily, verily" (KJV), or the more modern, "I tell you the truth" (NIV). In Greek, the word used here is *amen*, which means "this is the binding truth."

Take It home

In Jesus' day, those who were simply hoping for a conquered Rome missed the important truths of God's kingdom. There was a cost to following in Jesus' footsteps: a death to self. This is a message for us today. What are we expecting from our faith? Miracles? Life made easier? Answers to prayers? Or humble obedience as Jesus' disciples? Throughout history, humanity has tried with all sorts of religious acts to please God in the hopes of a variety of returns, but only in death to self, and a complete devotion to Jesus, is God truly pleased.

📄 **12:27–36**

THE POWER OF THE CROSS

After speaking about the importance of giving up one's life, Jesus now faces that very sacrifice. He is deeply anxious, and asks if He should pray for deliverance. Instead, Jesus basically says to God the Father, "If My death and agony bring You glory, then I'll do it" (12:27).

After Jesus declares His desire to the Father, the Father speaks to Him in an audible voice (12:28). There are only two other times in the Gospel accounts in which God speaks audibly—at Jesus' baptism (Matthew 3:17; Mark 1:11; Luke 3:22; compare John 1:29–34) and His transfiguration (Matthew 17:1–8; Mark 9:2–8; and Luke 9:28–36). When God spoke at Jesus' baptism, He expressed His approval, authenticating His Son. Why? Because people around Jesus were thinking about a great Jewish nation, and Jesus was talking about His own death.

When Jesus says that God is speaking for the people's sake (12:30), He means that the Father did not speak from heaven because Jesus needed confirmation, but because the crowd needed confirmation that Jesus' death will bring glory to God. That is the centerpiece of God's plan. In verses 31–33, Jesus explains.

Critical Observation

The background of Jesus' description of the "prince of this world" (12:31 NIV) being driven out is found in Genesis 3, the story of the fall of Adam and Eve. God promised a struggle between Eve's seed (that which would be born of her, her descendants) and the seed of the serpent who had tricked her (Genesis 3:15). Jesus is the fulfillment of this promise. The cross is the place where we see God, but it is also the place where Satan's power will be broken.

Notice that Jesus says that He will draw all people to Himself (12:32). The words we translate as "all people" don't mean that Jesus will draw to Him everyone ever created. It means that He will draw all those who put their faith in Him throughout history.

Look at the response. The people understand that Jesus is saying He must die, but they can't reconcile that with the idea that the Messiah will live forever (12:34). They miss the simple reality that the Old Testament says both about the Messiah, that He will die but that He will also live forever.

Jesus' reply points them to the urgent necessity to act on the light that they have (12:35–36). They must give up their preconceived notions and act on the revelation that Jesus is giving them, and then their questions will be answered. In essence, you must first become a child of the light if you are going to walk in the light.

The next public revelation will come at His crucifixion. Jesus spends the remainder of His days preparing the disciples for what is to come.

📄 12:37–50

THE UNBELIEF OF ISRAEL

John inserts verses 37–50 to show his readers that the rejection of Israel is all a part of what God had said would happen, and therefore, it is not a reason to deny that Jesus is the Messiah. Instead, it is a sign confirming that Jesus is the Messiah (12:38–41). He quotes from two passages of Isaiah: 53:1 and 6:10. Both of these passages talk about the blindness of Israel in relation to the Messiah. That blindness was produced by God as a form of judgment. There is a segment of people who believe, but they are afraid of the stigma of admitting it (12:42–43).

Verses 44–50 summarize Jesus' teaching and public ministry. This is not a literal response to the leaders mentioned in verse 42. It is probably from a series of messages that Jesus had preached to the leaders and is now condensed for the readers of this Gospel. The idea that Jesus cries out these words (12:44) means that whenever they are spoken, they are shouted out. This signifies their importance.

The point in verse 47 is not that Jesus will never judge sin or faithlessness, but that His mission for the time being is not about judgment. Judgment will happen in the future (12:48–49).

JOHN 13:1–38

FINAL WORDS

Love in Action	13:1–17
A Traitor in the Camp	13:18–30
The Distinguishing Mark of the Church	13:31–38

Setting Up the Section

Chapter 13 begins a very concentrated description of the love of God as seen through the sacrifice of Jesus.

The Passover was a celebration that pointed in two directions. It pointed backward to the great exodus from Egypt, God's deliverance. But it also pointed forward to God's final salvation. Isaiah and other Old Testament prophets described a new and greater exodus that God will accomplish when He delivers His people and establishes His kingdom (Isaiah 11:10–16; 40:1–5).

Jesus is that once-for-all Passover Lamb who will accomplish this new exodus. Jesus knows that He is about to die and become the fulfillment of what the Passover meal pointed to. John tells us that Jesus is fully aware of what is taking place (13:1).

📄 13:1–17

LOVE IN ACTION

In verse 1, the word "hour" (NIV) refers to the whole period of the crucifixion, not just the hanging on the cross. John is making the point that Jesus knows He is ending His full-time public ministry and, therefore, will die, then ascend into heaven, completing the task of redemption.

For Jesus to love His own "to the end" (NASB) is another way of saying that Jesus loves them with a complete love, a love that will carry them through to the end. To love someone to the end means to love someone to perfection. It's unconditional love. The cross is the place where Jesus' perfect and complete love is manifested.

John refers to Judas's betrayal but leaves out any details concerning it (13:2). Jesus is in the room with a man who is in a conspiracy with Satan to seek His execution.

When Jesus lays aside His outer garment and takes the towel to wash the disciples' feet, He is putting on the clothes and taking on the role of the lowest of servants (13:3–5). This is why Peter is so unsettled (13:6). His view of leadership would have rejected a leader doing such a thing. His interpretation of leadership was that of being served, not of serving. Once Peter understands the cross, the foot washing will make more sense (13:7).

Critical Observation

In that day people usually wore sandals. Walking on dusty, sometimes filthy, roads would make their feet dirty. It was the role of the lowest slave to actually clean the feet of the guests as they arrived. At the home the disciples used for this meal, there were no servants, and therefore, their feet did not get washed.

In verse 10, Jesus responds to Peter's request for a bath (13:8-9) with a principle of forgiveness. If a person has taken a bath before he goes to a gathering at someone's house, when he arrives he does not need to get an entire bath again. All he needs is to have the dust of his feet washed off. The rest of his body is already clean. The point—you do not need to go beyond what Jesus offers for salvation. His work is enough for a lifetime. That is why it is a perfect love.

The point of Jesus' explanation of the foot washing is for these men to understand their roles in a new way (13:12-17). The example that Jesus has set is that of humility. True love is an enduring love that seeks to serve others at expense to self. The only way for the world to see what Jesus did to save mankind is for His followers to model before the world that kind of humility.

13:18–30

A TRAITOR IN THE CAMP

In verses 12-17, Jesus explains to His disciples that they are to show true love by their humble service to each other. In the midst of this lesson, Jesus changes gears and begins to talk about Judas. John has already mentioned the betrayal of Judas in his Gospel as early as John 6:70-71.

Jesus' point in verse 18 is simple: The commands and the blessing of obedience do not apply to Judas. As He said in verse 10, one man in the room is not really a true disciple and therefore does not or will not ever receive any blessing from God. Yet Judas fits into the divine design that God established for the redemption of mankind.

Jesus tells the disciples that His betrayal was predicted in the Old Testament; it fulfills scripture (13:18). He's referring to Psalm 41:9, a psalm of King David. David says in essence, that "his betrayer has lifted up his heel against him." This phrase can carry the idea of an attacker who, after wounding a person until he or she is defenseless, picks up his foot and drives it into the person's neck to inflict more damage. It also can refer to the heel of a horse, raised for a swift kick.

Demystifying John

King David had a son named Absalom with whom he was in conflict. Absalom tried to overthrow David's kingdom with the help of Ahithophel. Ahithophel was a counselor to both David and Absalom, and so Ahithophel betrayed David in favor of the rebellious Absalom (2 Samuel 15–17). David wrote Psalm 41, from which Jesus quotes here, in light of this betrayal.

In verse 19, Jesus once again refers to Himself as the *I Am*, the name God called Himself when commissioning Moses. His revelation of a betrayer will one day serve as a confirmation that He is who He claims to be. Verse 20, then, follows the chain of command. If Jesus and God are one, then those that Jesus sends out are included in that connection.

Note the response of the disciples to Jesus' announcement about a traitor. These men have labored together, yet they don't immediately suspect Judas (13:22). They are at a loss. This reminds us that their lives and relationships were as complicated and mysterious as our own can sometimes be.

While people of this day often ate sitting on the floor, it was also the custom at special meals to eat reclining at the side of a table. Each person reclined on his left arm, and ate with his right arm. In this way, since John was in a place of honor beside Jesus, John's head would be close to Jesus. This is why he would have been in a position to observe Jesus and to ask about the identity of the betrayer (13:23–25).

Jesus offers the bread dipped in sauce to Judas, signifying to John that Judas is the betrayer (13:26–27). Ironically, offering bread to a guest was a sign of friendship.

John mentions Judas's being possessed by Satan (13:27). This highlights the fact that the conflict is not between Jesus and the Pharisees, or the Romans, or even Judas. It is between Jesus and Satan. So when Jesus speaks to Judas, He gives Satan the approval to start the chain of events to bring about His crucifixion, though the disciples still don't understand the significance of those instructions and come to their own conclusions (13:28–29).

Light and darkness are a constant theme in John. It is symbolic that when Judas leaves, the Gospel makes it clear that it is night (13:30).

📄 13:31–38

THE DISTINGUISHING MARK OF THE CHURCH

In this passage, Judas has already left the room, and Jesus is talking with the remaining disciples.

Son of Man (13:31) is a historical phrase that Jesus uses in the Gospels to refer to Himself. It is a title introduced in the Old Testament book of Daniel (7:13–14). In Daniel 7:13 (NIV), Daniel speaks of "one like a son of man" (meaning a human figure) who comes before the Ancient of Days (God Himself) and is given authority, glory, sovereign power, and an eternal kingdom. It is this portrait of the exalted Messiah that Jesus is drawing on when He refers to Himself as the Son of Man.

The word "glorified" (13:31 NIV) means to reveal with honor. Contemporary English describes a son who looks just like his father as a glorified version of his dad. Notice that, in this case, Jesus ties His glory in with His death. It is in the death of Jesus that His glory, the presence of God, is revealed. God will put Jesus on display (13:32).

Critical Observation

Keep in mind that on the cross Jesus performed a great act of love. By doing this, He manifested the Father and therefore was glorified. Consider this:

- On the cross Jesus redeemed mankind from hell.

- On the cross Jesus disarmed Satan and destroyed the power of sin.

- On the cross Jesus paid the price that God's justice demanded for humanity's sin: death.

- On the cross Jesus offered His body as the perfect sacrifice to God.

- On the cross the justice of God and the law of God were fully satisfied.

Jesus tells the disciples that they are not allowed to come with Him (13:33). He had told the Jewish leadership this same thing in an earlier confrontation (8:21). There is a difference in the meanings, though. Jesus told the Jews that they would die in their sins and could not come with Him into eternal life. He is telling the disciples that they cannot come with Him to the cross.

Then, in verse 34, Jesus gives the requirement of the mission with which He will leave the disciples. He calls this a new commandment, though God had already commanded the Jews to love each other (Leviticus 19:18). This is a new commandment because of the standard of this love. Jesus says that they are to love each other even as Jesus loves. The result will be that the disciples are recognized as followers of Jesus by the way they love (13:35).

All four Gospels record the claim Peter makes to lay down his life for Jesus (13:37; Matthew 26:35; Mark 14:31; Luke 22:33). His words echo those of Jesus when He describes the work of the shepherd laying down his life for the sheep (10:11, 15, 17). As bold as Peter's claim is on behalf of Jesus, Jesus predicts here Peter's denial (13:38)—which happens that very night (18:17, 25–27).

JOHN 14:1–31

HOPE FOR THE DISCOURAGED

Hope for the Hopeless   14:1–3
Clarity for the Confused   14:4–31

Setting Up the Section

Jesus is giving His final address before His death. Some have compared His words to Moses' last address to his people before his death (Deuteronomy 31–33).

In this passage, Jesus offers some very specific encouragement regarding the Spirit of God, and the role He will play in the lives of the disciples. Then, in the following chapters (15–16), He offers instructions on how He wants them to act, and speaks of the persecution they are to expect from this point on.

📄 14:1–3

HOPE FOR THE HOPELESS

Jesus first tells His disciples what not to do: Don't be troubled (14:1). He does not want the current situation to create fear and sadness. This is actually a night of rejoicing.

Next He tells them to believe in Him. Jesus is redirecting their faith and focus from their circumstances to the God who controls those circumstances. First, Jesus tells the disciples that He is preparing a place for them; second, that His return is as sure as His departure; third, Jesus tells them that they will be unified with Him as a result of His return (14:2–3). Being united with Jesus in heaven will be the full consummation of the disciples' faith. His leaving is not a sign that He is out of their lives, but rather a sign of His desire to be with them forever.

Critical Observation

Jesus' comment about God's house having many rooms (14:2) has sparked many images of a heaven with specific dwellings in it. Another understanding of Jesus' words has less to do with a place in heaven and more to do with the access that we have to God through Jesus' work. Jesus is providing a way for His followers to be *with* God. The way we do that as people is to go to someone's house.

📄 **14:4–31**

CLARITY FOR THE CONFUSED

Jesus tells the disciples they already know both the place and the way to where He is going, and that both the location and the way to that location are bound up in Him. When Thomas asks about this, Jesus makes another *I am* statement, identifying himself as the way, the truth, and the life (14:4–6). In Jewish wisdom literature following "the way" meant living life by God's standards. The "truth" and the "life" further that explain the way. Jesus is the only true path that leads to eternal life with God.

The disciples do not recognize Jesus for who He truly is (14:7). When He tells them they will eventually know who He is, He is referring to all that is to come—His resurrection, ascension, the coming of the Spirit—then they will fully know Him, and in knowing Him they will know the Father.

Philip's request reveals that he wants his confidence to be grounded in his physical and earthly experience (14:8). Jesus' rebuke reiterates His same point—Jesus is the revelation of the Father on earth. Jesus is not enough for Philip because Philip does not truly understand or believe this (14:9).

Jesus makes three key points in verses 10–12:

1) His unity with the Father. Jesus asks a question that forces the point (14:10): Do they believe He is one with God?

2) A call to faith. Only God could do the works that Jesus has done (14:11).

3) Those who believe in Jesus will do His same works and even greater (14:12). The word *greater* indicates the idea of "greater in depth." What could be greater than raising the dead? Preaching the gospel of eternal life.

Jesus shares with them in verses 13–14 that the gap between the Father and the disciples is closed by Jesus. They now have access to the Father. They have the resources of heaven at their disposal.

Verse 15 carries the idea that a person cannot say that they love Jesus and disobey Him. Intrinsic to faith is obedience.

Jesus says that He will intercede before the Father and ask that the Helper, or Counselor, be given (14:16). The word translated *helper* or *counselor* means one who "comes alongside to intercede or to support." This is not the idea of a therapist's role, but more like a lawyer who pleads a case for you. The helper is the Spirit of truth (14:17). He reveals the truth to those who believe.

In verses 18–19, Jesus moves on to the eternal relationship His followers will have with Him. Because of His resurrection and departure, He is giving them the Spirit, access to God, the ability to work the miracles of heaven, and a promise of abundant life on earth and eternal life in heaven. They are not orphans; they have a new home in heaven. When the Spirit comes, they will understand these things (14:20).

In verse 21, Jesus goes back to the importance of obedience. True love is marked by obedience. Those who truly obey are one with Jesus, one with the Father, and truly understand who Jesus is (4:21). Jesus reveals Himself to those who obey Him.

There were two Judases in the original twelve disciples. John is clear here which is asking the question (14:22). Judas's question probably comes from a misunderstanding of prophecies such as Isaiah 11, which describe the coming of the Messiah in terms of worldwide recognition and a change in the entire world system. He is wondering why Jesus wouldn't be revealed to the whole world.

To answer Judas's question, Jesus explains the nature of salvation (14:23–24). Those who do not obey out of faith will not come to the realization of who Jesus is. The disclosure is not an automatic reality for everyone; it is only a reality for those who are truly devoted.

Then Jesus reminds them that when He goes, things will get a little more difficult but He will send the Holy Spirit to empower them (14:26). They are required to obey, preserve, guard, and protect all that Jesus has taught. That is something that is impossible in the flesh. Yet, with the Spirit's help, it can be done.

The discouragement of the disciples initiated this conversation, so Jesus reminds them of the peace that only He can give (14:27).

Critical Observation

One idea of *peace* is the absence of war—knowing that your nation and your home are secure. Peace was to be the supreme result of the Messiah's coming. The *Pax Romana*, peace of Rome, was achieved through military power, and the Jews of that day easily thought that the messianic peace would have to come through a mightier military power than that of the Roman army. Yet the peace of Jesus was achieved through the death of a righteous man.

Jesus refers to His departure for the sixth time in this chapter (14:28). Each time, He has shown the disciples some theological error in their belief. In this case, Jesus directly challenges their love for Him. Why? To produce faith (14:29).

Take It Home

In this text, Jesus gives us two great descriptions of what it means to be a Christian:

First, to obey Jesus' words. Obeying Jesus is more than just a series of dos and don'ts. It's a way of life in which all that you do and believe is conformed to the image and character of Jesus.

Second, to be devoted to Christ's glory. A true believer seeks to glorify Jesus even at expense to himself.

JOHN 15:1–27

FINAL INSTRUCTIONS

Abide in Jesus   15:1–11
Abide in Love   15:12–17
The Cost of Abiding   15:18–27

Setting Up the Section

Central to the heart of Jesus' message, and especially clear in the Gospel of John, is the fact that Jesus declares that He is what the Old Testament longed for. Jesus is the resolution. He is the one promised as early as Genesis 3:15, the great redeemer of humanity.

Chapter 15 moves from Jesus' first discourse of encouragement to His second discourse of instruction.

📖 15:1–11

ABIDE IN JESUS

Jesus says, "I am the true vine" (15:1 NIV). (This is the seventh time Jesus makes an *I am* statement in John's Gospel.) The disciples are already connected to the vine, not on the basis of their works or adherence to the law, but based upon the Word Jesus spoke to them (15:3). The idea around the word "clean" (15:3 NIV) is that of being purified from sins in order to be used by God. Unlike Old Testament Israel, who failed to produce the fruit of obedience, the disciples' hearts are cleansed from their sin so they can produce fruit.

Demystifying John

Jesus explains the Father is the vinedresser. The role of a vinedresser is to care for and protect the vine and the branches. The act of pruning the dead branches is the act of protecting the good branches to ensure that they get the maximum amount of sap for growth (15:2). The Father is actively a part of the fruit-bearing process.

Jesus reiterates His point that the disciples must maintain their faith in Him (15:4; see John 8:31-32). The idea of maintaining means not breaking fellowship. The disciples must keep an undivided heart and an undivided faith. They cannot bear fruit without being connected to the vine. Therefore, it is essential that they completely trust Jesus, or they will not be connected to the source of life (15:6).

Verse 7 declares that if we are in this union with Jesus, our prayers will be heard and answered. Because of our union with Jesus, He is able to hear and answer us. God intended for His character to be manifested through the fruit that is produced by a person who is in union with Him (15:8).

Jesus has shown His disciples the same love that the Father has shown to Him. He wants the same relationship between His disciples and Himself as He has with the Father. That relationship is marked by Jesus' complete devotion to the commandments and love of the Father. In the same way, if a person keeps His commandments, that person abides in Jesus (15:9-10).

Jesus tells the disciples all this so that they might experience the joy that He possesses (15:11). If they abide in Jesus, then they will have that perfect joy.

📄 15:12-17

ABIDE IN LOVE

Jesus gives the commandment that His disciples should love one another as Jesus loved them (15:12). This is the application of verse 10—abide in Jesus' love by loving others the way that Jesus loved.

Verse 13 reveals God's definition of love. At one level, this verse lays out the standard of love Jesus' disciples are to show to one another; at another level, it refers to Jesus' death on behalf of His friends. It is this level of sacrifice that Jesus wants the disciples to associate with love. Jesus shows these men that they have been the recipient of this type of selfless love, and it is upon that basis that they are to love each other. The implication in verse 14 is obvious—Jesus is going to lay down His life for them.

In verse 14, it might appear that Jesus is saying that you are a friend of Jesus if you are obedient. Notice the last part of this verse: Jesus tells them that they are His friends "if you do what I command" (NIV). It's not their obedience that makes them friends, but rather their friendship is characterized by obedience. The point is that Jesus lays down His life for them, and they, as a result of this love, become completely devoted to Him.

How have they been a recipient of Jesus' love?

1) They've gone from being called a slave to being called a friend (15:15).

2) They will produce lasting fruit (15:16).

Jesus, out of His love, chose these men. Their relationship with God is a result of *His* choice, not theirs. Not only were the disciples chosen, but they were chosen for a purpose: that they should be sent to bear fruit. The idea around the word "appointed" (15:16 NIV) is the word *ordained*. They have been set apart for a particular purpose. Inherent to their salvation is their mission. This is true for every believer.

📄 **15:18–27**

THE COST OF ABIDING

In order to help the disciples deal with the fear of the future persecution that awaits them, Jesus instructs them about suffering. In verses 18–21, Jesus identifies two reactions that the world (in this context, anyone who is not devoted to Jesus) will have to the disciples: hatred and persecution.

The second half of verse 20 shows a division. Everywhere that Jesus went there was a mixed reaction—those who hated what Jesus said and those who believed. The disciples will receive the same mixed reactions.

Jesus sums up His point by telling the disciples why they will face persecution (15:21)—because they are associated with Jesus and because their opposition does not know the Father. It is clear in verse 22 that Jesus is talking about the Jewish leadership. It is not as if the coming of Jesus introduced sin and guilt to these people. Rather, by coming and speaking to them, Jesus revealed the most central and most controlling sin, that of the human heart to choose the darkness over the light. Jesus not only revealed God, He revealed humanity's heart.

The sin that Jesus is referring to in verse 22 is the sin of rejection. If Jesus had not come, the rejection in the Jewish leaders' hearts would have never been made evident. Jesus' coming caused people to either accept or reject Him—which is the same as rejecting the Father (15:23). Jesus did works among them that displayed the glory of the Father to the Jewish leaders, and in rejecting Jesus they rejected the Father (15:24).

Demystifying John

Verse 25 is a quote from two psalms: Psalm 35:19 and 69:4. These are psalms of David, in which David is being hunted down because he was the chosen king of Israel. Jesus connects Himself to these psalms. If David, the lesser king, was hated without a cause, how much more would Jesus, the greater king of Israel, be hated without a cause?

When Jesus goes to heaven, His testimony on earth will not go to heaven with Him, but will stay and be proclaimed by the Holy Spirit. Not only will the Spirit bear witness, but the disciples will bear witness as well. In the face of these witnesses, Jesus' opposition will continue to reject the message just as it did when He walked the earth (15:26–27).

JOHN 16:1–33

A HELPER FOR DIFFICULT DAYS

A Final Word on Persecution	16:1–4
Better Days Are Yet to Come	16:5–15
The Transforming Work of the Spirit	16:16–33

Setting Up the Section

In the last several chapters, Jesus has warned the disciples about the difficulties they will face. John 16 continues on this same topic. This way, when these men face the persecution Jesus has described, they will not be surprised. In fact, it could confirm their faith.

📄 **16:1–4**

A FINAL WORD ON PERSECUTION

The Jewish leaders had already expelled from the synagogue those who believed in Jesus (9:22; 12:42). This will certainly continue and will happen to the disciples (16:1–2). By the time John was writing this Gospel, the Christian movement had broken ties completely with the synagogues, which once had been the conduits for Jesus to speak to His countrymen.

Critical Observation

Stephen became the first Christian martyr (Acts 7:54–60), with Saul, the yet unconverted Paul the apostle, looking on. Saul's perspective was very much what Jesus describes in verse 2. He saw his persecution of Christians as his service to God (Galatians 1:13–14; Philippians 3:6). These deaths happened for the very reason that Jesus described—the persecutors didn't know the Father and didn't understand the connection between God the Father and His Son, Jesus.

📄 **16:5–15**

BETTER DAYS ARE YET TO COME

In verses 5–6, Jesus identifies a major problem in the heart of the disciples: their self-focused minds. Sorrow has filled their hearts because it seems they are going to lose everything when Jesus goes away. This is the second time that Jesus has shown the disciples their self-centeredness (14:28). They can't see past the persecution that is to come to see the bigger picture of what Jesus is accomplishing through His departure.

Jesus focuses now on one aspect of His departure, that of the Holy Spirit (16:7). The role of the Holy Spirit on earth cannot be understated. The Spirit is the Helper, or advocate, of those who believe and the accuser of those who don't. He duplicates the work of Jesus on earth.

The ministry of the Spirit to the world centers on conviction of sin (16:8–10). The word *convict* means "to expose, refute, or convince." The Spirit will also proclaim the end of Satan's reign (16:11). The Spirit will testify that Satan and his system have already been condemned by God.

Jesus is beginning to draw His instruction to a close (16:12). It is time for them to endure the next few days. After that, the Spirit will work on their behalf (16:13–15).

📄 16:16–33

THE TRANSFORMING WORK OF THE SPIRIT

Jesus' point, that He will go and then return (16:16), confuses the disciples (16:17–18). They are trying to reconcile all that Jesus said to them. This is the first that we have heard from the disciples since Judas's question in chapter 14, but in this case they are only wondering among themselves out of earshot of Jesus. Aware of their confusion, Jesus articulates the question that they do not ask Him (16:19).

Demystifying John

The King James Version (also NKJV) includes the phrase, "Because I go to the Father," at the end of verse 17. This phrase, which does not occur in the earliest Greek manuscripts, was probably added by a later copyist to help the reader understand verse 17. Jesus has said throughout His instructions that He was going to the Father.

Jesus tells the disciples their sorrow will be turned into joy (16:20); notice not *replaced with joy* but *turned into joy*. This means the very event that plunges them into grief will be what lifts them into joy. What is the thing that will plunge them into sorrow? The cross.

Jesus illustrates this principle with childbirth (16:21). Before the baby is born, there is sorrow. The pain is astounding. But once the baby is born, the focus suddenly shifts from the pain to the joy of having a baby. The event becomes a day of celebration, where once a year the birth of this child is remembered, not as a day of pain but a day of joy. The event did not change, only the focus of the event. And the birth becomes a greater day than the sorrow. And the sorrow is only temporary, but the joy is eternal (16:22).

Critical Observation

Jesus continues to explain. There will come a time of understanding. They will be able to approach God directly in the name of Jesus and He will answer them (16:23). This is a tremendous change from the Old Testament Judaism that required a mediator between humanity and God (16:24). This is not a rebuke; rather, Jesus is explaining to the disciples that they will have this new relationship with the Father, and He encourages them to go the Father and receive His response. And the result: full joy.

It is one thing to have joy; it is another thing to have *full* joy. Full joy comes from a person who has an active prayer life with the Father. Those who are in such a relationship, where the Father is granting their prayers, have their joy strengthened because they are experiencing a relationship with the Father.

Some translations have the world *parable* in verse 25, others say *figurative language*. The meaning is "a veiled or hidden truth." Because Jesus speaks in this kind of language, the disciples will be dependent upon Him for the understanding.

The point of verse 26 is that Jesus does not need to do all of the requesting for them anymore. Now they can pray on their own because they will pray in accordance with God's will—because they know God's will. They now have the understanding to be able to come before God and pray.

The reason that Christ will not intercede for His disciples is that the Father Himself loves them. The Father does not need to be persuaded to be gracious to them (16:27-28). Because they place their faith in Jesus and are completely devoted to Him, they are able to enjoy a relationship with the Father in which they can now approach Him on their own.

In verse 28, Jesus restates the truth that must be believed: Christ came from heaven, therefore, He manifests God. He'll return to heaven, completing the perfect work of salvation. Christ's heavenly origin is important, else He would not be our Savior. But His heavenly destination is also important, for it is witness to the Father's seal on the Son's saving work.

Verse 29 is the first public response of the disciples since chapter 14. In verse 30, they ascribe their understanding to the fact that Jesus is from God because He knows everything. They think that because they understand His answer that they now understand what is going on. But this is not the case. If they truly understand, then they will not have such a fearful reaction when Jesus' trials start.

Observe Jesus' response to their aggressive answer (16:31-32). In less than twenty-four hours they will experience their first set of trials, and those trials will continue for the rest of their existence. But Jesus wants them to fully understand that His peace will allow them remain stable in the turbulent world around them. And the reason that His peace will do this is because His peace has overcome the world (16:33).

Take It Home

Just as Jesus promised the Spirit's help to the disciples, that help is here for us. We are not alone, left to fend for ourselves. God's Spirit still points us to Jesus. And it is upon His power that we become His witnesses.

We must continue to look to Jesus to live the Christian life and to accomplish the work that He set out for us to do. We must believe in the presence of the Holy Spirit, here to give us the strength to continue on in that work, no matter what we face.

JOHN 17:1–26

JESUS' PRAYER

Jesus Prays for Himself   17:1–5
Jesus Prays for His Disciples   17:6–19
Jesus Prays for All Believers   17:20–26

Setting Up the Section

This chapter offers a pre-cross preview of the post-cross work of Jesus: the work of intercession—praying on behalf of believers. Jesus prays for Himself, for His disciples, and for believers of every age and every generation. His prayers reveal even more about the beautiful relationship between Jesus and the Father.

📄 17:1–5

JESUS PRAYS FOR HIMSELF

Today we often bow our heads in reverence when we pray. In the first-century Jewish culture, a common prayer posture was standing with eyes lifted to heaven (17:1). It signifies two things:

1) that the person praying acknowledges God's place in heaven on the throne, and

2) that the person praying is coming to God with a clean and pure heart.

Jesus prays that the will of God will be done in His life. He acknowledges that God's plan, appointed in eternity past, is ready to be carried out. He prays:

1) That the cross would bring God glory

2) That the cross would save people

Jesus also prays for the consequence of the cross (17:2). The essence of this prayer is that Jesus desires that eternal life be given to all of those who have been given to Him.

In verse 3, Jesus speaks to an essential element of salvation: the understanding of God. Eternal life is not a measure of time; it is the life of God in man or woman. This is why Jesus has told the disciples that they are to have His peace, His joy, His love, and all that Jesus has. Jesus' role is to dispense all that He is to those whom the Father has given Him.

Verse 4 reveals the perfect obedience of Jesus. He finished the work that God called Him to do. Because of that, He prays that He will return to the union that He shared with the Father before He came to earth (17:5).

JESUS PRAYS FOR HIS DISCIPLES

In verse 6, Jesus prays for the specific followers who were commissioned to bring the message of the Messiah to the world. These followers are described as those who kept the Word of God. Jesus made known to them the Word of God, and they responded to it and upheld it as a way of life.

Critical Observation

Some translations of this verse mention Jesus revealing God's name to His disciples. To reveal the name of God simply means to show the full character of God. This is one of the key roles of Jesus particularly highlighted in John's Gospel: to reveal the Father. Jesus revealed God to these people, and ultimately, they came to believe that Jesus was indeed from heaven as He claimed (17:7–8).

Jesus is saying that these disciples are a part of His family (17:9), true believers. He then prays for their unity.

There is a reason that this is a specific prayer for a specific group of people, and that reason is found at the end of verse 10 and at the beginning of verse 11. Jesus is preparing to leave the world, and His disciples are going to put Jesus on display to the world as He has displayed the Father.

In verses 11–12, Jesus prays for protection for these men. The idea is that the Father will protect them in the same way that Jesus did while He was on earth. But even more than protect them, He will uphold them so that they will remain an ever visible representation of Jesus Christ on earth.

Jesus calls God "Holy Father" (17:11 NIV). The word *holy* means "to be separate, or set apart." In this context, it means someone who is set apart from sin and this world. The idea is "holy and separate Father, protect them from the world that You are not bound to."

In verse 12, the one that was lost is a reference to Judas Iscariot. Judas's betrayal was predicted in the Old Testament (Psalm 41:9; 109:4–13). He was given to Jesus to fulfill the role of betrayer. In 17:12 the word "perdition" (KJV), or some translations use "doomed to destruction" (NIV), refers to someone who is utterly lost with no hope of ever being saved. A subtle point here is that the will of the Father was accomplished in both Judas and the other eleven disciples.

In the midst of all of the persecution and hatred, Jesus prays that His joy would fill these men (17:13). Not only does Jesus want them to have joy on the basis of the Father's care for them, He also wants them to be sanctified as a result of the Father's protection.

Because they, like Jesus, are not a part of the world's system, they will be hated (17:14). Jesus is not asking that they be taken away from the hatred (17:1–5). Instead of escape, they need protection from Satan so that they will be set apart from the world (17:16).

Verse 17 is the other side of the coin of protection. Not only are they to be protected from Satan, they are also to be holy, or sanctified. To be *sanctified* is to be set apart for a specific purpose. It is the idea of being a holy vessel in the hands of the Master. How does a person become sanctified? By the Word of God.

In verse 18, Jesus, in prayer, sends the disciples out. Then in verse 19, Jesus sets Himself apart. Upon His work the disciples were sanctified and are sent out to continue His mission.

📄 17:20–26

JESUS PRAYS FOR ALL BELIEVERS

Jesus prays a three-fold prayer for future generations of believers (17:20)—unity, glory, and love.

1) Unity. That the disciples would know the oneness that exists between the Father and the Son (17:21). This oneness is revealed when the life of God is living in a person (17:22–23). Because of Jesus' work with the disciples (revealing the Father), they have His life within them and are to be unified just as the Father and the Son are one.

2) Glory. Jesus prays to the Father that we will experience the full glory of Himself in heaven (17:24).

3) Love. Jesus prays that we will have His love within us. One of the functions of the revelation of the Father was to place the unending love of God within those who believe (17:25–26).

Take It Home

Jesus' prayer makes it clear that Christians need to be one in the perfect unity of God so that they will have a testimony in this world. Without this unity, there is no testimony. Our ability to be unified in thought, mind, word, and deed shows the world that Jesus is from God.

How are the Father and the Son one? They are both separate from sin, and they both are devoted to the revelation of the other. And in that sense, we are to be one in this body. We are to be holy, and we are to be devoted to each other's best interests.

JOHN 18:1-40
JESUS' TRIALS

The Sovereign Control of Jesus   18:1–11
Humanity's Corruption and Jesus' Innocence   18:12–27
What Is Truth?   18:28–40

Setting Up the Section

Chapters 18–21 make up the final section of the Gospel of John—the death and resurrection of Jesus. John's focus in this account remains true to the rest of the Gospel—even in the account of the crucifixion, Jesus reveals the Father. This is not the picture of a weak and feeble man who is being taken by surprise by the events. Instead, the point here is that Jesus is actually in control of all of the events that are going on.

This is Jesus' moment. It is God's plan and not the plan of the Jews. The death of Jesus was ultimately the will of God—John's Gospel makes this clear.

📄 **18:1–11**

THE SOVEREIGN CONTROL OF JESUS

Verse 1 transfers us from Jesus' prayer to His walk to the garden where He is going to be betrayed and arrested. The Garden of Gethsemane is the place where Jesus went often to pray.

Judas knew that this is where He would be (18:2), and Jesus would have been aware of that. Jesus is not being taken by surprise; He is giving up His life. Jesus knew that Judas was plotting to turn Him over to the Jews. He went to the garden because it was His time to die.

Verse 3 reveals what Judas was doing when he left the Passover meal (13:30). The Jews now have Judas working for them, and the leaders put an entire army together to arrest Jesus. There are two groups of people mentioned:

1) The Roman cohort. This represents about six hundred soldiers. During Passover, the Romans would usually double their guards to create a show of force to eliminate the beginnings of any insurrection.
2) Officers from the chief priests and the Pharisees. The chief priests hired a group of temple police to enforce the Jewish laws. These officers were the ones who arrested Jesus.

At this point in the year there would have typically been a clear sky and a full moon, which means there would be need for just a few lanterns. These people came with torches, lanterns, and weapons—this implies that they were prepared for a search and, if necessary, a fight.

Instead of putting up a fight, Jesus goes to these men before they can come to Him (18:4). Notice that the Gospel writer makes it clear that Judas is standing with the guards, not the disciples (18:5).

Jesus responds with another *I am* statement, confirming His identity as God, who introduced Himself in the Old Testament as "I AM." Jesus is not simply saying that He is Jesus; He declares Himself the revelation of God. When He does this, close to seven hundred people fall to the ground because of the power of His name (18:6). This detail is a continuation of John's theme of Jesus as the revelation of the Father. It also further emphasizes that Jesus is offering Himself. It is God's will that He be arrested, not human will.

Jesus asks a second time who these men are looking for. The essence of this question is, "Whose name is on the arrest warrant?" (18:7–8). These officers may have wanted Jesus' disciples arrested as well. But there was, in essence, only one name on the warrant; and so Jesus, the one to be arrested, instructs the officers to let the others go.

In His prayer Jesus had just claimed that He would lose none of the disciples. Here, Jesus is preserving the disciples (18:9).

In verse 10, Peter, at the height of passion, attempts to defend Jesus with his sword. The particular Greek word for *sword* used here implies a small dagger. This kind of dagger would have been used to gut fish and could have been used to defend oneself in close combat. Given that Peter was a fisherman, it was not strange for him to carry this kind of weapon.

There is a good possibility that Peter was not aiming for the ear, but rather swinging for the head. In Luke's Gospel, we are told that Jesus put the ear back on Malchus (Luke 22:50–51), but John focuses on Peter's mistake—Peter failed to see Jesus as being in control. Jesus rebukes Peter and tells him to put his sword away (18:11).

Critical Observation

Peter gets a lot of attention in this chapter because He goes from the height of passion in defending Jesus, to the depth of despair in denying Jesus. But both are equal in their disobedience. Neither is an act of faith.

Passion, zeal, and excitement for God are not pleasing to Him if not in accordance with the divine will of God. Peter is still trying to prevent the cross from happening. He is trying to protect his Friend and Teacher, but he is actually standing in God's way.

Notice the word *cup* in verse 11. In Jewish thought this word is sometimes associated with judgment—the cup of God's wrath, or the cup of judgment (Revelation 14:10). Peter missed the point. His flesh produced a zeal that tried to defend Jesus, but in all reality Jesus did not want or need to be defended by him.

📄 **18:12–27**

HUMANITY'S CORRUPTION AND JESUS' INNOCENCE

The Romans and the Jewish officers of the high priest worked together to arrest Jesus (18:12). Typically, these groups did not work together; in fact they were often in opposition.

Jesus is led to Annas, the father-in-law of Caiaphas (18:13). Annas was a powerful man. Annas, for several years, operated as the high priest, and then continued his influence through his son-in-law's role as high priest. Annas's control of Caiaphas was generally recognized by the people.

In verse 14, John reminds his readers that Caiaphas was the one who said that it is better to kill Jesus than to lose the entire nation (11:49–50).

John's Gospel moves us from an introduction of the leaders to the failure of Peter, a failure that reveals that even with the best of intentions (13:37–38), it is impossible to be faithful to God in one's own power. Peter is following behind (18:15). In addition to Peter following, there is another disciple who is not named. This disciple might not be one of the eleven. Other followers of Jesus are also referred to as disciples, for instance Nicodemus (7:50) or Joseph of Arimathea (19:38).

This other disciple was known in the court of the high priest and is able to get Peter in to see what will happen (18:16). As Peter goes through the door, he is questioned, and he denies his association with Jesus (18:17). Then he goes to the fire to warm himself with the officers who have just been part of the arrest (18:18).

When the high priest questions Jesus about His teaching and His disciples (18:19), Jesus responds by asking why He is being questioned. He has already spoken openly before hundreds (18:20–21). Jesus' comments expose two things—His innocence and the illegalities of the trial. They should not be questioning Him without confirmed witnesses.

It was also illegal to strike a prisoner. The wording used for the officer striking Jesus (18:22) carries the idea that the officer hit Jesus hard, as one would strike an insubordinate criminal who was mouthing off to the authorities. There is a possibility that the officer did not use his hands, but actually used a stick. The wording used to describe the blow that Jesus received could be translated as a punch or a hit with a stick. There was no evidence offered to warrent Jesus' being hit in this situation (18:23–24).

Jesus is sent to the high priest for the next phase of the trial (18:24). While all of this is going on, Peter is still mingling in the courtyard. When asked if he is a disciple, again he says no (18:25). Then, one of the servants of the high priest, a relative of Malchus, recognizes Peter and asks him if he is a disciple (18:26), and Peter says no a third time (18:27). When this happens, the rooster crows, just as Jesus had predicted (13:38).

18:28–40

WHAT IS TRUTH?

It is at this point that Pilate is brought into the story. The Jews did not have the authority to enforce the death penalty. Therefore, they needed to have the Romans find Jesus guilty, and then the Romans could put Him on a cross.

The Praetorium, or palace (18:28), is the Roman court, the hall of judgment. It is early when they lead Jesus to Pilate. This was a hurry-up process. Jesus has been up all night in an illegal trial, and now they bring Him before Pilate early in the morning before anyone can stop them.

Observe the hypocrisy in verse 28. The Jews are illegally running Jesus through a false trial, they are seeking to murder an innocent man, yet they do not want to go to into the house of a Gentile and be considered ceremonially unclean. (This is an example of John's Gospel highlighting the corruption of the process and the innocence of Jesus.)

Pilate's inquiry about the charges against Jesus exposes the motives of the Jews (18:29). They respond, in essence, with "Take our word for it" (18:30). They want Pilate to work for them and to execute Jesus on the basis of their judgment. They are not interested in a trial, only an execution. The Jews want death by crucifixion because it will portray Jesus as a lowly criminal, not someone to be followed. Another consequence might turn Jesus into a martyr and increase His following (18:31–32).

John gives us some important information in verse 32—the desire to crucify Jesus is not a cause for discouragement. The leaders are falling into God's plan. Jesus had told Nicodemus that He would be lifted up (3:14). The idea is that He would be lifted onto the cross. Psalm 22, considered a psalm about the Messiah, speaks to the crucifixion (Psalm 22:1, 18).

Pilate launches his own investigation (18:33). He's been led to believe that Jesus is an insurrectionist, declaring Himself king and, therefore, is leading a mass rebellion against Rome. This would have fed into the thoughts Rome had of the Jews all along. Rome feared any insurrection and, therefore, had guards and soldiers around Israel to minimize any attempts of rebellion.

The exchange between Pilate and Jesus reveals that Pilate doesn't have any idea why Jesus is being accused. The interview does provide Jesus an opportunity to explain that He is a king, but the kingdom of which He is a part doesn't exist within earthly boundaries (18:34–37). Jesus is not subject to the affairs of this world. Even His wording—that He came into this world—implies that He existed outside of it.

When Pilate asks about the truth, it is as if he is saying the truth cannot be found, that there is no absolute answer. Yet Jesus spoke the truth. Pilate finds no fault in Jesus, but the custom that makes releasing Barabbas a possibility, negates Pilate's view of Jesus' innocence (18:38). The Jewish leaders choose a robber over God's Son (18:39–40).

Pilate's role in the trial of Jesus reminds us that we all have to answer the same question: What are we going to do with Jesus? Will we trade Him for someone more like us? Will we wash our hands of Him rather than deal with the havoc His reign might wreak in our lives? Will we acknowledge who He is and surrender our lives? Will we make our choices based on that truth?

JOHN 19:1–42
JESUS' DEATH

Behold the Man   19:1–16
The Culmination of History   19:17–42

Setting Up the Section

Pilate will try over and over again to get rid of Jesus. He has already tried in chapter 18. He put Jesus up against a real insurrectionist named Barabbas, but the accusers chose Barabbas. Therefore, Pilate will attempt to avoid having to face Jesus and having to come to a point of action concerning Him.

📖 19:1–16

BEHOLD THE MAN

Pilate's first attempt to rid himself of Jesus is centered on punishment (19:1). Maybe if he gives Jesus the most severe punishment, short of execution, that would satisfy accusers.

The Roman scourge was a stick wrapped in leather with long leather strips hanging off the end. Attached to the leather strips were bits of brass, lead, and bones filed to sharp points. The victim was strapped to the ground with his back up, tied to a post, or actually hung in the air. Scourging involved forty lashes on the back. This process could expose the arteries and even the internal organs. It shredded the skin. This was such a horrendous torture that no Roman citizen could ever legally be scourged, only the enemies of Rome. Many did not survive.

Critical Observation

Luke's Gospel records that before Pilate ordered Jesus to be scourged, he sent Jesus to Herod in the hopes of moving the case. Herod was the governor of the entire region of Palestine. Herod sent Jesus back, finding no fault in Him (Luke 23:6–12). It was at this point that Pilate ordered Jesus to be scourged, hoping that this would be enough punishment to satisfy His accusers.

Jesus is mocked as well as whipped (19:2–3). The idea in the description is that the soldiers keep mocking Jesus while they continue to beat Him.

Pilate again declares Jesus' innocence (19:4). At this point, Jesus has been beaten almost to death. His face would have been swollen, His body shredded, and He would have been covered in blood. There is also a crown of thorns on His head (19:5), piercing His skull and causing even more blood to pour down His face. He is also wearing a purple robe to signify that no one who is in the position to decide believes that Jesus is a king.

In displaying Jesus (19:5), Pilate tries to make the point that this man is no threat and certainly no king. Perhaps Pilate hoped this would satisfy the Jewish leaders. But nothing will keep Jesus from the cross.

The leaders call again for Jesus' crucifixion, hearkening back to the accusation of blasphemy. While Pilate reiterates that he has no official grounds on which to execute Jesus, the people explain their view on blasphemy (19:6–7). Pilate, scared and confused, makes His second attempt to free Jesus (19:8).

Critical Observation

Matthew's Gospel adds the detail of Pilate's wife. According to her dream, Pilate's dealings with Jesus would only bring suffering (Matthew 27:19). She sent a message to this effect to Pilate, increasing his discomfort with the situation.

Pilate wants to know if Jesus is a god (19:9). Jesus sits quietly, reminiscent of the lamb silent at his slaughter as described by the Old Testament prophet, Isaiah (Isaiah 53:7).

After Pilate reminds Jesus of his own power, Jesus responds, but only to put Pilate in his place (19:10–11). Any authority Pilate has is a delegated authority. Therefore, Jesus is not concerned about the outcome. The future of Jesus does not rest in the hands of Pilate; it ultimately rests in God.

From that point, Pilate moves from trying to persuade Jesus, to trying to persuade the Jews in the face of their threats to paint him as an enemy of Caesar (19:12).

Demystifying John

History records that the Jews had already complained to Caesar once about Pilate. Pilate had brought Roman votive shields, which the Jews viewed as idols, into Herod's palace in Jerusalem. When the Jews complained to Caesar, Caesar ordered Pilate to remove the shields, humiliating him.

If the Jews went to Caesar again and said that Pilate refused to execute a man who was trying to take over the Roman kingdom, Pilate might lose his position.

Pilate resorts to political pressure. He goes to the place where official judgments were made. Once a judgment was made from this place, it was permanent and binding. Pilate puts Jesus on display one more time in the robe, thorns, and with wounds and blood (19:14). John's Gospel points out that it's almost the sixth hour. The Passover celebration is at hand. A judgment needs to be made.

Pilate wants to put the pressure of the decision on the Jewish leaders. If Jesus is going to be crucified, it will be because they made the decision. And thus in a hypocritical expression of loyalty to Caesar, the Jewish leaders call for Jesus' death (19:15–16).

📄 **19:17–42**

THE CULMINATION OF HISTORY

In verses 17–18, John shows the crucifixion simply and clearly. John's focus is the glory of Jesus, not the horror of the cross.

Demystifying John

The crucifixion of Jesus is a central event in human history. Jesus came so that God would be made known, and He died so that man would have eternal life.

The Gospel of John's main purpose is to present Jesus as the manifestation of God. Therefore, in writing the Gospel, John highlights accounts that speak to the issue of Jesus' deity. As we come to the account of Jesus' crucifixion, John will show us the majesty of Jesus in the midst of what His enemies hoped was His humiliation.

The "place of the skull" (19:17 NIV) is *Golgotha* in Hebrew and *Calvaria* in Latin. It is, of course, from the Latin that we use the English word *Calvary*. This was a hill, so the crucifixions would be seen by many. The public nature of Calvary was a visual reinforcement of Rome's power to control.

Jesus carries His own crossbeam. The vertical posts were already in the ground. Victims were led through the streets with the crossbeams on their backs.

Critical Observation

We are told in other accounts that before Jesus got to the foot of the hill, He became so weak that a man named Simon was asked to carry Jesus' crossbeam. When Jesus got to the place of execution, the crossbeam was nailed to His hands, He was hoisted up on to the vertical post, and the crossbeam was set into a notch on the horizontal beam already in the ground. (For other accounts of Jesus' crucifixion, see Matthew 27:27–54; Mark 15:25–39; Luke 23:26–47).

On this hill Jesus is hung between two thieves. This is significant because Isaiah 53:12 prophesied that the Messiah would be "counted among the rebels" (NLT).

Pilate's sign, made for the top of the cross, becomes a center of controversy (19:19). Pilate believes Jesus to be innocent, yet, for political reasons, he gives in to the crucifixion. It was a

Roman custom to place the offense of the person being crucified on the top of the cross to announce what the person did to warrant execution. Pilate's sign simply identifies Jesus as the King of the Jews, and is written in Aramaic, Latin, and Greek (19:20) so that all onlookers will be able to read it. Verse 20 tells us that the place where Jesus is crucified is near the city, and therefore, everyone can see the sign.

It is unusual that the sign has no disgrace to it, at least none for Jesus. But it does have some disgrace for the Jews. The leaders look guilty because they just crucified their king. In light of this, these Jews want the sign changed to put the offense back on Jesus—that He only *claimed* to be king (19:21). Pilate refuses (19:22), which may be a way of retaliating for the difficult position they put him in.

The next aspect of Jesus' glory relates to scriptures that He fulfilled.

Jesus' outer garments would have been His shoes, the belt, the headdress, and the outer cloak. The inner garment is one piece, therefore, the soldiers gamble to see who will get it (19:23–24). These soldiers fulfill Psalm 22:18.

There are four ladies at the foot of the cross (19:25), but almost all of the disciples are nowhere to be found. The first lady mentioned is Mary, Jesus' mother. When Mary brought Jesus to the temple as a baby, she was told by Simeon that there would come a day when her own heart would be pierced. The other ladies there are Mary's sister, Mary's sister-in-law, and Mary, the one in which Jesus cast out seven demons. All of these ladies loved Jesus and are there to be with Him until His death.

Even on the cross, Jesus fulfills His duty as Mary's son in seeing to it that she is cared for (19:26–27). Jesus places her into the care of John. From that point on, John treats Mary as his own mother and cares for her.

After Jesus completes His duty to His mother, He knows that everything that was to be accomplished has been (19:28). He then fulfills the final prophecy concerning what He would say on the cross and says, "I thirst" (19:28; Psalm 69:21). In response He is given sour wine—vinegar (19:29).

Jesus is given the vinegar with a branch of hyssop, a reedlike branch significant in Jewish culture. The hyssop was used in the first Passover in Egypt to spread lamb's blood on the doorpost of the house so that the angel of death would spare the firstborn son. Each time hyssop is used, it would remind a Jewish person of this event. And so in this moment the Passover is coming to life in the death of Jesus.

Finally, Jesus exclaims, "It is finished" (19:30 NIV). This does not simply mean that His earthly life is over. Rather it means His task is accomplished—the plan is fully realized. Therefore, with that, Jesus physically dies.

Exodus 12:46 declares that the Passover lamb is not to have any broken bones. Therefore, since the Passover is a picture of the cross, Jesus was not to have any broken bones, and He does not (19:31–37). Jesus dies before they need to break His legs.

Demystifying John

The custom of breaking a crucified person's legs functioned to hasten death. To die by crucifixion was actually to die by asphyxiation. As the person hung, he could breathe in, but it became increasingly difficult to breathe out. In order to do so, he would have to gather his strength to push himself upward on feet that had been pierced. That effort would have also scraped his back, already raw from flogging. If a person was surviving too long on the cross, breaking his legs took away any ability to support himself in order to breathe.

The piercing of Jesus' side (19:34) is the completion of what was prophesied in Zechariah 12:10.

Often in this day, victims of crucifixion were buried in a common grave. In Jesus' case, though, Joseph of Arimathea and Nicodemus, two Jewish leaders that had become disciples of Jesus, ask Pilate for the body and take care of the funeral arrangements (19:38–42). Even in this, the scriptures are fulfilled. Isaiah 53:9 says that the Messiah would be a rich man in death. Though Jesus died the death of a wretched man, in a twist of circumstances, He was allowed to be buried in a rich man's tomb.

Take It Home

Jesus' deity is evident in the sign that Pilate made, the scriptures fulfilled, the selfless love, the supernatural knowledge, and the final scriptures concerning His death. What this shows us is that Jesus is God, and as God He perfectly redeemed us. Jesus is the perfect sacrifice for humanity.

JOHN 20:1-31

JESUS CONQUERS DEATH

The Empty Tomb	20:1–18
Jesus and the Disciples	20:19–31

Setting Up the Section

Jesus controlled death; death did not control Jesus. He died in humanity's place and then rose from the dead, conquering the bondage of death. John's Gospel offers evidence that Jesus rose from the dead and, therefore, if we believe in the person and work of Jesus, we will have life.

📄 20:1–18

THE EMPTY TOMB

John records Mary's trip to the tomb (20:1). This is not an exhaustive picture of the event—just a snapshot. When Mary discovers that Jesus' body is gone, she runs to get Peter and John to tell them that someone has taken the body of Jesus away (20:2). When John, Peter, and Mary arrive at the tomb, they find the burial clothes of Jesus lying there (20:3–6).

If Jesus' body had been moved by someone, then the burial clothes would not be lying there. They would still be around the body. If someone stole the body, he or she would not likely unwrap it. Something else happened to the body—this is the first evidence of the resurrection.

The second piece of evidence John offers is Jesus' face cloth (20:7). While the body of the deceased is wrapped in strips of cloth, somewhat mummy-like, the face cloth is laid over the head. This piece of cloth is folded up and placed away from the wrappings. Again, this is unlikely to be the work of grave robbers, who would not likely take the time to fold up the cloth even if they chose to unwrap the dead body.

This is evidence of not only the spiritual resurrection of Jesus, but the bodily resurrection. Jesus doesn't just rise as a spirit. He rises from the dead in a body that is able to pick up the head covering and fold it and place it in another part of the room.

John enters the tomb with Peter, and when he sees the burial clothes, he believes (20:8). When John sees the cloths lying there and the head piece folded up, he is convinced that Jesus has risen from the dead.

At this point, the disciples still have not understood all that Jesus had spoken about His resurrection. John believes the prophecies, but does not fully understand that they are being fulfilled before his eyes (20:9–10).

John's next piece of evidence regarding the resurrection is the claim of Jesus. Mary sees two angels, one by the head and the other by the feet of where the body had been lying (20:11–12). John's Gospel does not focus on Mary's reaction to the angels, but rather focuses on their question (20:13). The presence of angels confirms this as a divine moment. They ask Mary a question, not because the angels need the answer—Mary needs to know it. Mary thinks Jesus' body has been stolen. She thinks that Jesus is gone, and has no idea what has taken place. The implication of the angels' question is that there is nothing to weep about. This is a day of rejoicing, not of tears.

Jesus had said that the disciples would be in a state of deep sorrow while the world is in a state of rejoicing (see John 16:20). But Jesus said that He would not leave them in a state of sorrow. Mary finds herself face-to-face with Jesus, but she has no idea that it is Him (20:14). Mary does not recognize Him because He looks different after the resurrection (1 Corinthians 15:35–49).

Critical Observation

Mark 16:12 says that Jesus appeared to the disciples in a different form after the resurrection. He had a glorified body. While we know He had a physical body, it was in a different form than what He had before He died.

Jesus asks Mary a question: "Why are you crying?" (20:15 NIV). Jesus asks the same question as the angels. Mary has all love and no faith.

In John 10, Jesus said that His sheep know His voice, and He, as the good shepherd, calls them by name. That is what happens to Mary (20:16). Jesus speaks her name, and suddenly she sees that it is Jesus. She responds to Jesus and calls Him *Rabboni*, a title of great respect. It is like calling someone master, or even supreme master. It could even be used to describe God. She sees that it is Jesus, and she automatically humbles herself before Him. She also clutches Jesus, and will not let Him go.

In verse 17, some translations describe Jesus as saying, "Do not touch me," but a better translation would be, "Don't cling to me." Jesus must ascend to the Father. The relationship is going to change, and Mary cannot cling to Him physically. She must now learn to cling to Jesus spiritually.

Mary is to announce Jesus' ascension to the disciples (20:17–18). Remember, Jesus had told the disciples in chapters 14–16 that He would ascend to the Father. Notice that Jesus calls the disciples "brothers." Now that He has risen from the dead, their relationship has changed. They have a new life in Him and are in the family of God.

Take It Home

Jesus calls the disciples brothers because they are now a part of the family of God. Hebrews 2:11 tells us that we, by the virtue of Jesus' death, also become siblings of Jesus. His life is placed within us, and we, therefore, can call His Father our Father. We do not fear death anymore because of our new life in Him.

📄 **20:19–31**

JESUS AND THE DISCIPLES

When Jesus appears to the disciples, they are locked in a house because they are still afraid of being arrested and tried as Jesus was (20:19). Jesus says to them, "Peace be with you!" (20:19 NIV). To wish someone peace was to wish them all of the fullness and happiness that God intended. When Jesus uses this greeting, it carries a deeper significance because Jesus wishes the disciples the fullness of life and peace that is found in Him. It is within this context that Jesus gives them the precursor to their great commission (20:20–21). Just as God sent Jesus on a mission, so Jesus is sending the disciples on a mission. They are to be the manifestation of Jesus on earth, continuing the work He started.

The Holy Spirit is essential to the disciples' mission (20:22). The Spirit is the power and ability to accomplish what needs to be done. Jesus had promised the Holy Spirit would come after He ascends to heaven, but this event is not exactly the same as the coming of the Holy Spirit described in Acts 2. Here, it is Jesus connecting the Holy Spirit with the mission of the disciples in anticipation of what will happen after His ascension.

Verse 23 describes the disciples' right to speak on behalf of God. The disciples are not able to forgive sins, but they are charged with telling those who believe, that their sins have been forgiven through Jesus' sacrifice.

Thomas was not with the other disciples in the room when Jesus gave the commission, though the other disciples obviously explained it to him. He responds in his famous skepticism (20:24–25), wanting physical confirmation. Jesus does appear again, announces peace, and then offers the physical evidence that Thomas has been looking for (20:26–27).

Jesus knows Thomas's doubts even though He wasn't in the room when Thomas voiced them. This is another way in which John's Gospel emphasizes Jesus' sovereignty over everything. He knows Thomas's doubts, and He meets Thomas at his point of need (20:28).

Take It Home

In verse 29, Jesus lays out a principle: It is one thing to believe when you have seen Jesus; it is a greater thing to believe if you have never actually seen the physical resurrected body of Jesus. Since that day, there have been millions of people who have believed without seeing, only trusting in the Word of God. That is real, undeniable faith.

John states his purpose for writing this Gospel here. He wants the reader to believe that Jesus is God manifested, that on the cross He bore all people's sin, and that when He rose from the dead He gave humanity life (20:30–31).

JOHN 21:1–25

EPILOGUE

Fishing Instructions	21:1–14
Breakfast by the Sea	21:15–25

Setting Up the Section

Chapter 21 is the epilogue of this great Gospel. Jesus gives His disciples a living illustration that He is their provider, and that He is the sovereign Lord of the universe.

In Peter's restoration, we learn what it means to love Jesus and what it means to follow Jesus. This becomes a fitting conclusion of the Gospel of John.

John offers this final account of one of Jesus' post-resurrection appearances to not only confirm the resurrection of Jesus, but to also illustrate one last time the fact that Jesus is truly the manifestation of God.

📖 21:1–14

FISHING INSTRUCTIONS

After Jesus' resurrection, He is in His glorified body, and only appears to those who know Him.

Seven disciples are fishing (21:1–3). They are not returning to their old trade, but they are continuing to fish in this transition time. They are no longer with Jesus daily, and yet the Holy Spirit has not come and empowered them to preach. They are waiting for their mission to start.

They have fished all night and have caught nothing. After Jesus offers instructions, they are unable to haul in the load because there are too many fish. John realizes that the man on the shore is Jesus. Who else controls the fish in the ocean? (21:3–7).

Note Peter's zeal in verses 7 and 8. The rest of the disciples are left to carry the load of fish in by themselves as Peter is swimming to the shore.

Jesus serves the disciples with a hot breakfast. There are 153 fish in the catch—Jesus has provided abundantly (21:9–11).

By the time Jesus invites the disciples to eat breakfast, they all recognize Him (21:12). When this Gospel was written, years later, these kinds of statements offered proof for those who questioned whether the resurrection was a reality. John tells us that this is the third manifestation of Jesus to the disciples, and it is an experience filled with service and compassion (21:13–14).

BREAKFAST BY THE SEA

When breakfast is over, Jesus is ready to deal with Peter. In John 13:37, Peter had declared he would lay down his life for Jesus. Since this was said in the context of Jesus' recognizing Judas's potential betrayal, Peter's words had the implication that he would be faithful even if the rest of the disciples were not. Yet later that same night, his failure—in denying Jesus—was monumental.

Jesus' question addresses the heart of the problem (21:15). Peter does not understand the nature of love. He loves Jesus with passion, enthusiasm, and emotion, but his love is lacking simple obedience. Peter's answer declares Jesus as the center of His affection. Jesus wants that love and affection channeled through tending His lambs.

The idea around the word *tend* is that of feeding. Peter is to be sure Jesus' flock is kept healthy. If Peter truly is devoted to Jesus, then it will show when he cares for the lambs of God in the same way Jesus cares for His disciples. The point is, if Peter loves Jesus then he will love and value the things that Jesus loves and values.

Jesus asks the question again (21:16), and this time His directive to Peter has to do with nourishing, caring for, and treating the sheep as if they are an extension of his own body. It is more than just pet-sitting; it is engaged nurture.

Jesus asks the question a third time, which grieves Peter (21:17). He takes it personally that Jesus has not trusted his responses, but Jesus is restoring Peter. For each time Peter looked out for himself at the expense of obedience by denying Jesus, he will be restored. This last time, Jesus charges Peter to make sure he take Jesus' lambs as his primary responsibility.

Jesus begins verse 18 with the final, "Verily, verily" (KJV), or, "I tell you the truth" (NIV) statement of the Gospel of John. Remember, this is Jesus doubly affirming His point. The idea is that this is binding and absolute truth.

In Peter's denial he showed compassion only for himself, and in his subsequent denials he showed that he was afraid of death. Jesus now addresses Peter's death (21:19). We know that Peter was indeed crucified. Church tradition claims that he went to the cross and asked to be crucified upside down because he did not want to die in the same way as Jesus.

In light of this information, Jesus calls Peter to follow Him. The implication of the Greek word for "follow" (21:19 NIV) is that Peter is to follow Jesus constantly and consistently as opposed to the sporadic nature in which he had followed in the past.

Peter turns and sees John and asks Jesus a question that we would all be prone to ask, "What about John?" (21:20–21). Is John going to have a violent death as well? Jesus simply states that His plans for John are of no concern to Peter.

At one time, it was believed that Jesus' response to Peter's inquiry (21:20–21) about John meant that John was going to live forever. Here, as Gospel writer, John clears up the rumor and says that Jesus is not giving a prophecy (21:22–23).

Take It Home

This Gospel account ends here (21:24–25) to illustrate to us that we must follow Jesus as Lord, and follow Him wherever He has called us. In following Jesus we will all be called into one body, but into different places in that body. Some will have a difficult struggle in their walk, and will constantly be under attack for faith. Some will experience prosperity on earth, and will be used to advance the kingdom. Some will die early, and some will live long.

The key is to follow God where He has planted you. Do not seek what He has not given you, and do not be ungrateful for what He has given you. Rather, follow God whatever the cost, wherever the location. That is what Jesus wanted Peter to know.

CONTRIBUTING EDITORS

Robert L. Deffinbaugh, Th.M. graduated from Dallas Theological Seminary with his Th.M. in 1971. Bob is a teacher and elder at Community Bible Chapel in Richardson, Texas, and a regular contributor to the online studies found at Bible.org.

Dr. Stephen Leston is pastor of Kishwaukee Bible Church in DeKalb, Illinois. He is passionate about training people for ministry and has served as a pastor at Grace Church of DuPage (Warrenville, Illinois) and Petersburg Bible Church (Petersburg, Alaska).

CONSULTING EDITOR

Dr. Mark Strauss is a professor at Bethel Seminary's San Diego Campus. He is the author of *Distorting Scripture? The Challenge of Bible Translation and Gender Accuracy*; *The Essential Bible Companion*; and *Four Portraits, One Jesus: An Introduction to Jesus and the Gospels*. He is presently revising the commentary on Mark's gospel for Expositor's Bible Commentary.

WITH SPECIAL THANKS TO BIBLE.ORG

Bible.org is a non-profit (501c3) Christian ministry headquartered in Dallas, Texas. In the last decade, bible.org has grown to serve millions of individuals around the world and provides thousands of trustworthy resources for Bible study including the new NET BIBLE® translation.

Bible.org offers thousands of free resources for
- Spiritual Formation and Discipleship
- Men's Ministry
- Women's Ministry
- Pastoral Helps
- Small Group Curriculum
  and much more

Bible.org can be accessed through www.bible.org

Watch for All 12 Volumes
in the
QUICKNOTES SIMPLIFIED
BIBLE COMMENTARY SERIES

Volume 8: Matthew and Mark
Good News for Everyone

ISBN 978-1-59789-774-7
Available Now

Volume 10: Acts thru
2 Corinthians
What About Church?

ISBN 978-1-59789-776-1
Available May 2008

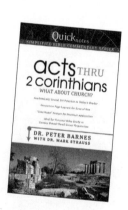

Other Volumes Planned for the Series:

Volume 11: Galatians through Philemon, August 2008
Volume 12: Hebrews through Revelation, November 2008
Volumes 1–7: The Old Testament, beginning February 2009

Available wherever Christian books are sold.